WORKS ISSUED BY
THE HAKLUYT SOCIETY

———————

THE DISCOVERY OF THE SOUTH SHETLAND ISLANDS
(1819–1820)

THIRD SERIES
NO. 4

Plate 1. Brig *Williams*: most southerly position 23 February 1820. From a painting by Commander G. W. G. Hunt, RN.

THE DISCOVERY OF

THE SOUTH SHETLAND ISLANDS

THE VOYAGES OF THE BRIG *WILLIAMS*
1819–1820
as recorded in contemporary documents

AND
THE JOURNAL OF MIDSHIPMAN C. W. POYNTER

Edited by

R. J. CAMPBELL

THE HAKLUYT SOCIETY
LONDON
2000

Published by The Hakluyt Society
c/o Map Library
British Library, 96 Euston Road,
London NW1 2DB

SERIES EDITORS
W. F. RYAN
ROBIN LAW

ISBN 0 904180 62 X
ISSN 0072 9396

British Library Cataloguing-in-Publication Data
A catalogue record for this book is
available from the British Library

Typeset by Waveney Typesetters, Wymondham, Norfolk
Printed in Great Britain at
the University Press, Cambridge

For Sconadh

CONTENTS

LIST OF ILLUSTRATIONS

ABBREVIATIONS

BL   British Library, London
DNB   *Dictionary of National Biography*
IOR   India Office Library and Records (British Library), London
NMM   National Maritime Museum, Greenwich
PRO   Public Record Office, Kew
SPRI   Scott Polar Research Institute, Cambridge
UK HO   United Kingdom Hydrographic Office, Taunton

PREFACE

Note on the Sources

The brig *Williams*, under the command of William Smith, made three voyages in 1819, during which the first discovery of the South Shetland Islands was made. There appear to be no surviving original documents from these three voyages, but there were published accounts which are listed below and which are partially or fully reproduced in this book as supporting the main text and completing the story of the discovery.

The central text of this book is Midshipman Charles Poynter's manuscript journal of the fourth voyage (1819–20), under the command of Edward Bransfield. The manuscript, entitled 'His Majestys Hired Brig Williams on discovery towards the South Pole' (reference number MSX–4088) is held in the Alexander Turnbull Library, National Library of New Zealand, Te Puna Mātauranga o Aotearoa, which kindly supplied a microfilm. Poynter's spelling has been used as far as practicable and where it is not discernible modern spelling has been used. There is a number of pencil emendations, which appear to be in Poynter's hand, which are included either in square brackets or in footnotes. The journal contains seventy-three pages of text, a drawing, three charts and three sheets of views (two of which appear to be unfinished). Reproductions of all these graphics are included at Plates 10, 11, 14, 22 and 30.

Accounts of the preceding three voyages were published between 1820 and 1825, in the *Edinburgh Philosophical Journal*, the *Literary Gazette and Journal of Belles Lettres, Arts Sciences, &c.*, various newspapers and Sailing Directions and in James Weddell's *Voyage towards the South Pole performed in the years 1822–24*. There are also versions in the manuscript report forwarded to the Admiralty by Captain Shirreff and in the Memorandum forwarded by Captain Smith himself to the Admiralty. The journals and newspapers are all held at the British Library. No copy of Purdy's *Memoir Descriptive and Explanatory, to accompany the New Chart of the Ethiopic or Southern Atlantic Ocean, etc.* could be located in Britain; copies are in the Library of Congress, Washington DC, and the New York Public Library. A copy of Norie's *Piloting Directions for the East and West Coasts of South America and the River Plate to Panama &c. also for the South Shetland, Falkland Galapagos and other*

Islands etc. was already in the possession of the editor. Blunt's *American Coast Pilot*, eleventh edition, and various other editions, are available in the Admiralty Library, Taunton, as well as in the Library of Congress. Weddell's voyage is available in a number of libraries and the manuscript sources are in the Public Record Office at Kew.

All charts reproduced are from the UK Hydrographic Office with the exception of those from Poynter's journal and the track chart which has been redrawn from modern British Admiralty charts with the positions of the *Williams* inserted. The original charts produced by Bransfield were not available for inspection and photographic copies were used.

Names

Place names are given using current conventions, i.e. in the form used by the country having sovereignty. A few conventional names, which are frequently referred to in the various documents quoted, are given in their standard English form e.g. Cape Horn for Cabo de Hornos (both forms are indexed). Names in the Antarctic are those agreed by the Antarctic Place-names Committee and used on British Admiralty charts. Names from original documents are given in the form in which they appear in that document (with a footnote if their modern form is not obvious); references to them are in the same form. Poynter's journal presents a far greater problem since he is inconsistent in his usage – for example Cape Valentine appears as Valentine's Head, Valentines Head, Cape Valentine and Cape Valentines. The track chart has been prepared using the form which Poynter states was used to name the feature, or, if this is not given, the name on the 1822 Admiralty chart. Names from the modern Admiralty chart are used for features which were not named at the time. Names on the illustrations and in Chapter 7 are the same as those used on the track chart.

Acknowledgements

The Alexander Turnbull Library, National Library of New Zealand, Te Puna Mātauranga o Aotearoa, most generously gave permission for the publication of Midshipman Poynter's journal. All published journal and newspaper articles and copyright material are reproduced by permission of the British Library. Crown copyright material in the Public Record Office is reproduced by permission of the Controller of Her Majesty's Stationary Office. Material from other original documents in the United Kingdom Hydrographic Office, and crown copyright material from Admiralty charts and publications are reproduced by permission of the Controller of Her Majesty's Stationery Office and the United Kingdom Hydrographic Office. The Library of Congress, Washington, D.C., provided the text of the extract from Purdy's *Memoir Descriptive ... of the Ethiopic or Southern Atlantic Ocean*. I am most grateful to all these authorities for their help and permissions.

I have also had considerable help from a number of people the foremost of whom was Lieutenant Commander Andrew David, Royal Navy, who drew my attention to Poynter's journal in the first place and has since given me a vast amount of his time and expertise. I have also great pleasure in recording the help of Mr D. Colquhoun, the Curator of Manuscripts and Archives at the Alexander Turnbull Library and Mrs Jocelyn Chisholm, who have answered my queries on the manuscript; of Dr D. J. Goodman, Professor A. Clarke, Dr J. P. Croxall, Dr R. I. Lewis-Smith, Dr A. R. Martin (Sea Mammal Research Unit), all of the British Antarctic Survey who have helped me with the natural history aspects of the journal; of Mr C. J. Gilbert, British Antarctic Survey Library of Photographs, and Dr J. L. Smellie, also of the British Antarctic Survey, who very generously allowed me to use some of his excellent photographs; of Dr R. K. Headland and Ms Philippa Hogg of the Scott Polar Research Institute; of the staff of the Public Record Office, of the staff of the Data Centre at the United Kingdom Hydrographic Office; of the staff of Taunton Public Library who have been most patient in getting me items from various journals; of Mr P. J. Woodman and Miss J. Moore of the Permanent Committee on Geographical Names for British Official Use; of Mr G. Armitage of the British Library, Map Library; of Mrs S. Malloch of the Canterbury Cathedral Archives; of Mr Derek Leask, a co-lateral descendant of C. W. Poynter, who has helped with my research into his life and provided me with much relevant information; of Commander G. W. G. Hunt, Royal Navy, who painted the picture of the brig *Williams* used as the frontispiece; of Mr T. N. Snow, who gave me considerable assistance translating articles from Spanish; of Mr A. G. E. Jones, Mr F. E. Wooden, Dr G. Hattersley-Smith and Professor Glyndwr Williams who also helped in various ways, and finally of Professor W. F. Ryan, of The Hakluyt Society, who edited my work for publication. I would add my apologies to anyone whom I ought to have mentioned, but have not done, and say that I am none the less most grateful for their help.

INTRODUCTION

The South Shetland Islands are situated south of Drake Passage, about 450 nautical miles SSE of Cape Horn or 600 miles south of the Falkland Islands, on the northern flank of the Antarctic Peninsula, from which they are separated by Bransfield Strait.

Today the first impression tends to be one of awe – reverential fear or wonder – on sighting the magnificent scenery of the Antarctic. The fearful aspect is in general overridden by that of wonder since the area is no longer unknown, and visiting it is by no means the dangerous undertaking it once was. Ships are well found and, if need be, can operate in defiance of the weather. In the early nineteenth century and before, however, ships were subject to every whim of the wind, and sailing off a lee shore was fraught with danger, made considerably more so if that shore were iron bound[1] and unknown. Robert Fildes, who was captain of the brig *Cora*, wrecked off the islands in January 1821, recording his first impression stated that it 'had a most forbidding appearance' and 'displayed the most horrid picture I ever beheld' (see also p. 108, n. 1).

The Southern Ocean Current circles the Antarctic continent setting eastwards. It sweeps through Drake Passage and forms eddies and counter-currents along the coast of the continent; currents near the land are very variable, but generally set westwards. One such current circles Joinville Island and enters the eastern end of Bransfield Strait flowing westward along its southern side.

The climate is appreciably less severe than farther south, and in the summer months, December to March, the average temperature is above freezing. The weather is dominated by a circumpolar trough of low pressure situated between 60° and 65°S in which frequent depressions move eastward at high speed. With a cold southerly wind the visibility can be exceptional, but with a moist airstream slightly warmer than the sea, fog occurs which can last for a considerable time.

During the winter the islands are entirely icebound. Pack ice fills Bransfield Strait carried eastward on the current; stranded icebergs are common in areas

---

[1] A coast is said to be iron bound where the shores are of rock, generally rising perpendicularly from the sea and where there are no anchorages. It is therefore dangerous for vessels to approach.

with depths of less than about 200 metres (100 fathoms). The ice is usually clear of the western and northern parts of the strait by November, and the eastern and southern parts by late December although the bergs off Trinity Peninsula frequently remain throughout the season. The current from the Weddell Sea round Joinville Island, may retard the clearance of ice from the eastern end of the strait and in some seasons the eastern and southern parts remain closed altogether.

The sea is particularly rich in krill (*Euphausia superba*) which is the principal form of food for the whales, penguins, seals and fish which abound. The islands are inhabited by Adélie (*Pygoscelis adeliae*), gentoo (*Pygoscelis papua*), chinstrap (*Pygoscelis antarctica*) and macaroni (*Eudyptes chrysolophus*) penguins and numerous other birds, while seals are frequent visitors. The fur seals (*Arctocephalus gazella,*) having been exploited to the point of extermination in the early nineteenth century,[1] are returning.

The South Shetland Islands lie in the area covered by the Antarctic Treaty[2] and are in the territories claimed by Argentina, Britain and Chile. However, since the Antarctic Treaty was signed in 1959 (and entered into force 23 June 1961) all territorial claims have been frozen. The text of the Treaty starts, after listing the contracting Governments (which include Argentina, Chile and the United Kingdom of Great Britain and Northern Ireland), by 'Recognizing that it is in the interest of all mankind that Antarctica shall continue for ever to be used exclusively for peaceful purposes and that it shall not become the scene or object of international discord.' It goes on to prohibit the establishment of military bases, testing of military weapons, nuclear explosions etc. and allows for the setting up of scientific bases which may be inspected by other nations.

Bases are currently (1997) maintained in the South Shetland Islands by Argentina, Brazil, Chile (two), China, Korea, Poland, Uruguay and Russia, which are manned throughout the year. There is also a number of stations and refuge huts which are not permanently manned.

In 1972, 1973 and 1975 a group of biologists from the University of Concepción collected samples of sea bed flora and fauna from Admiralty Bay (Bahía

---

[1] Commander Henry Foster in HMS *Chanticleer*, who passed west of Smith and Low Islands, 5 January 1829, and then landed at Cape Possession, Hoseason Island, on his way to Deception Island stated: 'No Seals were seen by us on the Islands or places visited by us, nor were any met with at Sea, and during the whole time of our Stay at Deception. Eight Sea-Leopards only were seen, the whole of which were killed and five preserved for Specimens.' The ship remained at Deception Island from 9 January to 8 March, and then passed between Smith and Snow Islands the next day on the way north. UK HO, OD 39; Webster, 1834, I, pp. 137–71.

[2] Defined by Article VI of the Treaty as 'the area south of 60° South Latitude, including all ice shelves'.

Almirantazgo), King George Island, and Discovery Bay (Bahía Chile), Greenwich Island. These samples were examined in 1977 and among the benthic material were found two stone age projectile heads of aboriginal manufacture.[1] They were dated to between 1500 BC and AD 1000, however detailed examination led to the conclusion that they had been inserted in the samples subsequent to their collection in the South Shetland Islands,[2] and the thought of an early aboriginal discovery was laid to rest (although, of course, this does not exclude the possibility that future evidence of such a discovery may yet come to light).

The islands were first discovered in 1819, by William Smith in the brig *Williams*. When the news of this discovery appeared in the American newspapers a number of the New York and Boston papers[3] carried reports that they had been discovered by American sealers at an earlier date, but an exhaustive search of records by Thomas Stevens has failed to substantiate this story and indeed demonstrated that not one of the vessels which went sealing between 1812 and

[1] Now in the Instituto Antártico Chileno, Registration numbers c.d/423 and c.d/424, from Discovery Bay and Admiralty Bay respectively.

[2] Three different types of examination were carried out on the projectile heads by the Chilean authorities. The first included a study of existing collections of stone tools from Tierra del Fuego, together with interviews with relevant specialist archaeologists and historians, and interviews with the descendants of the Fuegians at Puerto Williams and with the biologists who took part in the find. The second included further field work. Samples were taken from the reported site in Admiralty Bay in January 1983, and compared with that on the projectile head and a search was made in the area for additional archaeological evidence. Thirdly laboratory analysis was carried out. This was to determine the derivation of the projectile heads and if they had been in the sea. These indicated that this type of projectile is extremely uncommon in the collections of the tribes of Tierra del Fuego, and that the material of which they were made is rarely used by the people of Patagonia. Similar types of tool are, however, common in parts of the southern Andes and central southern Chile, especially along the coast between Valdivia and Concepción. Surface analysis of one tool showed strong chemical weathering (i.e. patina) consistent with prolonged exposure in a temperate or warm climate, but unlike that to be expected in the Antarctic. The other had a shiny surface without patina and a sharply serrated edge. The quartz in it was of a different type to that found in Admiralty Bay. Neither showed any indication of marine erosion, salt encrustation, benthic organisms or anything else which might indicate a prolonged stay in sea water. Microgeological analysis showed that the material adhering to the tool said to be from Admiralty Bay was totally different from that found in Admiralty Bay and without any geological relationship to it, indicating that it was practically impossible that it had come from Admiralty Bay. The other tool had no material adhering to it. The conclusion of the Chilean authorities was that it could be categorically stated that the projectile head said to have come from Admiralty Bay, had not done so, and that, while they could not be so certain about the other, it was improbable that it had been immersed in Antarctic waters and that therefore both had been placed in the samples after they had been dredged from the sea bed. Stehberg, 1983.

[3] E.g. *New England Palladium and Commercial Advertiser* (Boston), 15 and 19 September 1820; *New York Evening Post*, 16 September 1820; *Niles' Weekly Register* (Baltimore), 16 September 1820; *Boston Daily Advertiser*, 27 September 1820 etc.: Stevens, 1954, pp. 10–14.

1819 returned with a cargo of seal skins the size of which might have indicated a visit to the area.[1]

The news of Smith's discovery spread rapidly and within three years the fur seals had been virtually exterminated.

Archaeological investigation of the remains of the sealers' huts have located human remains. A skull found at Cape Shirreff has been identified as probably being that of one of the indigenous people of the southern end of Chile from the beginning of the nineteenth century. It is thought to be a female, about twenty-one years old. Various other artifacts were located on Desolation Island which appear to be of aboriginal origin from Tierra del Fuego, indicating that the sealers may have made use of labour from Chile to help them in their work.[2]

This book is about the initial three voyages of William Smith in the brig *Williams* and the subsequent voyage of William Smith and Edward Bransfield, Master RN, who were sent by the Senior Naval Officer on the west coast of South America, Captain William Henry Shirreff, RN, to survey the Islands, and in particular includes the text of Midshipman Charles Wittit Poynter's journal, the only currently known manuscript first-hand account of this voyage.

PRINCIPAL PERSONNEL

Captain William Smith

William Smith (1790–1847) spent his early life in the vicinity of Blyth, and according to John Miers 'was brought up in the Greenland whale-fishery',[3] a fact of which he presumably informed Miers himself. He subsequently spent some time trading between England and Buenos Aires in the brig *Williams*, which had been built at Blyth in 1811–12 for a consortium of four owners of whom Smith was himself one (three of them had been baptized William, hence the brig's name). He returned to England in September 1821, after a sealing voyage to the South Shetland Islands during which he embarked a full cargo of 30,000 skins, to find that his partners had failed financially while he had been away and that he had been joined with them in bankruptcy. The *Williams* and her cargo were seized. Under these circumstances he wrote his 'Memorial to the Right Honorable the Lords, Commissioners of His Majesty's Admiralty' requesting a financial

---

[1] Stevens, 1954, pp. 17–29.
[2] Constantinescu and Torres, 1995; Stehberg and Lucero, 1995.
[3] *Edinburgh Philosophical Journal*, 3, 1820, p. 370, see p. 50.

reward for his discovery (pp. 63–6). It is undated but bears the date stamp of 31 December 1821, signifying when it was received. Smith received no reward and finally gave up trying to get one in 1838. He obtained his discharge from bankruptcy in June 1822 and took service as a Trinity House pilot on the River Thames. He subsequently commanded a vessel for three seasons whaling in the Davis Strait.[1] In 1839 he was superannuated by Trinity House and in 1840 he was admitted to one of the Corporation's almshouses. The date of his death is not certain but his will was proved in May 1847.[2]

Edward Bransfield, Master, Royal Navy

Edward Bransfield was born in about 1785,[3] in Cork, Ireland. He was pressed into the naval service in 1803 and in July appears on the muster book of HMS *Ville de Paris*, 110, Captain T. R. Ricketts, and wearing the flag of Admiral the Hon. William Cornwallis (after whom Cornwallis Island was to be named) where he served with Midshipman William E. Parry.[4] He worked his way up to master in HMS *Goldfinch*, 10, Captain E. Waller. In January 1816 he relieved James Weddell in HMS *Cyndus,* 38, Captain the Hon. F. W. Aylmer, but he was later to answer a query from John Brown Esq[5] that he had no knowledge of Captain Weddell's service career, so they apparently did not actually meet. He was serving as master in HMS *Severn*, 50, Captain Aylmer, at the bombardment of Algiers in August 1816, from which vessel he was paid off in February next year. During this period his Remark Book[6] (see p. 36, n. 2) records that he observed the latitude of various places using both artificial and sea horizons; he observed for latitude from the top of Genoa lighthouse (height 450 feet) obtaining values of

---

[1] The log books of the *William and Ann* of Leith 23 May–5 Oct 1830 and *Caledonia* of Kirkaldy 25 March–4 October 1834, of which William Smith was master, are in the SPRI, Cambridge.

[2] These remarks are based on Miers 1820, Gould 1941 and Jones 1975 where considerably more information can be found.

[3] Date calculated from Bransfield's age and date of death on his death certificate.

[4] PRO ADM 36/16010. I am indebted to Mr F. E. Wooden for drawing my attention to this information. William Parry subsequently had a distinguished naval career. He sailed with Captain John Ross in command of the brig *Alexander*, on his voyage to discover the North West Passage, 1818, and then commanded four voyages to the Arctic himself. He was also, among other appointments, Hydrographer, Comptroller of the Steam Department of the Navy and finally Captain-Superintendent of the Royal Naval Hospital at Haslar.

[5] SPRI MS 501/1 D. Letter dated Worthing 1st March 1839: 'In reply to your letter of 26th ultimo. I have to acquaint you that I have not the slightest knowledge of Mr Weddell's early career, either of the ships he sailed in or the Captains he served under … I have only been twice in his company, and that since his last voyage …'.

[6] UK HO, Misc. Papers, vol. 75, C4.

44°23′52″ with the artificial and 44°25′02″ with the sea horizon, which, considering the refraction errors likely in the latter, speaks very highly of his observation. He was then appointed to, and joined HMS *Andromache*,[1] 44, Captain W. H. Shirreff, on 9 September 1817, and sailed in her for the South America station in December. It was during his period in *Andromache* that the voyage to the South Shetland Islands in the *Williams* was carried out. He was paid off on 18 September 1821 and remained on half pay for the rest of his life. He served in the merchant service until going to live in Brighton in 1848 where he died, aged sixty-seven, on 31 October 1852.[2] His widow Anne lived on her widow's pension (£50 per annum) at the same address, 61 London Road, until she too died, aged seventy-three, on 9 December 1863.[3]

Midshipman P. J. Blake, Royal Navy

Patrick John Blake was the second son of Sir James Henry Blake, Bart. and Louisa Elizabeth, daughter of General Sir Thomas Gage who commanded the British forces in the American War of Independence. He was also a nephew of Admiral Sir William Hall Gage who had been one of the Lords of the Admiralty, and first cousin of Viscount Gage.

He entered the Royal Navy as a first-class volunteer in HMS *Scipion*, 74, in July 1812 subsequently joining HMS *Indus*, 74, Captain W. H. Gage, on the North Sea and Mediterranean stations. In May 1813 he became a midshipman. He served in a number of different ships before joining HMS *Tyne*, 24, Captain G. T. Falcon, where he was passed for lieutenant by Captains Falcon, Dashwood and Bridgeman of HMS *Tyne*, *Amphion* and *Icarus* on 2 February, 1819.[4] He then joined HMS *Andromache*, 44, Captain W. H. Shirreff, on the South America station whence he was appointed to the brig *Williams* on her voyage of discovery under Edward Bransfield. He was promoted lieutenant 19 July 1823. Thereafter he served in HMS *Conway*, 26, Captain Basil Hall, HMS *Creole*, 42, Commodore Sir Thomas Masterman Hardy, still on the South America station. In February

[1] Former French vessel *Junion* captured 16 June 1799, named *Princess Charlotte* and renamed *Andromache* 6 January 1812. College, 1987, I, pp. 32 and 274.

[2] According to Bransfield's death certificate the date was 30 October, but his grave has 31 October. I am grateful to Mr F. E. Wooden for this information, for the date of Anne Bransfield's death and for directing my attention to *The Times*, 5 November 1852. This carried a brief statement under Deaths – 'On the 31st Ult., at his residence, 61 London-road, Brighton, Edward Bransfield, Esq., R.N., aged 67, the first surveyor of the South Shetland Islands, &c., lying to the southward of Cape Horn.'

[3] The above is, except where stated otherwise, based on Gould 1925 and 1941, and Jones 1966 where further information can be found.

[4] PRO ADM 6/116.

1824 he joined HMS *Tweed*, 28, Captain F. Hunn, and returned to the South America station. In December 1825 he joined HMS *Warspite*, 74, and then HMS *Java*, 52, on the East India station where he spent most of his time as flag-lieutenant to Rear Admiral Gage until promoted commander on 15 January 1830. On 9 March 1837 he was appointed to command HMS *Larne*, 18, and returned to the East Indies for the next five years. He took part in the campaign in China in 1841, and was promoted to post rank 6 May 1841. On 3 September 1845 he was appointed to the command of HMS *Juno*, 26, in the Pacific. He became a rear admiral 4 June 1861, on the Reserved Half-pay List, vice admiral 2 April 1866, and admiral on the Retired List, 20 October 1872. He died in 1884.[1]

Midshipman T. M. Bone, Royal Navy

Thomas Mein Bone was the son of Henry Bone (1755–1834), an artist well known for his work in china decoration, watches and fans, but principally for his skill in enamelling. He had three other sons, Robert Trewick (1790–1840) and Henry Pierce (1779–1855), who followed their father in artistic careers while the third went into the army.[2]

Thomas Bone entered the Royal Navy at the age of thirteen in HMS *La Hogue*, 74, Captain The Hon. T. B. Capel, as a volunteer (and later as a midshipman) on 3 January 1812. He remained there until October 1814 working off Brest and on the Home station. He joined HMS *Clorinde*, 38, Captains T. Briggs and S. G. Pechell, on 16 October 1814, where he served until July 1816 in the East Indies, and on the Mediterranean and Home stations. He then joined HMS *Andromache*, 44, Captain W. H. Shirreff, on 5 October 1817 and passed his board for promotion to lieutenant on 29 May, 1819, at Valparaíso. His certificate is signed by Captains Shirreff, O'Brien and Bridgeman of HMS *Andromache, Slaney* and *Icarus*.[3] In December he was sent in the brig *Williams*, with Edward Brans-field, to survey the South Shetland Islands. HMS *Andromache* paid off on 18 September, 1821. After a little time on shore, on 14 March 1822 Bone joined HMS *Racehorse*, 18, Captain W. B. Suckling, as master's mate.[4] The ship was working out of Plymouth and round the west coast of England. On 14 December the same year she sailed from Holyhead for Douglas, Isle of Man. The pilot mistook a light for the harbour light and at 6 p.m. breakers were sighted ahead and almost immediately *Racehorse* struck a rock off Langness Point. Despite their best efforts

---

[1] O'Byrne, 1849, p. 88; PRO ADM 107/74; *Navy Lists.*

[2] *DNB*, s.v.

[3] PRO ADM 6/116.

[4] PRO ADM 107/74, ADM 37/6470; *Navy Lists.*

'at 7 the sea getting up on the Flood Tide, ship Striking heavy, rudder gone & making much water' hope of saving the ship was given up and efforts were devoted to saving the crew. The cutter and galley got away and finally made the shore a long way off, the jolly boat was swamped in lowering; eventually a boat put off from the shore to help them. Three trips were made in safety to a creek about half a mile off; at 'about eleven the Sea then making a fair breach over the Poop the boat returned & took off the remainder of the Officers and Crew who Consisted of the Captain, 1st Lieut, Master, Master's Mate, Boatswain, Pilot & six seamen.' On entering the creek the boat struck a rock, filled and was upset. Midshipman Bone with four seamen from *Racehorse* and three of the Manx boatmen were drowned, the remainder all made it safe to the shore.[1]

Midshipman C. W. Poynter, Royal Navy

Charles Wittit Poynter, the sixth child[2] of James Methurst Poynter, sometime commander with the Hon. East India Company[3] and Captain of Sandown Castle, and Elizabeth youngest daughter of James Peck Esq, surgeon of Deal, was baptized on 22 March 1798.[4]

He joined the Navy as a first-class volunteer on 28 August 1811 in HMS *Inconstant*, 36, Captain E. W. C. R. Owen (who was a friend of his father), at the age of fourteen and then joined HMS *Cornwall*, 74, Captain J. Broughton, on 3 March

[1] PRO ADM 52/4580: 'Log of the Proceedings of His Majesty's Sloop *Racehorse* Wm Benjn Suckling Esq Commander from 30 August to 14th day of Decr 1822 the day the sloop was wrecked. Kept by Henry Hodder – Master'.

[2] The eldest child, baptized 11 May 1789, was Elizabeth Bower, who married the Reverend George Henry Teal Farbrace and died, without issue, 30 May 1878; Ann Lyon was baptized 22 August 1791 and died in 1795; James Peck was born in 1791, married Sarah Westall Meredith in Tasmania 30 April 1836, died 21 June 1847 leaving four children: Benjamin Lyon was baptized 5 November 1792 and was buried four days later; Benjamin Lyon was baptized 17 January 1794, became a Captain in the Brigade of Royal Horse Artillery and died, unmarried, in 1837. Then came Charles Wittit and finally Henry Ambrose who was baptized 12 September 1799. I am indebted to Mr Derek Leask for this information (letters January to May 1998).

[3] The index of maritime service officers of the East India Company for the years c.1600–1834 (IOR L/MAR/A–B) shows him as fifth mate *Marquis of Rockingham* (824 tons) 1775/6, fifth mate *Resolution* (836 tons) 1778/9, and captain *Trial* (160 tons) 1781/2 and 1785/6.

[4] PRO ADM 107/49. The Navy Lists and Coast Guard records give Willit as the second baptismal name and O'Byrne has Willet. Poynter's signature, on his certificate of passing for Lieutenant, has a dotted 'i' not 'e' for the second vowel, but crosses all three verticals with a single stroke. His will uses Wittit, as does the entry in BL Add MS 38050 (his formula for O'Byrne). However in the entry in the baptismal register of St Leonard's Church, Deal, and on the copy of his baptismal certificate supplied by the Reverend John Barnes Backhouse (Rector of Deal 1795–1838), both 'i's are dotted and the three 't's are crossed individually; so that there can be no doubt that WITTIT is the correct form. This is also confirmed in his father's will.

1813, working in the North Sea and off Flushing. He became a midshipman and in May 1814 joined HMS *Nymphen*, 36, Captain M. Smith, in the Channel and Bay of Biscay and, amongst other duties, was involved blockading two French frigates in Brest, suspected of waiting to take Napoleon to America after the battle of Waterloo. While on the books of HMS *Albion*, 74, *Queen*, 74, and *Northumberland*, 74 (August 1815–November 1817), at Sheerness he served twice with Captain Owen in *Royal Sovereign*, yacht, and passed for lieutenant on 5 November 1817. He joined HMS *Andromache*, 44, Captain W. H. Shirreff, on 20th of the same month and sailed in her for the South America station where he was sent as mate and second in command to Edward Bransfield in the brig *Williams*, on discovery in South Shetland Islands. He left *Andromache* 14 July 1821, and became acting master in HMS *Morgiana*, 18, sloop, Captain W. Finlaison, on the South America station.[1] On 14 November he removed to HMS *Doris*, 42, Captains T. Graham and F. E. Vernon,[2] and then served as master's mate and acting lieutenant in HMS *Alacrity*, 10, Captain T. Porter all on the South America station,[3] where he remained until July 1823. He was confirmed lieutenant, with seniority 26 July 1823, in HMS *Alacrity* and left her the following month, when she returned to England. From January 1824 until March 1825 he served as a supernumary lieutenant in HMS *Ramillies*, 74 and then until October the same year in HMS *Hyperion* 42, Captains W. M'Culloch and W. J. Mingaye, operating off The Downs and Newhaven and employed on the Coast Blockade.[4]

[1] HMS *Morgiana* was in Bahia from 21 May to 12 June and arrived in Rio de Janeiro on 7 July, where she anchored close to HMS *Andromache,* (arrived 21 June). Lieutenant M. B. Jones was transferred to HMS *Andromache*, for invaliding home and Poynter joined HMS *Morgiana* on 14 July, the day before HMS *Andromache* sailed for Spithead. PRO ADM 37/6075, ADM 51/3012, ADM 51/3309, ADM 53/865.

[2] The transfer took place in Bahia. PRO ADM 53/865. HMS *Doris* remained on the South America station visiting Rio de Janeiro, 15 December 1821, to 24 January 1822; Bahia 8 to 16 February; Rio de Janeiro 24 February to 10 March; thence round the Horn passing 158 miles south of Islas Diego Ramírez at which time Captain Graham died; Valparaíso 28 April to 19 May; Arica 27 to 29 May; Callao 4 June to 24 August; Valparaíso 14 September 1822 where Poynter transferred to HMS *Alacrity*: PRO ADM 51/3147.

[3] HMS *Alacrity* visited Callao 2 November to 9 December 1822; Callao again 11 December to 9 February 1823, Valparaíso 28 February to 30 March; then called at Rio de Janeiro 15 to 28 May on the way home, arriving at Spithead 19 July and entering Portsmouth Harbour the next day. On 7 August 1823, 'Sunset hauled down the pendant' and paid off: PRO ADM 51/3010.

[4] HMS *Ramillies* remained at anchor at the Downs throughout this period with a visit to Sheerness from the end of November 1824 until mid-January 1825. HMS *Hyperion* was anchored off Newhaven throughout the period Poynter was on on her books: PRO ADM 51/3399, ADM 51/3215. Captain William M'Culloch, who was employed in HMS *Gannymede,* 20, on preventive work, had formed the Coast Blockade (see p. 10, n. 3 below) in 1816 initially with 92 officers and men. These were so successful that he was transferred to HMS *Severn,* 40, on 20 May 1817, with 1200 officers and men. The members of the Coast Blockade were borne as supernumeraries and

He then went on half pay and applied for leave of absence to reside in France, 18 December 1825,[1] and lived in Honfleur, Normandy, probably until the end of 1830. Poynter applied for a post in the Coast Guard[2] and, on 22 April 1831, was appointed chief officer at Pelter Brig (Dover, Folkstone district).[3] In June 1836 he was moved to Cushendun (Coleraine) in Ireland, and was moved again next month to Portrush, where he served from 9 July 1836 until 13 March 1840. He

employed as shore patrols. Their duties were to catch the smugglers as they came ashore with contraband: Webb, 1976, pp. 18–20. Captain M'Culloch transferred his headquarters to HMS *Ramillies,* on 31 May 1823, and by the time Poynter joined, as a supernumerary lieutenant for the Coast Blockade, he was employing about 100 lieutenants on that duty. HMS *Hyperion* joined the force early in 1825 and in the subsequent reorganization Poynter was transferred: *Navy Lists.* PRO ADM 12/224 digest 95.1 under 27 August 1824, describes a letter from the Master Gunner at Newhaven which refers to Poynter as the 'officer in charge of the Coast Stockade occupying quarters in the Battery', and ADM 1/2195 contains a letter from Poynter, dated 24 August 1825, at Cuckmere, requesting that he be superseded from the Coast Blockade 'family affairs making it necessary I should be immediately removed.'

[1] PRO ADM 1/3083. Letter dated 18 December 1825 from No 10 Lyons Inn: 'I have to request you will be pleased to move their Lordships to grant me Twelve Months leave of absence to reside in France.' This letter is minuted 'To have leave of absence' with the date of 21 December 1825. Poynter's last application, 'for a renewal of my Twelve Months leave of absence' was dated 16 December 1829 (PRO ADM 1/3086), no applications to extend the period overseas between these two letters appear to have survived, but since the last request was for a renewal they had presumably been made and granted). Poynter was in Deal in February 1831 (note 2 below), it would therefore seem probable that he returned to England at the end of 1830.

[2] Application for an appointment to the 'Coast Guard Preventive Service: or any other that My Lords Commissioners of the Admiralty may think fit,' sent from Deal on 20 February 1831. He was nominated on 18 April 1831 for the Coast Guard. PRO ADM 1/3086, ADM 175/5.

[3] The principal function of the Coast Guard when it was set up was the prevention of smuggling. This had been a problem since the first imposition of duty on imported goods in Saxon times, although the worst period was in the eighteenth and first half of the nineteenth centuries. A parliamentary report at the end of the eighteenth century estimated that 50% of the spirits drunk in the country had been smuggled. Furthermore, during the Napoleonic wars, smugglers did inestimable damage carrying spies, information and escaped prisoners: Webb, 1976, pp. 3–4.

Various organizations had been set up to combat the problem. In the early nineteenth century these consisted of Riding Officers (set up 1698), Preventive Water Guard (1809) and Coast Blockade (1816); Revenue Cruisers under the Admiralty, Cruisers under the Revenue Boards and a number of HM ships were also employed. A report to the Prince Regent, in 1820, gave these a total of 6708 men at a cost of over £520,000. In 1822 these, with the exception of the Coast Blockade, were amalgamated to form the Coast Guard under the Board of Customs. The Comptroller General and all the officers were nominated by the Admiralty. The first Comptroller General, who served from 8 July, 1822, until 23 November, 1841, was Captain William Bowles, Royal Navy (recently returned from his appointment as Commodore of the South America Squadron). Prize money was payable on seizures.

A major review of the Coast Guard was carried out in 1831. The Coast Blockade was subsumed and the Coast Guard became, in addition to its other functions (which by now included life-saving and management of wrecks), a reserve for the Royal Navy. Service was made to equate with service in the Royal Navy (time in Revenue vessels counted as sea time for pension, shore service in

then moved to Sennen Cove, Cornwall, until 22 March 1844 when he was appointed in command of the Revenue Vessel *Sylvia*. He joined her on 6 April 1844, and left on 30 April 1847, transferring to *Harpy*, 6, 138 tons, another Revenue vessel, which he joined the following day, and remained in her until 4 December 1848.[1] He then returned to be chief officer at Sennen Cove again until removing to Mothecombe, Devon, on 4 May 1850, where he continued until 10 January 1854. He was then promoted inspecting lieutenant at Patrington, Yorkshire, where he remained until his retirement on 3 November 1860[2] (under Order in Council dated 1 August 1860, which provided that 'Lieutenants on the Active List, who have attained or who may hereafter attain the age of 60, to be placed on the Retired List with the Rank of Retired Commander…')[3] as retired commander with seniority 1 October 1860. On his retirement he was relieved in the post at Patrington by Lieutenant Auchmuty T. Freese who had arrived early the previous month from a similar position at Burghead.

He lived with Harriette Sophia Desmond in Honfleur[4] and then married

---

the Coast Guard counted as one third sea time: Order in Council dated 1 August 1860: *Navy List 1866,* p. 317.

By 1839 there were 4553 officers and men employed in the Coast Guard at a charge of £528,387 (a very similar figure to that in the 1820 report). The coast of England was divided into 37 districts, Scotland 10 and Ireland 28. Each district was under an Inspecting Officer, normally a naval commander, and divided into stations. These were under the command of a Chief Officer, normally a naval lieutenant, whose principal duty was organizing the patrolling and guarding of the coast by night: he also had control of boats for offshore work. In addition there were 49 cruisers and 21 tenders attached to the various Divisions under the control of their respective Inspecting Officers.

After the Crimean War, in which some 3000 Coast Guards served as reserves in the fleet, a further review was carried out. The principal role of the Coast Guard now changed from combatting smuggling to that of a reserve for the navy. In order that it could fulfill this function properly it was placed under the full control of the Admiralty on 1 October 1856, (where it remained until 1 April 1923). However, the reorganization of the districts, and other major changes which resulted, would appear not to have been fully implemented before Poynter retired: Webb, 1976, pp. 14–37.

[1] Dates of arrival and departure from these ships are taken from their respective Muster Lists in PRO ADM 119/127 & 119/53, which do not agree with other records, but since they were kept on board would seem likely to be the most accurate.

[2] Poynter's Service Record, PRO ADM 196/2, starts his service with the Coast Guard on 18 April 1831 (the date of his nomination) and shows it as continuous, including his time in *Sylvia* and *Harpy*, until 8 November 1860.

[3] *Navy List*, 1866, pp. 317 and 436.

[4] James Methurst Poynter's will has a codicil dated 15 June 1830, which reads 'As I consider that my son Charles Wittit Poynter has already received a larger proportion of my property than either of my other children and I think it would be unjust that they should suffer by his Imprudence and Misconduct I make this codicil to my will (which is dated 25 August 1819)' and directs that, on the death of his wife, £300 be deducted from his estate and divided £100 each to his other three children to make their shares equate with that of Charles. I am indebted to Mr Derek Leask for this

Louisa, daughter of John Illenden, Esq, at Dover, on 8 August, 1835,[1] and had a large family,[2] dying at Sydenham in Kent, 21 December, 1878. Louisa moved to Teignmouth and died at her daughter's home in Mutley, Plymouth on 11 August 1885.[3]

Assistant Surgeon Adam G. Young

Dr Adam Young was an experienced assistant surgeon whose seniority was 26 May 1810. He served in HMS *Undaunted*, 38, until 14 November 1815, principally on the Mediterranean station and then in HMS *Slaney*, 20, Captain D. H. O'Brien, from 11 September 1818, until she paid off, 12 June 1822. He was then on half pay and in November 1825 was granted six months sick leave due to ill health. This was extended as a result of numerous certificates for a number of years and he finally died, 24 September 1834, without going to sea again.[4]

---

information (letter March 1998). From this it would appear possible that this liaison may not have been regularized and was regarded as misconduct by his family and that he was given £100 and packed off to Honfleur to hide the family shame. A search of the Canterbury diocesan records shows that no marriage licence was issued and although it may be that bans were read they were not read at St Leonard's Church in Deal, which was his parents' parish church. On the marriage licence (dated 7 August 1835 recorded in the Canterbury diocesan records) for his marriage to Louisa Illenden, Poynter is described as 'bachelor'. While none of this is conclusive, it is suggestive and would tend to confirm the hypothesis offered above.

[1] O'Byrne, 1849, p. 920 and Poynter's formula (BL ADD MS 38050) have 1833, but the date in the parish records, and on the Diocesan licence is 1835 (see note above).

[2] Mr Derek Leask (letters January to May 1998), has located evidence of sixteen children. The details are from records of varying authority – mainly official registrations (England, France and Australia) and censuses. The eldest son, Charles James was born in East Dean (Sussex) in June or July 1825 and died in Honfleur 7 May 1826. A second Charles J. was born in France in about 1828; Henry Benjamin and Horatio Francis (Horace) were both born in Honfleur in 1829 and 1830 respectively. Tempest March William was born about 1834 (according to his age in the census records, the Merchant seamen registrations, PRO BT 113/253, has 5 March 1836) and Fanny Eliza Jane in Folkestone about 1836. The family was in Portrush, Ireland, from 1836 to 1840, where two sons, William M. and George W. were born in about 1838 and 1839, and then at Sennen Cove 1840 to 1844, where James Gordon and Albert Trembath were born in 1840 and 1842. With Poynter's move to the Revenue cruisers the family appears to have moved to Paul, near Newlyn, where Louisa Charlotte and Eliza Ann (Elise) were born in 1844 and 1846. Poynter was again at Sennen Cove from 1848 to 1850, but the next known children were born at Mothercombe in Devon, where he served from 1850 to 1854 – Anna Emily Flora in 1850 and Edith Decima in 1853. Edmund Frederick and their last known child, Helen Sophia Laura, were born at Patrington in 1854 and 1857.

[3] O'Byrne, 1849, p. 920; Jones and Chisholm, 1998; PRO ADM 107/74, ADM 175/5, ADM 175/6, ADM 175/7, ADM 175/17, ADM 175/18; House of Commons Sessional Papers, 1857, XXVII 253; *Navy Lists*; BL ADD MS 38050.

[4] PRO ADM 104/20, ADM 104/33.

Captain W. H. Shirreff, Royal Navy

William Henry Shirreff was born in 1785, the only son of General Shirreff. He entered the Navy as first-class volunteer 1 January 1796 on board HMS *La Juste*, 80, Captain The Hon. Thomas Packenham. He continued on the Home station in various ships until wrecked in Vigo Bay 6 September 1800. He remained at sea on the East Indies and Irish stations and was promoted lieutenant 3 March 1804. In March 1805 he was in HMS *Circe*, 32, taking despatches to the fleet off Cape St Vincent when they captured a Spanish privateer, *La Fama*. He was given charge of this vessel and sent to the West Indies with despatches, but was caught and captured by the French. On his release he was promoted commander and appointed to HMS *Lily*, 18, sloop, 5 March 1806. He remained on the West Indies station and saw action at the reduction of the island of Deseada. He was promoted to post rank 15 November 1809, and continued to serve at sea until invalided in July 1814. He was appointed to HMS *Andromache*, 44, 10 September 1817, and served in her on South America station until September 1821. He had a number of further appointments before becoming Captain-Superintendent of the Victualling and Dockyards at Deptford and Chatham in March 1838. He was promoted rear admiral 9 November 1846 and became Admiral Superintendent at Portsmouth 24 August 1847 where he died on 1 December that same year.[1]

J. Miers

John Miers, the son of a London jeweller, was born on 25 August, 1789. His early life was spent working with his father and following various scientific pursuits. In 1818 Lord Cochrane, who was preparing to assist the South American republics in their struggle for independence, invited Miers to join him in a copper-refining venture in Chile. He reached Buenos Aires in March 1819 and proceeded to Valparaíso where he selected a site for his operations at Concón, which the Chilean government undertook to purchase on his behalf. He hired Captain Smith, in the brig *Williams* to carry his equipment to Concón and it was at this stage that Captain Shirreff, with Miers's agreement, hired the vessel and her master for the exploration of the South Shetland Islands, and Miers wrote his article for the *Edinburgh Philosophical Journal* (pp. 48–61).

Miers's operations were beset with troubles from the start. Although he had the support of the Supreme Director, Don Bernardo O'Higgins (who resigned in 1823), endless difficulties were placed in his way by the authorities. The owner of the land on which he had established himself changed her mind and refused to sell; an earthquake in 1822 destroyed most of Valparaíso and did considerable

---

[1] O'Byrne, 1849, pp. 1064–5.

damage to his works, as well as setting back the legal problem of the ownership of the land. Ultimately, six years later and considerably worse off ('I invested in machinery and implements no less a sum than 40,000 dollars, besides an equal sum which I expended in forming my establishments in Chile'), due to the 'impediments that naturally exist in the country, together with the absurd obstacles opposed by the general and local authorities, as well as by the obstinate jealousies of the natives', Miers gave up the struggle and left Chile.[1]

After his Chilean experiences Miers agreed to set up a mint in Buenos Aires, which he did in 1826, moving to Rio de Janeiro in 1831 for a similar operation before returning to England in 1838. For his services to Brazil the emperor decorated him first with the Cross and then the Grand Cross of the Order of the Rose. During his stay in South America he spent a lot of time making observations on geological structures and earthquakes, as well as collecting specimens of animals and insects, but his principal interest was botany. On his return to England he devoted himself to his scientific interests. In 1839 he became a Fellow of the Linnaean Society and in 1841 a Fellow of the Royal Society. When he died, in his ninety-first year, on 17 October, 1879, he had published nearly eighty papers on South American plants and left an herbarium of more than 20,000 sheets to the British Museum.[2]

---

[1] Miers, 1826, II, pp. 276–87.
[2] Miers, 1826, *passim*; Carruthers, 1880.

CHAPTER 1

ANTARCTIC BACKGROUND

The ancient Greeks could look up and see the bright stars circling in the sky. The constellation rotating round the axis, which never set, they called *Arctos* – the Bear – and the point round which it circled the Arctic Pole. Aristotle demonstrated that the world was spherical. Eratosthenes (about 250 BC) measured the size of the earth[1] with surprising accuracy and it was immediately apparent that the known world actually took up a very small part of the whole. Symmetry required that the land mass to the north be balanced by a land mass to the south and the concept of an Antarctic continent came into being. By no means everyone believed the earth was spherical but the majority did believe in an impassable zone, due to the heat in the tropics, to the south of them, and so the Antarctic was unattainable – if it did indeed exist. Ptolemy (ca. AD 90–168) placed Terra Incognita across the bottom of his world, joining Africa round the Indian ocean to Asia.

In due course the theory of the impassable zone was disproved,[2] for in 1487 Bartholomew Diaz crossed it and returned to tell the story. Ten years later Vasco da Gama sailed round Africa to India, proving that if Terra Incognita did exist it was not connected to Africa. Columbus sailed for America in 1492 and in 1521 Magellan sailed round the southern extremity of the mainland, through the strait that

---

[1] Eratosthenes, knowing that at the summer solstice the sun passed directly overhead at Syene, measured its elevation at Alexandria using a vertical gnomon, and the distance between the two places in stades. Then assuming the sun's rays at both places to be parallel, the difference in angle, 7°12′, represented the same angle at the earth's centre, and since its length on the surface was known, simple multiplication provided the circumference of the earth.

[2] Although this was a general belief it had apparently been demonstrated incorrect long before. Herodotus (ca. 489–425 BC) states that on the orders of Nechos, king of Egypt, 609–594 BC, Africa was circumnavigated. A Phoenician expedition sailed from the Red Sea into the Indian Ocean, landing every autumn to sow crops. The sailors then waited and, having harvested the crops, put to sea again. During the third year they entered the Mediterranean through the Pillars of Heracles, and returned to Egypt. Herodotus says that they made a statement, which he himself did not believe, though others might, that as they sailed on a westerly course round the southern end of Africa, they had the sun on their right hand – i.e. to the northward of them: Herodotus, *The Histories,* 4.42.

now bears his name, showing that it was not connected to Terra Incognita either. Maps of the period, however, continued to show it connected to Tierra del Fuego.

Francis Drake sailed round the world in 1577–80 in the *Pelican*, later renamed the *Golden Hind* (100 tons). He started in company with the *Elizabeth* (80 tons), John Winter, and the *Marigold* (30 tons), John Thomas, with two other vessels. They passed through the Strait of Magellan (Estrecho de Magallanes) and were then driven southwards by a terrible storm in which the *Marigold* was lost with all hands and the *Elizabeth*, having been separated from Drake, returned home. Drake found an anchorage in 57°S (which later gave rise to 'Drake's Harbour' which appeared on a number of eighteenth-century charts in about 67°S).[1] They also recorded that 'The uttermost cape or hedland of all these Ilands, stands neere in 56 deg. without which there is no maine, nor Iland to be seene to the Southwards: but that the Atlanticke Ocean, and the South Sea, meete in a most large and free scope.'[2] Modern determination puts Cape Horn (Cabo de Hornos) in 55°59'S, 67°16'W and the waters between South America and Antarctica are now known as Drake Passage.[3]

[1] De Lisle, *Hemisphere Meridional pour voir plus distinctment les Terres Australe*, Paris, 1714. P. Buache, *Carte des Terres Australes comprises entre le Tropique du Capricorne et le Pole Antarctique*, Paris, 1736.

[2] Drake, 1628 (reprinted 1966), p. 44. It was accepted in the nineteenth century that Drake discovered Cape Horn. This view has been queried, however, and while it is unlikely ever to be positively confirmed, it seems likely that it was indeed Cape Horn where this incident took place. See Aker, 1998.

[3] There are three accounts of the voyage in Hakluyt, 1598–1600, III. The first, p. 734, reads:

The 6. day of September we entred the South sea [Pacific Ocean] at the Cape or head shore.

The seventh day wee were driven by a great storme from the entring into the South sea two hundred leagues and odde in longitude, and one degree to the Southward of the Streight: in which height and so many leagues to the Westward, the fifteenth day of September fell out the Eclipse of the Moone at the houre of five of the clocke at night: but neither did the Eclipticall conflict of the Moone impayre our state, nor her clearing againe amend us a whit, but the accustomed Eclipse of the Sea continued in his force, wee being darkened more then the Moone seven fold.

From the Bay (which we called The Bay of severing of friends) wee were driven backe to the Southward of the streights in 57 degrees and a terce: in which height we came to an anker among the Islands, having there fresh and very good water, with herbes of singular vertue. Not farre from hence we entred another Bay, where wee found people both men and women in their Canoas, naked, and ranging from one Island to another to seeke their meat, who entred traffique with us for such things as they had.

We returning hence Northward againe, found the 3. of October three Islands, in one of which was such plentie of birdes as is scant credible to report.

The 8. day of October we lost sight of one of our Consotrs [*sic*] wherein M. Winter was, who as then we supposed was put by a storme into the streights againe, which at our returne home wee found to be true, and he not perished, as some of our company feared.

The other accounts are by Nuño da Silva (pp. 742–8) who was left 'in the Bay where they wintered before they entred the Streights' and so was not actually present although his account covers

In 1598 five ships sailed from Holland for the East Indies, through the Strait of Magellan, under the command of Jacob Mahu who died on 23 September 1598. In the subsequent reorganization of the command structure Dirck Gherritz (Dirck Gerritsz, Theodore Gerrards) became commander of *De Blijde Bootschap*, a yacht of 150 tons with a crew of 56 men. The expedition wintered in Cordes Bay (Calleta Gallant) where they suffered great hardship (120 men died), and sailed on 23 August 1599. In September *De Blijde Bootschap* damaged her foremast and became separated from the fleet in a fog. It was subsequently stated that she 'was carried by tempestuous weather to the South of the *Strait* to 64°S latitude, where they discovered a high country, with mountains, which were covered with snow like the *land of Norway*. Gherritz afterwards sailed to the coast of *Chili*, in hopes that he should there rejoin some of the fleet, but he missed the *Island Santa Maria* (which had been appointed as a rendezvous), and was taken by the Spaniards at *Valparaiso*'.[1] Although modern scholarship has shown that in fact Gherritz never went south of 60°S, one of his shipmates, Laurens Claess, did indeed go to 64°S on a different voyage without sighting land.[2] The story of

the storm, and Edward Cliffe (pp. 748–53), mariner in the *Elizabeth*. Neither differs in any essential from the first and both give the greatest latitude reached as 57°S.

Drake, 1628, (title page), states that it was 'carefully collected out of the notes of Master Francis Fletcher, Preacher in this imployment, and divers others his followers in the same'. It tells a slightly different story, but is similar in the essential points and again, at p. 40, records 57° as the furthest south.

[1] Burney, 1803–17, II (1806), p. 198. The sentence dealing with the discovery in 64°S was taken from *Recueil des navigations de l'Estroit de Magellan*, Amsterdam, 1622.

[2] The following remarks on this, and similar statements in other volumes of voyages of the period, are based on Balch, 1902, pp. 40–51. The earliest accounts of this voyage written by Barent Jansz and Van Noort make no mention of this discovery. It is first mentioned in 1622, in *Novus orbis, sive descriptio Indiae Occidentalis*, by Antonio de Herrera, which had been translated from the Spanish by Caspar Barlaeus and was published together with French and Dutch versions in Amsterdam. Folio 80 reads: 'Liburnica que Theodorum Gerardi vehebat, tempestatum vi versus Austrum propulsa fuit ad gradus usque 64. in qua altitudine posita ad Australem plagam solum monto sum & nivibus opertum eminus conspexit, qualis Norvvegiae esse solet facies. Versus insulas Salomonis exporrigi videbatur'. The passage does not appear to have been in the original Spanish version. Based on this it was generally believed, and recounted in most collections of voyages until the end of the nineteenth century, that Gherritz had discovered land south of Cape Horn. Bruce, 1894, p. 58, mentions it, as does Fricker, 1900, p. 22, adding that Gerritz had transmitted the information to Van Noort in a letter. Fricker uses the name Dirk Gerritz Archipelago to refer to the land separated from the South Shetland Islands by Bransfield Strait.

A manuscript at the Hague, *Instructien en Journaalen van Brasiliaansche en Oostindische Rysen. Zaedert 21 April 1623 tot 28 Augustus 1681, behoorende tot het archief der Westindische Compagnie*, contains *Bijlagen tot de Instructie voor Jacques l'Hermijte* in which are a declaration by Jacob Dircxz, and a statement by Laurens Claess, boatswain of *De Blijde Bootschap*. The former states that it was made by Jacob Dircxz, aged 30 years, of Purmerlant, gunner and finally under-pilot of *Vliegende Hart* (the name given to *De Blijde Bootschap* before her arrival at Valparaíso), on 17th March 1603. It reads:

On the 4th of September 1599, they ran out of the Strait of Magalhaês into the South Sea,

Gherritz's discovery was generally accepted until the end of the nineteenth century and was quoted by Edmund Fanning[1] when he gave the *Hersilia* her instructions (pp. 187–8).

In 1616 Schouten and Le Maire rounded the southern tip of South America, passing through the strait between Staten Island (Isla de los Estados) and Tierra del Fuego, which they named the Strait of Le Maire (Estrecho de Le Maire), and round Cape Horn (Cabo de Hornos) which they named for their home port. They were driven south by a storm and recorded 'The 3, [February 1616] wee were under 59 degrees 25 minutes, with indifferent weather, and a hard west winde, and guessed that we were that day under 59 degrees and a halfe, but saw no lande, nor any signe thereof in the South.'[2]

Tierra del Fuego was definitely cut off from Terra Incognita, which now could reach only to Staten Island. In 1643 Hendrik Brouwer, one of the directors of the Dutch West India Company, rounding South America on passage to Chile arrived at the Strait of Le Maire on 5th March. 'It happening to be a very clear day, we had the satisfaction to behold, that this *Staaten Land*, which hitherto has always been taken for a part of the continent, was an island of about nine or ten leagues long … we were forced to change our course on 9th of March, and resolved to sail round the said island'[3] – which they did. Again in 1680 Bartholomew Sharp sailing from the Pacific sailed round South America in 60°S without passing through the Strait of Le Maire.[4] Terra Incognita was thus finally cut off from South America.

on the third day thereafter they were separated by a great storm from the other ships, came three times to within 50°, and were driven twice to 55° and once to 56°. From there they came to the Island of Chiloe in 44 degrees, and then came to the Island of St Maria, which is situated at the heighth of 37 degrees.
The other document states:
   Laurens Claess of Antwerp, aged about 40 years, has served as boatswain on the Magalhaês ship, called *De Blijde Bootschap*, which sailed with other ships from the harbour of Goree on Saint Johns day of the year 1598 under Admiral Mahu, has served under the Admiral Don Gabriel de Castiglio with three ships along the coast of Chili towards Valparaiso, and from there towards the Strait, and that in the year 1603, and he went to 64 degrees where they had much snow, in the following month of April they returned to the coast of Chili… (translations from Balch, 1902, pp. 47–50.)
Neither of these accounts mentions sighting land, which would seem to mean that while it is possible that the statement added to the history in 1622 refers to an actual voyage, it cannot be attributed to Dirck Gherritz in *De Blijde Bootschap*. Mill, 1905, has suggested that in fact an error was introduced by Caspar Barlaeus when he translated Herrera's work in 1622 and that the reference is actually to Laurens Claess who did indeed go to 64°S on a different occasion without seeing land.
   [1] Fanning, 1834, p. 428.
   [2] Schouten, 1619 (reprinted 1966), p. 24.
   [3] Callander, 1768, II, p. 382.
   [4] Callander, 1768, II, p. 525. Captain Bartholomew Sharp (Sharp's Journal) 'On the 12th we killed two fishes, or two birds, with the harpoon, for they were formed like the one and the other,

The southern land continued to appear on globes and maps under various names such as 'Terra Australis Nondum Cognita' and 'Terra Australis Incognita' in varying shapes joined to varying known land masses. As late as 1763, Buache, of Paris, showed 'Terres Antarctiques' as two land masses which included the then known coast of New Zealand.[1]

Alexander Dalrymple, 1770, strongly asserted the existence of 'Terra Australis Incognita' and recommended a renewed search for it,[2] which was taken up by the Royal Society. He also published a chart of the Southern Ocean which showed

with two fins, like a tortise before, and the rest of the body shaped like a bird. Five days after, we saw two large islands of ice, which stood far above the water, and were two leagues in circumference.' There is no mention of sighting land.

[1] Buache, 1763.

[2] Dalrymple, 1770–71. This includes accounts of the earlier voyages, e.g. Juan Fernandez, of whom he said 'Juan Fernandez is better known by the islands to which he gave his name in 1572, than by the more important discovery he made of the SOUTHERN CONTINENT.'
In about 1576 he sailed:

from the coast of Chili about the latitude of 40 deg. little more or less, in a small ship, with some of his companions, in courses between W. and S.W. was brought in a month's time to a coast, from what he could judge of the *continent*, very fertile and agreeable, inhabited with white people, mighty well disposed, of our stature, cloathed with very fine cloths and so peaceable and civil, that in every manner they could express, they offered every thing in their power, and of the riches and fruits of their country, which appeared very rich and plentiful...
He returned to Chili, intending to go back properly fitted, and to keep it a secret till they and their friends could return on the discovery. It was delayed from day to day, till Juan Fernandez died, when, with his death, this matter, so important, sunk into oblivion. (I, p. 53)
The ORANGE, one of the Nassau Fleet 1624; When this ship arrived at JUAN FERNANDEZ, it was reported they had twice seen the *southern continent*; once in 50°S, and again in the latitude of 41°S.
The German relation, folio 1630, says, they lost by tempests two sails in 50°. and in 40°.S; but it does not mention a word of land. De Bry seems to be an exact translation of the German; however, the original journal, printed in Dutch, 4to. 1646, says, that after parting with the fleet, "the ORANGE lost two sails by tempests, and twice saw the continent; once in 50°.S, and again in 41°.S." (II, p. 121).
The final section is titled 'Conduct of the Discoverers in the track they made choice of' and pagination starts again and runs to p. 20. The last part of this is headed 'INVESTIGATION of what may be farther expected in the SOUTH SEA'. It contains a philosophical argument why the Southern Continent must exist based on proportion of land to water being similar in both hemispheres:

What has been said will naturally induce conviction, that from the tropick to 50°.S latitude there are extensive countries; and, from a view of the globe, it will naturally occur, that the most probable situations, in which those lands may be expected to approach nearest the equator, are not where the AMERICAN and AFRICAN continents project farthest into the southern hemisphere; but in the intermediate spaces between the CAPE OF GOOD HOPE and AMERICA, and to the westward of the last, between it and PAPUA. (II, final section pp. 14–15.)
It is not a necessary consequence that there must be an *exact* proportion of land in the two hemispheres; the different degrees of density may compensate for a deficiency of surface; but

to the east of the tip of South America a large tract of land surrounding Golfo de San Sebastiano,[1] taken from 'Ortelius's map, 1586',[2] which had been shown earlier on Mercator's world map of 1569.[3]

The instructions given to Captain Cook for his second voyage in 1772 ordered him to 'endeavour to fall in with Cape Circumcision,' discovered by Monsr Bouvet,[4] and ascertain if it was part of the 'Southern Continent which has so

there is ground for a probable conjecture, that the quantity of land in the two hemispheres is *nearly* equal. (II, final section p. 16.)

This is followed by a discussion of the winds ending: 'If there is no *Continent*, or extensive range of land in the SOUTH PACIFIC OCEAN, there can be no variability of the wind, but a constant SE and ESE *trade-wind* must prevail the whole year. If this *trade-wind* is not constant, there must, undoubtedly, be *land*.' (II, final section p. 17.)

Then came a new line of argument:

But at the same time it would be improper to omit entirely the argument of a *Continent* to the *south*, from the *fair-haired people* found in the islands, because nothing appears to be a more conclusive proof of the existence of the *Continent* than this fact, which is entirely contrary to the common circumstances within the tropic, but absolutely confirmed by the late voyages in this quarter. (II, final section, p. 19.)

The chapter concludes with a review of the voyages of Juan Fernandez, Gerrards (see p. 17, n. 2 above), the *Orange*, and other vessels which saw signs of land, which are covered in earlier sections, concluding:

It cannot be doubted from so many concurrent testimonies, that the SOUTHERN CONTINENT has been already *discovered* on the east side; and it appears more than probable, that TASMAN'S discovery, which he named STAAT'S LAND, but that is in the maps called NEW ZEALAND, is the *western* coast of this *Continent*.

The *north* coast of this *vast Continent* appears to be hitherto undiscovered; for although ROGGEWEIN for a space of 12°. of longitude, in the latitude of 28°.S, had *signs of land*, as *teal* and other *land birds* &c. and QUIROS also *signs* of the *Continent* farther to the *westward* in 26°.S, we have no relation of anyone having *seen* it.

Although the *signs of land* seen by ROGGEWEIN, previous to the *discovery* of EASTER ISLAND, denote the vicinity of the *Continent*, it is from his description of *that* island we are enabled to form some idea of the adjacent *Continent*; no voyage hitherto performed, points out so strongly the *original* of the PERUVIAN manners and religion. (II, final section, p. 20.)

[1] This was the chart a portion of which John Miers used to illustrate his article in the *Edinburgh Philosophical Journal*, see p. 52 (Plate 5). It is illustrated in David, 1992, p. xxxvii.

[2] Dalrymple, 1769, p. 5. Abraham Ortelius (1527–98) first published his atlas *Theatrum orbis terrarum* in May 1570. It ran through over forty editions to 1612, but there does not appear to have been one in 1586. This gulf is shown in the first and subsequent editions.

[3] See p. 55, n. 2, and p. 56, n. 1.

[4] Jean-Baptiste Charles Bouvet de Lozier sailed with M. Hays in *Aigle* and *Marie* in 1738 on a voyage of discovery, sponsored by the Compagnie des Indes Orientales, to find the land reported by de Gonneville in 1503–5 (now thought to be part of South America). On 1 January 1739 he discovered land which was named Cape Circumcision but, due to fog, could not tell if it was an island or part of the Southern Continent. It is now know to be an island and named Bouvetøya (Bouvet Island). His position was not good and the island was not sighted again until 1808: Burney, 1803–17, V (1817), pp. 30–37.

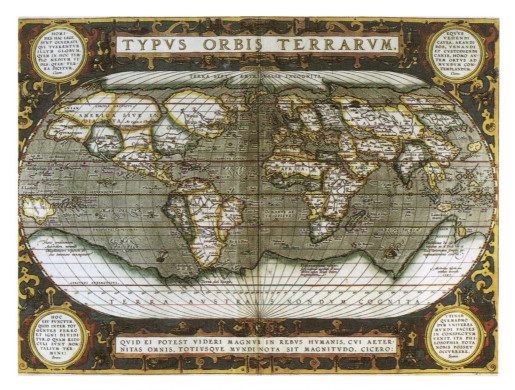

Plate 2. World map and map of the Americas from Ortelius, *Theatrum orbis terrarum*, 1606 edition. Admiralty Library, Taunton.

21

much engaged the attention of Geographers & former Navigators' or an island, and then in the event that it was an island, having surveyed it, proceed southward:

> as long as you judge there may be a likelyhood of falling in with the Continent ... then proceed to the Eastward, in further search of the said Continent ... keeping in as High Latitudes as you can & prosecuting your discoveries as before directed as near to the Pole as possible, until by circumnavigating the Globe you fall in again with Cape Circumcision.[1]

On completion of this mammoth task Cook was able to write:

> I had now made a circuit of the Southern Ocean in a high latitude, and traversed it in such a manner as to leave not the least room for the possibility of there being a continent, unless near the pole, and out of the reach of navigation ... That there may be a continent, or large tract of land, near the pole, I will not deny; on the contrary, I am of the opinion there is; and it is probable that we have seen part of it.'[2]

The land Cook had seen, 'which I named Sandwich Land was either a group of islands, or else a point of the continent'. The southern extremity of this land he named Southern Thule.

South Georgia had been sighted by Antoine de la Roché, a British merchant, in 1675,[3] and again by Gregorio Jerez in 1756, both of whom had been blown off course, and neither of whom landed. The latter called the island Île de St Pierre his ship having sighted it on 29 June, the feast day of Saint Peter. Captain Cook visited the island in January 1775, and having landed and taken possession, named it Isle of Georgia, in honour of King George III.[4]

Two French naval expeditions sailed under Yves-Joseph de Kerguelen-Trémarec in 1771 and 1773 to search for the continent, and discovered the islands which now bear his name. Another under Marc-Joseph Marion Dufresne in 1771 rediscovered Prince Edward Islands[5] and discovered Îles Crozet. Captain Cook carried out a third voyage during which he visited the earlier French discoveries. Apart from this there were no major expeditions to southern waters until the

---

[1] Beaglehole, 1961, pp. clxvii–clxix.

[2] Cook, 1777, II, p. 239.

[3] At one time it was supposed that Amerigo Vespucci had sighted South Georgia on his third voyage in 1501. This was based on letters allegedly written by him to Piero Soderini, Gonfalonier of the Republic of Florence (the house of Medici had been banished from Florence on the advent of Charles VIII on his passage through Italy to Naples, on 9 November 1494, and did not return until 1512, when Soderini was banished in his turn) and to Lorenzo di Piero Francesco de' Medici (who changed his name to Popolano for a time and escaped banishment). Historical research summed up by Christie, 1950, p. 563, has shown that, while expert opinion is not entirely in agreement on all aspects of this voyage, it is unanimous in ruling out the sighting of South Georgia.

[4] Cook, 1777, II, p. 218.

[5] Possibly discovered in 1663 by Barend Barendzoon Lam on a voyage from Cape of Good Hope to Batavia and named Maerseveen Island: Headland, 1989, p. 64.

Russian expedition under Thaddeus Bellingshausen (Faddei Faddeevich Belins-
gauzen), (1778–1852) in 1819–21.

Whalers from New England visited the Falkland Islands in 1774 and the next
year British whalers also went south. Subsequent reports from Captain Cook's
voyages led to the development of sealing and whaling operations on and in the
vicinity of the sub-Antarctic islands. Vessels sailed from Britain, America, France
and later on New South Wales for Tierra del Fuego, the Falkland Islands and
South Georgia as well as Île Saint Paul, Îles Kerguelen, Île Amsterdam and after
1803, when they were re-discovered by the sealers, for Îles Crozet. By 1801 fur
seals were reported to be very rare on South Georgia. Activity shifted to Foveaux
Strait and Stewart Islands in 1804 and increased when Macquarie and Campbell
Islands were discovered in 1810. On a number of occasions teams had to be left
behind on the islands to collect skins for recovery at a later date,[1] nevertheless by
1819 the numbers of seals had been so reduced that new locations were essential
if the operations were to continue to be commercially viable. The discovery of
the South Shetland Islands therefore came at a particularly opportune time.

---

[1] Headland, 1989, pp. 28–9, and chronological list of sealing voyages to 1820.

CHAPTER 2

SOUTH AMERICAN BACKGROUND

Spanish American Colonies

By the end of the sixteenth century the Viceroyalty of Peru included virtually all of South America with the exception of Brazil and Venezuela. The capital was Lima, through which all legitimate trade had to pass. When the Bourbons replaced the Hapsburgs in 1700 they started reforming the system. A Viceroyalty of New Granada, embracing the north of South America, was established and in 1777–8 the Viceroyalty of Río de la Plata covering Upper Peru and the countries now know as Argentina, Paraguay and Uruguay followed. Chile became an autonomous Captaincy General.

In 1804 Napoleon was declared Emperor of the French. Cape Colony, at the southern tip of Africa, which had been taken from the Dutch by the British, had been returned to them under the terms of the Treaty of Amiens, 1802. However, with Napoleon's occupation of the Low Countries, it became a part of the French empire and consequently a threat to British communications with India and the Far East. Commodore Sir Home Popham was therefore despatched to recapture it, which he did. Spain was at this time allied to France and the news of the defeat of their combined fleets at Trafalgar arrived on 9 January 1806, soon after the recapture of Cape Colony. Instead of keeping part of his force at the Cape to make sure France could not retake it and send the remainder on to India, as he had been instructed to do, the commodore, with General William Beresford and the 71st Highlanders sailed for Buenos Aires, then under Spanish rule, which they captured on 25 June, with a force of a little over 1600 men. It was lost again, on 12 August, to a small Spanish force assisted by local troops who, while they might have supported the British bringing them independence, were not prepared to exchange the Spanish for another foreign yoke.[1] Subsequently Montevideo was captured by a relieving force sent out from England which attempted to

---

[1] Commodore Sir Riggs Home Popham (1762–1820) was recalled and court-martialled at Portsmouth on board HMS *Gladiator*. He was charged with leaving the Cape in a defenceless state and undertaking an expedition to the Río de la Plata without authority, found guilty on both counts and 'Severely Reprimanded'. This would, under normal circumstances, have been the end of his

retake Buenos Aires in July 1807, but failed, and by their terms of surrender agreed to evacuate Montevideo as well.

Napoleon's establishment of Joseph Bonaparte on the Spanish throne, on 6 June 1808, left the Spanish American colonies on their own. Peru remained loyal to Ferdinand VII. But, with the example of the French Revolution and the ease with which the Spanish and then the British had been defeated in Buenos Aires, the local aristocracies in Río de la Plata, and then Chile, set up their own patriotic governments, initially in the name of Ferdinand VII, but which were subsequently to become independent states.

On 25 May 1810, the *Cabildo abierto*[1] in Buenos Aires set up an autonomous government to administer the Viceroyalty. However, when Ferdinand VII was returned to the throne of Spain, an assembly in San Miguel de Tucumán on 9 July 1816 declared the country independent as the United Provinces of Río de la Plata. In Chile a *Cabildo abierto* in Santiago, on 18 September 1810, accepted the resignation of the Captain General and appointed a junta of local leaders to rule in the name of Ferdinand VII. These were at odds with each other and in 1814 the Viceroy in Peru reasserted his authority. An army was sent and at the battle of Rancagua, 1 and 2 October 1814, the patriots were defeated and their leaders retired to Mendoza, in the United Provinces of Río de la Plata. The authorities in the United Provinces, fearing for their own position and believing that the best way to maintain themselves was by fomenting trouble in Chile to keep the Spanish occupied, lent their aid. José de San Martín and Bernardo O'Higgins (the son of an Irishman, Ambrose O'Higgins, a former Captain General of Chile) raised an army with which they crossed the Andes and at the battle of Chacabuco, 12 February 1817, defeated the Spanish forces and occupied the capital, Santiago. O'Higgins became the Supreme Director and on 12 February 1818, (the anniversary of the battle) Chile declared itself independent. The Viceroy in Peru sent more troops and surprised the patriot army in their encampment on the field of Cancha Rayada, near Rancagua, 19 March 1818, and defeated them.[2] O'Higgins was wounded (his arm was broken by a musket ball) but he rallied his troops and having been joined by reinforcements under San Martín, gave battle again on the

---

naval career, but four months later he was appointed Captain of the Fleet (i.e. the senior captain) in HMS *Prince of Wales*, 90, under Admiral Gambier, much to the chagrin of the captains of some of the other ships in the fleet who were considerably senior to him: Popham, 1991, pp. 145–78.

[1] The *cabildo* was an ancient Spanish municipal council which had existed in the colonies since the sixteenth century. It had little power but provided a form of local government. In times of emergency it could hold an open meeting, *cabildo abierto,* attended by the local landowners, and might then be the only form of government available.

[2] Miers, 1826, II, p. 17, refers to this as Canchayarada.

plains of Maipú, where the Spanish under General Osorio[1] were defeated and fled to Concepción, whence they took ship for Peru, leaving the patriots in control.

Ferdinand VII sent troops out from Spain to reinforce the Viceroy in Peru. They sailed from Cadiz on 11 May 1819, in four ships. The *Alexandro I*, 74, Captain Antonio de Tiscar, sprang a leak and had to return to Spain, while the remainder of the fleet was dispersed in a storm off Cape Horn. One vessel, the *San Telmo*, 74, Captain Don Joaquín Toledo, was lost with all 644 hands on board.[2] Pieces of this vessel were subsequently found on Livingston Island, giving rise to the possibility that some of her crew may have been the first to sight the South Shetland Islands. The other two vessels, the frigate *Prueba*, 40, Captain Melitón Pérez, and the *Primorosa Mariana*, Captain Manuel del Castillo, completed their voyage.[3]

The Chilean naval ships *San Martín*, 64, (ex-East Indiaman *Cumberland*) and *Lautaro*, 44 (ex East Indiaman *Wyndham*), under the command of Admiral Encelada, arrived off Concepción on 28 October 1818, and found the Spanish frigate *Maria Isabella*, 48, and four transports at anchor off Talcahuano, in the south-west corner of Bahía Concepción. After a token resistance their crews fled and the Spanish ships were taken by the patriots. The *Maria Isabella* was renamed *O'Higgins*.[4]

After the battle of Chacabuco the Chilean government had started looking for naval officers in Britain to assist them. As a result Lord Cochrane had been recruited. He sailed in August and arrived in Valparaíso at the end of November 1818. He hoisted his flag in the *O'Higgins,* 48, and, on 15 January 1819, proceeded to sea with the Chilean fleet to attack Callao. This was unsuccessful and after a return to Valparaíso he tried again, again without success, since his orders allowed only the use of fireships and rockets and precluded any direct attack by his ships. He then captured Pisco, and took two armed merchantmen in

[1] General Mariano Osorio, 1722–1818.

[2] She was last seen from the *Primorosa Mariana*, whose crew had tried for some time to take her in tow, but had ultimately had to abandon her, rudderless and dismasted drifting south in 62°S on 4 September 1819: Gould, 1941 and Barra, 1992.

Robert Fildes recorded in his description of 'Sherriffs Cove', 'If you walk over the Land you will find a fine sandy beach or bay ¾ of a mile in length in form of a Crescent and called the half-moon beach, here was found the half an Anchor stock of a 74 Iron hoopd & copper bolted, studsail booms & other spars were found here likewise, the Melancholy remnants of some poor fellows Misfortune.' And in a footnote 'This anchor stock Cap[n] Smith brought home to have a Coffin made of, it has been Identified & found to have belonged to a Spanish 74 that was bound round Cape Horn with 1400 men against the Patriots & has never more been heard of.': PRO ADM 55/143. See also Appendix 4, report in *The Courier*, 2 May 1820, p. 203.

[3] Barra, 1992.

[4] Miers, 1826, II, p. 20.

Guayaquil which he sent as prizes to Valparaíso and proceeded to capture the Spanish stronghold of Valdivia in the south of Chile on 2 February 1820. Then, on 20 August, he sailed with General San Martín and his troops to effect the overthrow of the Spanish authority in Peru – Lima was occupied on 14 July 1821, and Peru was declared independent on 28th of the same month.

The Chilean government, when it was initially established, was greatly assisted by loans from British merchants, secured on debentures which were received at the Custom House in payment of duty on imported goods.[1] The British government maintained a number of warships on the station whose officers had 'to perform the very difficult task of defending British property and British rights, to act the parts of regulators of customs-house, consuls and plenipotentiaries'.[2]

The senior officer performing this duty in 1819 was Captain William Henry Shirreff, in HMS *Andromache*, 44. His orders, from Commodore Bowles, the senior officer on the South American Station, gave him wide latitude to act on his own initiative, but stated

> You will, however, observe, as the general principle by which you are to be guided on all occasions, a perfect neutrality between the contending parties and a scrupulous avoidance of all political interference … requiring only that British subjects shall not be molested in their commercial pursuits as long as they conform themselves to the established laws of the country …. The protection of the persons and property of his Majesty's subjects actually in Chile will, of course, be one of the principal objects of your care, but while attending to this object it will require the utmost circumspection to avoid altercations with the Spanish authorities and the appearance of infringing the laws of blockade.[3]

It was to Captain Shirreff that William Smith reported that he had discovered a new land to the south of Cape Horn, on his arrival in Valparaíso on 11 March 1819.[4] Captain Shirreff was heavily involved in his duties, and bearing in mind that no soundings had been taken, believed that what Smith had seen was ice. He told him so, and took no further action.

One of the British merchants in Valparaíso at this time was John Miers. He subsequently wrote that:

> owing to the flattering inducements held out to me, and the promises of protection from the Government of Chile, which I received, I ventured to export, at incredible risk, an immense train of machinery for the purpose of refining and manufacturing copper into sheathing for the consumption of America and the East Indian market.[5]

[1] Miers, 1826, II, p. 166.

[2] Miers, 1826, II, pp. 60–61.

[3] PRO ADM 1/23, Enclosure to Commodore Bowles letter of 5 April 1818, to the Secretary of the Admiralty, John Crocker.

[4] *Gazeta ministerial de Chile*, 27 March 1819.

[5] Miers, 1826, II, p. 276.

He also says that he had embarked with a friend[1] a very considerable capital in speculation. He had sailed from the Downs, in a merchant brig called *Little Sally*, on 26 January 1819, having been delayed there two weeks. He took with him some 70 tons of equipment and a further 100 tons in a different vessel together with skilled workmen, engineers, millwrights and refiners.

He reached Buenos Aires on 22 March, and having arranged the transhipment of his equipment, set out for Valparaíso overland. Having passed through Mendoza his wife gave birth to their first child at Villa Vicencio and he had to return 45 miles to Mendoza where she remained while Miers hurried on across the Andes to Valparaíso to meet the vessel with his machinery. He located a suitable site for his operations at Concón, about 40 miles NNE of Valparaíso, and the Chilean government undertook to arrange its purchase for him. He arranged to build a jetty to land the heavy machinery, since it was impracticable to take it round by road, and then returned to Mendoza to collect his wife and son returning to Valparaíso again in November.[2]

It was at this stage, on 24 November, 1819, that William Smith, in the brig *Williams*, again arrived in Valparaíso with confirmation of his discovery of land to the south of Cape Horn. A message was despatched to Captain Shirreff, who was in Santiago, and Smith started to load some of Miers's machinery to transport it to Concón. This was unloaded again, with Miers agreement, when the report was accepted and the brig hired by Captain Shirreff to carry out a survey of the newly discovered land.

---

[1] Miers, 1826, I, p. 1. This was Lord Cochrane, Carruthers, 1880. This is corroborated by Grimbal, 1978, pp. 248–9, who quotes a letter from John Miers to Lord Cochrane of November 1820: 'Doubtless you will be gratified to hear that other parts of our Machinery have arrived in safety from England.'

[2] Miers, 1826, I, chs I–VIII.

CHAPTER 3

NINETEENTH-CENTURY NAVIGATION AND SURVEYING

Time

In Britain it had been customary to start the year on 25 March since the late twelfth century. Scotland changed to starting it on 1 January in 1600 and England followed in 1752.

Pope Gregory XIII reformed the Julian calendar in 1582 making 15 October follow 4 October. The vernal equinox thus fell on 21 March, thereby bringing the seasons, and hence the date of Easter, back into line with that intended by the Council of Nicaea in AD 325. This was accepted by the Catholic states in Europe but not by the Protestant. The same act of George II, in 1752, that started the year on 1 January, brought Britain into line with Europe the rest of which used the Gregorian calendar; 2 September was followed by 14 September.[1]

Civil time starts at midnight and runs through two sets of twelve hours, a.m. and p.m., until the following midnight. Astronomical time runs from noon to noon with the date the same as that in civil time in the p.m. Nautical time ran from noon to noon, with the date coinciding with civil time in the a.m. Thus at 2 a.m. on 2 January civil time it would be 2 a.m. 2 January nautical time but 2 a.m. 1 January astronomical time. Time was, in general, kept by ships at sea, until the nineteenth century, in nautical time. In 1806 the Royal Navy started keeping civil time (Admiralty Instruction dated 11 October 1805); the East India Company followed in the 1820s, but many merchant vessels retained the old system for a considerable period beyond this.

Apparent time is that told by the sun, i.e. as shown on a sundial, so that as the sun crosses the observer's meridian it is midday. Due to the earth's elliptical orbit round the sun, the inclination of the ecliptic and to a much lesser extent the variations in the earth's movement, this is not regular. The difference between this apparent time and a clock keeping perfectly regular time, i.e. Mean Time, is

---

[1] Russia, Greece and the Balkan states did not follow until the twentieth century.

known as the 'equation of time'. This can vary on either side of the mean with a maximum of about 16½ minutes in early November.[1]

It would appear that Poynter kept his journal in civil time as one would expect under Royal Naval regulations, but that Smith used nautical time and converted it to civil time in some of the extracts from his journal.

On board ship the day is divided into watches of four hours each, except for the period between 4 and 8 p.m. which is divided into two watches of two hours each. These are, from midnight, the middle, morning, forenoon, afternoon, first dog, second dog[2] (two hours each) and first watches. The ship's company was divided into two watches, the starboard and larboard or port watch, alluding to where their hammocks were slung. The dog-watches were divided so that the same men would not keep the same watch every night. Each man remained on deck during his watch, but when not actually required for duty the seamen were allowed to sleep; the officer of the watch, however, was required to remain alert throughout his watch. To allow the officers a reasonable period of rest it was customary for them to be in three watches while the seamen were in two. The ship's company might also be placed in three watches which meant less men were available on deck to trim the sails in case of emergency, but that they got considerably more rest.[3] Poynter records that on 22 December 1819 their company was placed in three watches (pp. 98–9).

Navigation

Towards the end of the eighteenth century a practicable method of finding longitude at sea produced as great an advance in the art of navigation as the advent of the magnetic compass had done at the end of the twelfth and start of the thirteenth centuries, or indeed satellite navigation in our own time.

At the start of the century navigation was largely by latitude and account (see below). The meridian altitude of a heavenly body (i.e. when it crossed the meridian, bearing due north or south, and reached its greatest or least altitude), normally the sun, could be observed with a back staff to an accuracy of about 10′, depending on the ability of the observer and the accuracy of his instrument, which, depending on the accuracy of his tables, gave the latitude to within about

---

[1] Sidereal time, which does not come into this work, is defined by the transit of the first point of Aries across the observer's meridian. By virtue of the earth's motion round the sun the earth completes one less revolution relative to the sun than to the stars in a year i.e. in the time it takes to get back to the starting position in its orbit. In the same way as for solar time there is apparent and mean sidereal time and the difference between them is known as the 'equation of the equinoxes'. The sidereal day is shorter than the solar day by a little under four minutes.

[2] Now generally referred to in the Royal Navy as the 'last dog watch'.

[3] Falconer, 1769, s.v. *watch*; Smyth, 1867, p. 720.

ten miles on the earth's surface. Finding the longitude was another matter. The situation in the sixteenth century was well put by William Bourne, and had not changed:

> I woulde not any Sea men shoulde be of the opinion that they mighte get anye Longitude with instruments. Therefore let no Sea men trouble themselves with anye such rule, but (according to their accustomed manner) let them keepe a perfite accompt and reckening of the way of their shippe, whether the shippe goeth to lewards or makith hir way good, considering alwayes what thinges be against them or with them: as tides, currents, winds, or such like.[1]

The ship's speed was observed by the log, which consisted of a line about 150 fathoms in length, marked at intervals, with a board at the outboard end. The board was weighted on one side and secured by a sling, with two or three legs, in such a way that it floated vertical with its flat side at right angles to the line of advance. A sharp jerk would pull one leg of the sling free so that the board could be recovered easily. The line was allowed to run out until it was running free; at the first marker the half minute glass was turned and the amount that had run out when the sand was all gone was recorded. The nautical mile is rather over 6,000 feet in length and the recommended markings were knots every 50 feet subdivided into ten fathoms of 5 feet each,[2] which gave a slightly greater observed than actual speed, in knots and decimals, since 'it is safer to have the reckoning before the ship than after it'.[3]

The current could be observed at sea:

> Let three or four men take a little boat away from the ship; and by a rope, fastened to the boat's stem, let down a heavy iron pot, or loaded kettle, into the sea to a depth of 80 or 100 fathoms, when it can be; whereby the boat will ride almost as steady as at anchor: Then heave the log, and the number of knots run out in half a minute will give the miles which the current runs per hour; and the bearing the log shows the setting of the current.[4]

---

[1] Bourne, 1573, edited Taylor, 1963, pp. 239–40.

[2] The log was subject to errors, detailed in Phipps, 1774, p. 90. Because of these mariners used various different lengths for the knots. 'The log line, from the first use of that instrument about the year 1570, was invariably marked forty-two feet to thirty seconds. Norwood, when he published his Seaman's Practice, stated the true measure to be fifty-one feet to thirty seconds': Phipps, 1774, p. 88. In due course this was altered to a glass of 25 seconds but some retained the 30-second glass and lengthened the line to 45 feet per knot. Phipps himself did experiments using 45, 49 and 51 feet with a 30-second glass (as well as experimenting with 'two perpetual logs', one by Russel and the other by Foxton which he found very useful but 'I doubt much whether it might ever be substituted entirely in the room of the common log. Machines easily repaired or replaced have advantages at sea, which should not lightly be given up for others more specious.'): Phipps, 1774, p. 98.

[3] More, 1814, p. 132.

[4] Robertson, 1764, II, p. 441 (pagination of vol. II follows on from that in vol. I.).

At best, if the kettle proved an effective sea-anchor, the measurement was the surface current relative to any water movement at the depth to which it was lowered. If time and the depth of water allowed the vessel could be anchored and the current observed by a direct reading of the log.

The course was steered by the magnetic compass. Variation was a well known phenomenon,[1] but a knowledge of the effect of iron on board, i.e. deviation, was still in the future, at the start of the nineteenth century. The variation was obtained by comparing a magnetic bearing with a known bearing, either a transit taken off the chart or more likely a bearing of the sun. The latter could be taken at the sun's rising or setting, when the zenith distance is 90°, and was then called an amplitude. However to make the zenith distance 90° the semi-diameter of the sun, the height of the observer's eye and the refraction of his line of sight have to be allowed for. The latter is dependant on meteorological conditions and tables are notoriously unreliable when the line of sight passes close to the sea's surface. This is of little importance when the sun is falling almost vertically into the sea, as in the tropics, but in high latitudes, when its trajectory approaches the horizon very slowly, it can give rise to quite appreciable errors. The navigation manuals, even at the start of the nineteenth century, were inconsistent in their advice on the sun's position, one saying when its lower limb is slightly more than a semi-diameter above the horizon (which is correct), another when its lower limb sits on the horizon, and yet another simply referring to rising and setting. It was also possible to take an azimuth of the sun, i.e. a magnetic bearing, at any time, and by measuring its altitude calculate the true bearing;[2] this was only practicable when the sun was reasonably low in the sky, about 10° to 15° maximum, due to the difficulty in observing an accurate bearing of an elevated object with a standard compass. The advantage of using the amplitude method was that tables were provided with latitude and declination as arguments giving the angular distance of the sun from the east or west cardinal point at rising and setting and hence the variation could be found without calculation. However, in general, a more accurate value could be obtained by using the azimuth method, which entailed some calculation.

The amount a ship went to leeward was a matter of opinion. Navigation manuals contained tables with the amount of sail which could be carried as the argument for leeway in points and fractions of a point. However they usually ended

---

[1] Variation is the angle between magnetic north and true north measured east or west as appropriate. Its existance had been appreciated since the mid-fifteenth century. A Nuremburg portable sundial dated 1451 has a magnetic needle for setting it in the meridian. The box is marked to show where the needle should point to allow for the variation. Taylor, 1956, p. 173.

[2] The true bearing of the heavenly body can be calculated from the altitude of the body, its declination and the latitude of the observer without knowledge of the longitude.

by advising observing the angle the wake made with the fore and aft line of the ship and using the seaman's experience.

All these uncertainties, together with the problem of steering a straight and steady course, made keeping an accurate record of the ship's movement far from easy.

The ship's log was written up every hour with columns for Knots and Fathoms (i.e. the amount the log ran out to give the ship's speed), Course, Wind and Leeway. The account was calculated by the traverse table with columns for Course (now adjusted for variation and leeway) and Distance; Current, if any, and if known, was treated as an additional leg and might be represented as a single direction and rate for the entire twenty-four hours. These were summed to give Distance in each of the cardinal directions, north, south, east or west and converted to difference of latitude and longitude. Finally using the previous days noon position the new noon position by account was calculated. If it had been possible to observe a meridian altitude it might then be necessary to make an adjustment to take this into account.[1] Normally both positions were logged.

The eighteenth century saw the introduction of John Hadley's octant, also sometimes known as a quadrant or Hadley, in 1731. This was modified, as a result of Captain John Campbell's work, by John Bird to produce the sextant, 1757, much as we know it today. The scales on these early instruments were divided geometrically by beam compass using computed chords so that great care was essential to produce an accurate instrument; they were fitted with verniers for reading to 1′ of arc. In 1775 Jesse Ramsden's dividing engine came into use for constructing the scale mechanically, producing consistent accuracy in this field.[2]

In 1675 King Charles II appointed the first Astronomer Royal, John Flamsteed, who was required to direct his attention to 'rectifying the tables of the heavens' in order that the longitude might be found. In 1714 a prize of £20,000 was offered to whoever could devise a method which, on a round voyage to the

---

[1] One method of making this adjustment was as follows: if the course was due north or south the latitude alone was corrected assuming the course to have been correct and the speed in error. If the course was less than 3 points, 33°, from the north-south direction, it was assumed that the course was correct and the speed in error. The correct speed was calculated to agree with the observed latitude and the longitude re-calculated at that speed. When the course was more than 3 points, 33°, and less than 6 points, 67°, from the north-south direction it was assumed that both course and speed were in error. Correction was made by calculating a value for the longitude in the same way as in the previous case, then the mean between this new value and the longitude by account was used as the new longitude to correspond with the observed latitude; finally a revised course and speed could be calculated. When the course was more than 6 points, 67°, from the north-south direction, the new position was assumed to be the observed latitude and the longitude by acount, and the course and speed were calculated: Haselden, 1765, pp. 130–31.

[2] Moskowitz, 1987.

West Indies and back, would give the longitude to within 30′ of arc, or two minutes of time.[1] The Board of Longitude was set up to evaluate proposals submitted and to allocate funds for their development. They considered a number of ideas the majority of which proved unsuitable, but eventually two provided the answer.

The sun apparently travels round the earth once every twenty-four hours passing over the meridians at a rate of one degree every four minutes. Thus if an observer knows the time the sun passes over a fixed meridian, e.g. Greenwich, and the time it passes over his own meridian the difference will give him the angular distance he is east or west of the fixed meridian.

Observation of the eclipses of the moon[2] (or of Jupiter's satellites, advocated by Galileo) can provide time at different locations which can be used for determining their difference in longitude, but this is a difficult operation requiring special instruments. Furthermore, lunar eclipses are infrequent phenomena, so that although this method could be, and was, used ashore, it was quite impracticable for navigation at sea.

The moon moves in the heavens and if its movement can be accurately predicted, and measured, it can be used as a clock. The movement is about one minute of arc in two minutes of time, which means that an error of 1′ in observation will produce an error of two minutes in time and hence ½° in longitude. The combination of Hadley's, Bird's and Ramsden's work had produced an instrument capable of measuring the necessary angles to the required degree of accuracy, which could be held in the hand and used on the moving deck of a ship at sea.[3] Tobias Meyer, a German astronomer and professor of mathematics at Göttingen, produced a set of tables of the moon's motion which were converted by Nevil Maskelyne for use at sea, and proved successful. When Maskelyne became Astronomer Royal he published the *Nautical Almanac and Astronomical Ephemeris for the year 1767* together with the *Tables requisite to be used with the Nautical Ephemeris for finding the Latitude and Longitude at Sea*. The form of the *Nautical Almanac* has gone through a number of changes, but it has been produced annually from that year to this.

To observe a lunar sight the angle between the moon and the sun, or one of

---

[1] Act 12 Anne *cap* 15 (1714). *An Act for Providing a Publick Reward for such Person or Persons as shall Discover the Longitude at Sea.*

[2] This method had been known in antiquity. Hero of Alexandria (first century AD), in his *Dioptra* (ch. 35), mentions that the great circle distance between Alexandria and Rome could be found by observing the same lunar eclipse in both places.

[3] Johann Werner (1468–1522) recognized the connection between longitude and time, although he did not suggest its use at sea. In 1514 he published what was essentially the lunar method. First by eclipses and in a subsequent note by 'means of the true motion of the Moon and by means of a fixed star which is not more than 5° in latitude from the ecliptic': Andrews, 1996, pp. 377–85.

ten fixed tabulated stars, is taken and at the same time the altitudes of the two heavenly bodies concerned are measured. There are restrictions on this in that for about half the month the sun is either too close to, or too far away from the moon for observation. Furthermore only about seven stars were tabulated in any month with rarely more than two choices available on any given day. This could present serious problems in high latitudes due to the length of daylight when of course the stars cannot be seen. Four observers were required, since the time has also to be recorded. Belcher remarks 'Those who know the value of their own observations prefer taking all themselves',[1] which possibly says more about the author than his method.

The angular distance between the moon and sun or star has to be corrected for the index error of the sextant and the semi-diameter of the body to give apparent distance as seen by an observer on the earth's surface, and then again for refraction and parallax to give the value at the centre of the earth. This was known as 'clearing the distance'. 'To reduce the apparent to the true angular distance, is a problem that has employed the pens of many mathematicians; and various tables have been computed and published, for the express purpose of clearing the distance from the effect of parallax and refraction, by such rules and computations as have appeared best adapted for nautical usage.'[2] There were indeed many methods and different special tables published, but whichever method was used it was a laborious process. The distance was then compared with those in the *Nautical Almanac* (tabulated for every three hours) and by interpolation the apparent time at Greenwich found. Local apparent time was calculated from one of the altitudes using spherical trigonometry and an assumed latitude, normally by account from the last observed value, and the longitude finally determined by comparison of the two times.

Gemma Frisius proposed the use of a portable time-keeper as a method for finding longitude at sea in 1553[3] – the difficulty at that time was finding a sufficiently accurate instrument. John Harrison, who started out as a Yorkshire carpenter, produced such a machine, which, in 1765, appeared to fulfill the requirements of the Act but failed to satisfy the Board of Longitude. In fact his Chronometer Number 4 completed the trip to the West Indies and back with an

---

[1] Belcher, 1835, p. 227.

[2] Robson, 1834, pp. 85–6.

[3] The idea of using a portable timepiece to establish the difference of longitude between two places was proposed by Gemma Frisius in 1530 in *De principiis astronomiae et cosmographiae*. The fifth edition, 1553, adds that the method could be used at sea, but goes on to suggest the use of 'clepsydras or water clocks or sandglasses' to correct the errors of the timepiece': Andrews 1996, p. 387.

error of less than two minutes in 1761, but the Board called for further trials. A second trip to Barbados had an error on return of 54 seconds in 156 days (allowing for a rate of 1 second per day and if the changes in rate predicted by Harrison are taken into account this reduces to 15 seconds), and then the Board called for a copy to be made by another clockmaker, which Larcum Kendall duly did.[1] However the final instalment of the £20,000 reward was not paid until King George III took an interest in 1772.

Longitude by chronometer was obtained by timed altitudes of the sun or stars, observed when the body was as near the prime vertical (due east or west) as practicable. Using spherical trigonometry and an assumed latitude, the hour angle of the body could be calculated and hence the local apparent time could be found which was compared with the Greenwich apparent time from the chronometer to give longitude using a similar calculation to that used in the latter part of the lunar sight.

The problem with this was that the error of the chronometer, and its rate of change, had to be known for the comparison to be realistic. This was achieved by lists of known, or accepted longitudes in the navigation manuals, for some of the principal ports, or by establishing the longitude of a given locality by a sufficient number of lunar observations (Vancouver took 220 sets, each consisting of six observations at Port Discovery in 1792; Parry took 692 sets of ten observations at Winter Harbour in 1820, but normally far less were considered adequate). The altitude of the sun could be observed accurately, ashore, using a sextant and mercury bath to provide the horizontal surface, from which local apparent time could be calculated, then the application of the known longitude would provide Greenwich apparent time and the equation of time Greenwich Mean Time and hence the chronometer error. Observations could be taken at fixed altitudes while the sun was rising and again at the same altitudes as it set. The mean of the times of these observations, adjusted for the change in the sun's declination, gave apparent noon, and if the observations were taken again a few days later the chronometer's rate could be determined.

The longitude of Valparaíso is listed in the tables available in 1819, although the value differs between them. However, an examination of the Remark Books[2]

---

[1] This copy, known as K 1, was carried by Captain Cook on his second voyage, who found it went very well.

[2] These were ordered to be kept in all HM ships in 1759. They were to contain reports on all places visited giving details of the approach, anchorage, facilities (wood and water), fortifications, tides, etc. PRO ADM 2/83. The captain and master kept separate books. They were subsequently used for the compilation of the *Admiralty Sailing Directions* and are retained at the UK HO, Taunton.

of the ships on the station at the time reveals that they all recorded the longitude of the anchorage which they had individually determined by lunar sights. HMS *Creole*'s, March 1822, records 33°02'S, 71°34'W by 'means of several lunars' and 71°28'25"W by 'two occultations'.[1]

Tables of declination for the sun had been provided since the end of the fifteenth century. These together with tables for the stars gave latitude from the observation of the altitude of the body as it crossed the meridian. Navigation manuals gave further examples for the calculation of latitude when the body was close to, but not exactly on the meridian, and from two ex-meridian sights. The latter involved calculating the change in altitude of one of the bodies occasioned by the ship's run, to reduce them both to the same time and place, and then, using spherical trigonometry, the latitude could be calculated without a knowledge of the longitude.

Latitude and longitude were still treated separately, as they had been at the start of the eighteenth century and indeed had been since the fifteenth century.[2]

One of the functions of the master in an HM ship at the time was the navigation, and he was normally expected to instruct the young gentlemen in the art. He also carried out surveys if and when required and kept a remark book.[3] It is therefore reasonable to suppose that Edward Bransfield himself carried out the survey work from the *Williams* and took the sights, probably with the assistance of the midshipmen. William Smith would in all probability have kept his own records and taken his own sights, comparing the results with those of the naval officers. No original documents for this part of the work appear to have survived.

Hydrographic Surveying

The surveys carried out in the late eighteenth and early nineteenth centuries can be divided into two basic sorts; small-scale running surveys, and large-scale detailed harbour and coastal surveys. The former were employed on voyages of exploration when relatively rapid results were required with the emphasis on laying down the coastline and identifying sites for anchorages and ports. Large-scale plans of the latter were sometimes produced at the same time, while

---

[1] UK HO, Misc. Papers, vol. 54, Ad 1.

[2] When Captain Thomas Sumner, in 1837, worked out his longitude from an astronomical sight, using different values for his latitude his positions all fell on a straight line, giving the first concept of a position line from such an observation. It was not until 1873–5 that Captain Marcq St Hilaire published his method which relies on the principle that the zenith distance of a heavenly body defines a position circle on the earth's surface centred on the point where the body is directly overhead. This principle was used by virtually all navigators for computing their sights until the advent of satellite navigation.

[3] Edward Bransfield's Remark Book for this period in HMS *Andromache* is held in the UK HO, but it contains no mention of his work in the *Williams*. UK HO Misc. Papers, vol. 54, Ad 1.

chronometers were being rated ashore or when the ship remained in harbour for a few days for water or for some other reason. Detailed surveys were carried out of harbours and anchorages, their approaches and adjacent coastal areas, when time was no longer a major consideration; there were of course any number of variations combining aspects of both basic types.

The method by which a running survey was carried out in the eighteenth and nineteenth centuries would have been readily recognized in the sixteenth century, although the navigational techniques had advanced considerably. The basic principle was the same as that described by William Bourne and Richard Hakluyt.[1] The ship's position was fixed by astronomical observations, while sailing along the coast and lying off at night. The principal features were located relative to the ship, by magnetic bearings, taken on transits if possible, and at known intervals, using the ship's track to provide the base, or by using magnetic bearings and estimated distances, while the detail was sketched in by eye and soundings positioned by dead reckoning between fixes. The advent of the sextant made latitudes more accurate, and a practicable method of finding the longitude together with the use of astronomical azimuths, rather than magnetic bearings, to control bearings made the results very much more reliable[2] – however distance at sea was still measured by the log and an unfavourable wind (or none at all) could throw the whole operation into jeopardy.

This method was perfected by James Cook and the surveys made during his three voyages show the standard it was capable of achieving. It was the method employed by Edward Bransfield.

Large-scale detailed harbour and coastal surveys were a much more complicated operation. The techniques were developed during the eighteenth century mainly as a result of the work of Murdoch Mackenzie,[3] but also on ideas put for-

---

[1] Bourne, 1574, ed. Taylor, 1963, ch. 14, p. 236.

Hakluyt, 1598–1600, I, p. 382. 'A Commission given by us Thomas Randolfe Ambassadour for the Queenes Majestie in Russia, and Thomas Bannister, &c. unto James Bassendine, James Woodcocke and Richard Browne … for searching of the sea, and border of the coast, from the river Pechora, to the Eastwards, as hereafter followeth Anno 1588. The first of August. Necessarie notes to be observed, and followed in your discoverie…' and p. 435, 'Instuctions and notes very necessary and needful to be observed in the purposed voyage for discovery of Cathay Eastwards, by Arthur Pet, and Charles Jackman: given by M. William Burrough. 1580.'

[2] If two ships were available it was possible to obtain the distance to an object ashore by simultaneous horizontal sextant angles between the other ship and the object while the distance between the two ships was calculated using a vertical angular measurement of the other ship's known masthead height. This method is advocated by Phipps, 1774, pp. 99–100, although the problem of taking the angles at the same time and to exactly the same object is likely to have made it of only limited practicability.

[3] Mackenzie, Murdoch (1712–97). Mackenzie, 1750, and Mackenzie, 1819.

ward by, among others, Edmond Halley,[1] John Michell[2] and Alexander Dalrymple.[3] By the nineteenth century, in simple terms, the work involved obtaining a position and azimuth by astronomical observation ashore; measuring a base; extending this by theodolite observation from each end through a system of triangles to fix the positions of hill tops and salient features to provide a system of control for the survey. The coastline was then delineated relative to the fixed positions and boats employed sounding the waters fixing the position of their soundings and any dangers located either by bearings to or from the shore, transits, horizontal sextant angle resection between the fixed objects,[4] or in some cases by eye or indeed any combination of these methods. It took a considerable time to do. Belcher estimated that making full use of the wind a boat could be expected to complete twenty lines of soundings, each one mile long, in one day.[5]

The various methods of surveying were covered in the navigation manuals of the day to enable charts to be produced by seamen without specialist training. These were then engraved professionally, usually on behalf of their originators, and sold by specialist dealers. This meant that when preparing a ship for sea the captain would normally have to obtain for himself the charts he needed or considered appropriate for the duties on which he was to be employed.

Alexander Dalrymple was appointed Hydrographer to the Admiralty and the Hydrographic Office was set up in 1795. Its original function was to provide charts for the fleet. However, relatively early in the nineteenth century the Hydrographer began sending ships to carry out specific surveys which frequently took years to complete, so that their officers became specialists in the work.

As stated above, carrying out hydrographic surveys was part of the normal duty of the master of one of HM ships. Bransfield recorded in his Remark Book for HMS *Andromache* that he had sounded Valparaíso Harbour[6] so that he had had a certain amount of experience in this field, but he had not been in a vessel employed on surveying duties and was not a specialist in that field.

---

[1] Letter from Edmond Halley to Sir Robert Southwell dated 27 Jan 1701/2 in MacPike, 1932, pp. 120–22.

[2] Michell, Reverend John, (1724–93); Michell, 1765.

[3] Dalrymple, 1786 (originally published 1771).

[4] Resection fixing employs the principle that the locus of a point which subtends a fixed angle between two fixed objects is a circle passing through all three. Thus if an observer measures two angles between four fixed marks either floating or on shore, two position circles can be plotted and the observer will be at their intersection. In practice one mark is taken common to both angles and the fix is plotted with a station pointer, an instrument invented by Murdoch Mackenzie, consisting of three arms, two rotating and one fixed, which can be set to the observed angles and used to produce a graphic solution to the geometrical problem.

[5] Belcher, 1835, p. 135.

[6] UK HO, Misc. Papers, Vol. 55 (Ad2). See p. 170 and n. 5.

CHAPTER 4

THREE VOYAGES OF WILLIAM SMITH

In 1819 William Smith, in the brig *Williams*, on passage from Buenos Aires to Valparaíso,[1] decided to pass well south of South America in hopes of finding favourable winds. On 19 February he sighted land bearing SE by S distant 3 leagues, in latitude 62°15′S, longitude by chronometer 60°01′W.[2] On his arrival in Valparaíso he reported his discovery to Captain Shirreff, HMS *Andromache*, the senior British naval officer on the station, who was not convinced and considered it most probably ice.

From John Miers's account it was at this stage that he 'learned of it from a young man, who took his passage during this voyage' (pp. 50 & n. 1). This young man may well have been Mr Herring, who returned to Buenos Aires and, having noted the locality of the land they had sighted, prevailed upon some merchants to fit out a vessel (probably the *Espírito Santo),* on speculation to go sealing (see pp. 190–91).

Smith sailed again on 16 May for Montevideo and, finding ice and poor weather in the vicinity of his discovery, proceeded on his way without sighting land. He sailed from Montevideo and sighted the land again on 15 October, in much the same place as on his first voyage. This time he sailed along the coast to the eastward as far as the end of the land, which he named North Foreland. Then finding a suitable landing place, on 17 October, he sent a boat ashore, and claimed the newly discovered land for His Majesty King George III,[3] calling it

---

[1] The records of the Port Captain of Buenos Aires show that the brig sailed on 16 January, 1819, with a cargo for the firm of McNeill, Dixon & Co., of: 272 cases of stores (*efectos*), 221 rolls of tobacco, 29 cases of medicine, 29 loads of paper, 18 loads of cloth, 7 loads of ponchos, 9 cases of pianos, 5 cases of hats and 1 case of eau-de-Cologne. The Port Captain at Valparaíso records the arrival of the brig, Captain William Smith, on 11 March, 1819, after 45 days with a crew of 22: Berguño, 1993.

[2] William Smith's Memorial, PRO, ADM 1/5029 (pp. 63–4 below).

[3] The island referred to in the extracts from the log of the *Williams* , due to its position, as given in the text, adjacent to North Foreland, and as shown on the map, would appear to be that which was subsequently named Ridleys Island, in which case the landing probably took place in Venus Bay. See p. 66 below.

New South Britain. He then proceeded some 150 miles west-south-westward along the coast before, 'having a Merchants Cargo on board, and perhaps deviating from the insurance',[1] sailing for Valparaíso. The next day he was surprised to see more land, so that he was confident the land extended at least 250 miles. He arrived in Valparaíso on 24 November 1819, and again reported his discovery. This time the reaction was very different, and steps were immediately taken to follow it up.

Documentation

The log of the *Williams* has not survived. There have, however, been several reproductions of the remarks section leaving out the weather, courses steered and all the normal data for re-constructing a passage.

1. Captain Shirreff forwarded a copy to the Admiralty[2] (pp. 46–8).
2. John Miers wrote an article for the *Edinburgh Philosophical Journal*, 1820, pp. 367–80[3] which contained extracts. It is the only published account that was illustrated with a chart and views (pp. 48–61 and Plates 5 and 6):
3. The *Literary Gazette and Journal of Belles Lettres*,[4] 14 October, 1820, p. 668, contains a copy (pp. 62–3):
4. *The Globe*, London, 2 November, 1820, printed a copy:
5. William Smith submitted a memorial to the Admiralty[5] which contained a copy, this account was accompanied by a chart (pp. 63–6 and Plate 7):
6. J. Purdy,[6] *Memoir Descriptive and Explanatory, to accompany the New Chart of the Ethiopic or Southern Atlantic Ocean etc,* R. H. Laurie, London, 1822, pp. 38–9, contains extracts, principally from the third voyage (pp. 193–6).[7]

---

[1] Account forwarded by Captain Shirreff to the Admiralty, p. 47.

[2] PRO ADM 1/2548.

[3] This account was reproduced in *Polar Record*, 5, 1950, pp. 565–75.

[4] The *Courier* of 20 July 1820 carried the following advertisement describing the *Literary Gazette*:

LITERARY NEWSPAPER – The Attention of the Public is respectfully invited to the Weekly Paper, entitled The LITERARY GAZETTE, and Journal of Belles Lettres, Arts, Sciences, &c. – This New Weekly Journal, containing 48 Columns of entirely Original Matter is regularly published every Saturday Morning, on a Single stamped Sheet, price One Shilling, and sent consequently free of postage, throughout the Kingdom, so that it may be received in the Country on Sunday, at the distance of nearly two hundred miles from Town; and unstamped, for circulation in London and the environs, at the price of Eightpence.

[5] PRO ADM 1/5029.

[6] John Purdy was an hydrographer employed by Messrs Whittle and Laurie, chart sellers of Fleet Street. He produced other navigational publications: Taylor, 1966, p. 403.

[7] Reprinted in Purdy, 1837, and later editions.

7. James Weddell[1] printed a copy in *A Voyage towards the South Pole performed in the years 1822–24*, Longman, 1825, pp. 129–31, (pp. 193–6):

8. J. W. Norie[2] printed an extract from the third voyage in *Piloting Directions for the East and West Coasts of South America from the River Plate to Panama &c. also for the South Shetland, Falkland, Galapagos and other islands etc.* London, 1825, pp. 10–11, (pp. 193–6).

Purdy's version was reprinted by Edmund Blunt in *The American Coast Pilot*, eleventh edition, 1827, pp. 520–21, (pp. 196–7) and it would seem probable that additional copies were printed in other papers at the time.

Captain Shirreff's report [1] is marked 'Duplicate' in the top left-hand corner in the original hand and dated 'Panama February 16th 1820'. The date is crossed through and another hand has written 'Valparaiso 19 Dec 1819'. The date in the receipt stamp is May 17 1820, however it was minuted to Captain Hurd[3] by J W Croker, the Secretary, on 2 May, indicating that it had been received and seen by the Board by that date (pp. 198–9, for covering letter). The Valparaiso date is presumably the date of the original copy which has apparently not survived. It can be accepted that Captain Shirreff's text is based on William Smith's original logbook since he states that it is.

John Miers's account [2] is dated 'January 1820 Valparaiso', and appeared in the October 1820 edition of the *Edinburgh Philosophical Journal* (an abbreviated version had already appeared in the *Edinburgh Magazine and Literary Miscellany* in August 1820, pp. 208–11). Miers starts by saying it was written during his last visit to Santiago 'to convey *Admiral* and Lady *Cochrane* to Valparaiso'. Since Admiral Cochrane was at sea off Valdivia on 18 January and did not return to Valparaíso until 27 February, it was presumably written early in January.

John Miers was acquainted with Smith and his mate and his account must also be based on original information, although he makes no pretence that it is a direct transcription of the original log. The information contained is similar to that in Captain Shirreff's account considerably augmented with additional material. The article also contains a map and views which again must have come from Smith although the originals do not appear to have survived.

A manuscript version of this chart and views (although not quite identical) is

---

[1] James Weddell (1787–1834) served in the Royal Navy, rising to the rank of master, as well as in the merchant service. He made his famous voyage in the *Jane* in 1825–27 (of which this volume is an account). He reached 74°15′ south and gave his name to the Weddell Sea.

[2] John William Norie (1772–1843) of the Naval Academy, 157 Leadenhall Street. He also produced various volumes on navigation and navigation tables: Taylor, 1966, p. 346.

[3] Captain Thomas Hurd, Royal Navy (1753–1823), Hydrographer to the Admiralty, 1808–23.

held in the Hydrographic Office[1] which is inscribed 'A View of the Land Discovered by Willm Smith Master of the Brig Williams of Blythe Feby 1819 and taken possession of in the name and on the behalf of His Britannic Majesty George III and called New or South Shetland. Henry Foster Mid^{n} HMS Creole Jany 1820'[2] (Plate 3).

The account in the *Literary Gazette* [3] states 'We have been favoured with the following extract from the log-book of the brig Williams, by a vessel just arrived from Buenos Ayres.' It is possible this refers to Captain Shirreff's account, but it seems unlikely that the Admiralty would have provided it, and the probability is that it too is based on original information, although at second hand.

The account in the *Globe* [4] is almost identical with that in the *Literary Gazette* [3]. The only differences are a sentence left out of the rubric and a latitude incorrectly printed.

William Smith's Memorial [5] is undated but the date in the Admiralty stamp is December 31 1821. It sets out the bare essentials of the voyages. Like the other accounts no attempt is made to reproduce remarks verbatim from the log. It was accompanied by a chart which was passed to the Hydrographic Office and marked 'Received from the Record Office 3rd January 1822.'[3] This chart

[1] UK HO, s 90/3 Shelf Ae1.

[2] Midshipman Foster is shown in HMS *Creole*'s Muster Book (PRO ADM 37/6339) as having been on board his ship throughout January 1820. HMS *Creole*, Commodore W. Bowles, was in Buenos Aires in January, 1820, sailing for Montevideo on 16 January and for Rio de Janeiro on 19 January. She remained in Rio 5 to 22 February and then sailed for England arriving at Spithead on 29 April where the Admiral, Sir George Campbell, was saluted with 17 guns and Commodore Bowles's broad pendant was struck (HMS *Creole*'s log, PRO ADM 51/3127). Commodore Bowles was relieved as senior officer on the South America Station by Commodore Sir Thomas Hardy in HMS *Tyne* who arrived in Buenos Aires on 2 January 1820. The probability is therefore that Captain Shirreff sent the first copy of his report, which does not appear to have survived, (duplicate copy PRO ADM 1/2548) to the Admiralty through Commodore Bowles who received it in Buenos Aires and had the map copied by Midshipman Foster, before taking the report home with him to forward to the Admiralty, where no doubt it arrived at much the same time as the duplicate – See Appendix 2.

Captain Shirreff's duplicate copy of his report is marked 'duplicate copy of a sketch and chart of land mislaid'. The subsequently published chart of *New or South Shetland* dated 30 November 1822 (UK HO, C74 shelf Gy), Plate 31, which is based on Bransfield's survey also includes Smith's Cape with fields of ice to the north of it and a sounding of 120 fathoms, from this chart, so that it may be that Captain Shirreff's chart was damaged and Commodore Bowles had it copied and this is the chart which was sent with the report to the Hydrographer, who retained it.

There is no date stamp on the chart to indicate when it arrived in the Hydrographic Office, but it has been folded in four reducing the size to 18 by 14 cms (7¼ by 5½ inches).

[3] UK HO, s 91 Shelf Ae1, currently (1997) not available for examination. A copy of this document was presented to the Scott Polar Research Institute by Vice Admiral Edgell, Hydrographer of the Navy, in August 1941 (SPRI MS 354), from which this information has been taken.

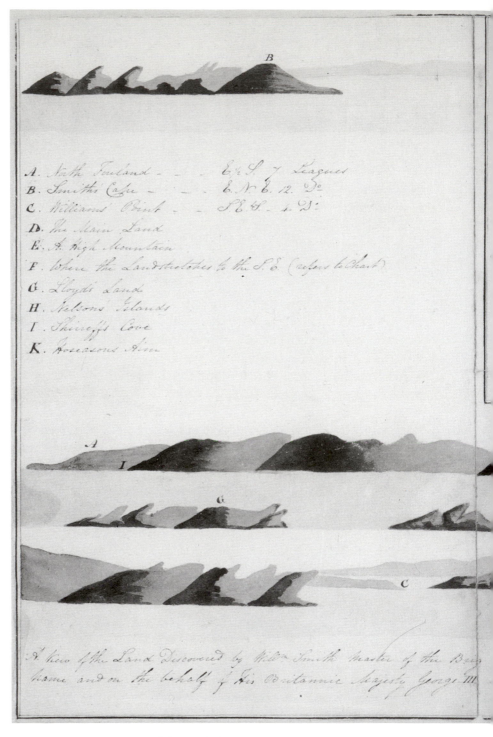

Plate 3. Charts and Views of the Land discovered by William Smith, February 1819.

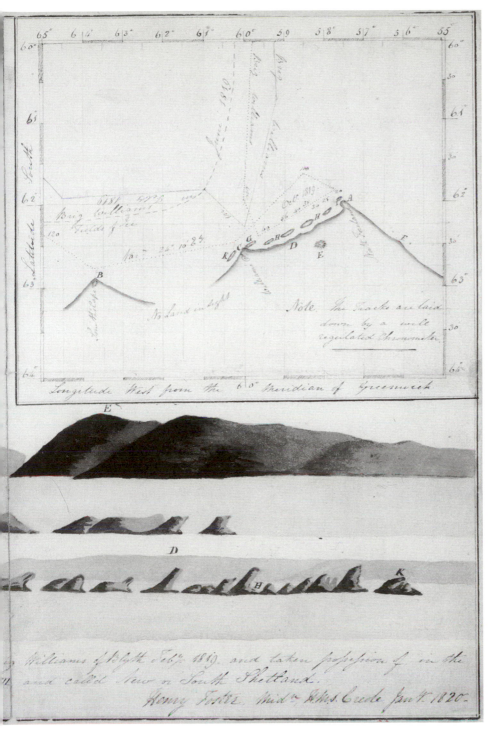

UK HO s. 90/3 – Aa1.

(Plate 7) shows the track of the *Williams*, in February 1819. The land mass is divided into individual islands, presumably the results of William Smith's work on his fifth voyage, i.e. that after the one with Edward Bransfield, and before his return to England (or copied from another sealers' work). It is titled 'A Chart of New South Britain Discovered by Captain Smith in the Brig Williams the 19th of February 1819' and written in very much smaller lettering, in manuscript, below the title 'Drawn by William Henry Goddard.' It is 80 by 52 cms (31½ by 20½ inches) and covers latitudes 50° to 70°S. and longitudes 20° to 85°W. On the right, within the border, are two plans, George's Bay and the coast between Start Point and Shirreff's Cape, similar to those in Poynter's journal, (Plates 14 and 11) which cover the area of the chart between 20° and 35°W. In the lower margin, and outside the border of the chart, there is a watercolour sketch of the *Williams* approaching the South Shetland Islands.[1]

Weddell states that the report was 'originally made known to the British Public in the Literary Gazette.' This is presumably a reference to the article published on 5 August, 1820, p. 505–6, (pp. 204–6) but could be to that of 14 October, [3] above.

Weddell's account [7], and Norie's [8], were published later than the others and include only the third track. They are very similar to Purdy [6] and are given, all three together in Appendix 1.

Norie's account [8], which has been changed from the first to the third person, includes the statement 'a remarkable point of land now bore E.½S. which he called the *North Foreland*, from its similarity in appearance to the *English* coast so named;'. This appears to be the only positive contemporary statement for the origin of this name.

Account 1. Captain Shirreff:

Extract from the William's Log Book from Buenos Ayres to Valparayso beginning February 19th. 1819.[2]

Having sailed round to the Eastward of the Falkland Islands and Keeping our wind to the Southward and Westward, wind variable from West to South West, in Latitude 62°.40′S and longitude per Chronometer 60°.00′ West, Land or Ice was discovered ahead bearing SEbS distant about two leagues, blowing hard gales with flying showers of snow, and the daylight breaking, at 6 AM. wore Ship to the Northward – At 9 AM more moderate and clear, a large field of ice, West distant 10 miles, Noon mod[te] & fine, latitude observed 62°.17′S. Longitude per Chronometer 60°.12′W. wore Ship and

---

[1] This chart was reproduced in Lee, 1913, in part in Hobbs, 1939, Plate I, (who remarks that it is 'obviously a forgery'!) and in Gould, 1941. It was described in detail in Hinks, 1939.

[2] Marked in top left-hand corner 'Copy' and initialled by Captain Shirreff.

made Sail for the land again – At 2 PM – the large body of ice bore West dist^{ce} 4 miles, 4 PM. tacked Ship the land or islands bearing SEbE to ESE distant about 10 miles, the weather fine and pleasant, when discovered to be land a little covered with Snow – made sail and Stood to the NW^d At 6 PM – the ice ENE distant 1 mile; round about a number of whales and Seals, made all sail on our intended voyage –

William's track from Valparayso to Monte Video. –

On my arrival at Valparayso this land being considered doubtful from my not taking the necessary precaution of sounding, which on taking my departure from this place on a voyage to Monte Video, and steering in a parallel of 62°.12′S with an intention of making the Islands again, but in longitude 67°W at 6 PM. June 16th in the above mentioned latitude, we found ourselves completely beset with loose ice, and hawling immediately to the Northward under easy sail going at the rate of 1½ to 2 miles per hour for fear of damage, At Midnight got clear water again and finding it not practicable to make farther researches at this season we abandoned our project and made the best of our way on our intended voyage – On our arrival and delivering of the cargo, notwithstanding all our precaution we found the ice had taken several sheets of copper of our bottom. –

William's track from Monte Video to Valparayso. –

After taking our departure from this place nothing material occurred excepting passing the latitude of Cape Horn on the fourteenth day with a fine wind to go to the westward, but we steered away in a SSE direction with an intention to make the islands again if possible – On the 15th October at 6 PM – we discovered land bearing SEbE distant about 3 leagues, Hazy weather, bore up and sailed towards it – At 4 miles distant sounded in 40 fathoms fine black sand, Island bearing EbS., When bearing SEbE sounded in 60 fathoms the same bottom, hawled off during the night to the Northward – Daylight stood in for the land again, at 3 leagues distance from the body of the islands sounded again in 95 fathoms Sand and Oaze – At 8 AM/ clear pleasant weather saw the main land bearing ESE, distance from the Islands 3 leagues, having run as far as the Cape we found the land tend off to the N^d and E^d, in coasting to the Eastward, the soundings found to be the same as the former – (fine sand.) – The point we called the North Foreland bearing E½S., hauled in for it, got the island to bear NW. distance 7 leagues, soundings regular from 35 to 20 fathoms, good bottom, sand and gravel, finding the weather favor us, down boat and succeeded in landing, found it barren and covered with snow, and seals in abundance called it the North Foreland, the boat returned on board, secured her and made sail off shore for the ensuing night, in the morning altered the course so as to keep the land to the Southward in view – At 11 AM. the North Foreland bore SEbE 5 leagues, the land then took a South Easterly direction, the wind varying to the Eastward with thick squalls of snow, I thought it prudent as having a Merchants Cargo on board, and perhaps deviating from the insurances to haul off to the Westward on my intended voyage, I again through variable winds made Cape Williams, and could perceive some trees on the land to the SW^d of the Cape, and stretching in a SW^y direction, the weather coming thick and squally made Sail to the Westward, after having sailed about 150 miles WSW, the weather being a little settled saw another head land bearing about ENE, distance 10 leagues, very high and by observation in latitude 62°.53′S. Long^{de} by Chronometer 63°.40′W from Greenwich

Plate 4. Smith Island bearing south-west, distant about 20 miles (1961). UK HO, *Antarctic Pilot*.

named this <u>Smith's Cape</u> found the land to extend from the Cape in a Southerly direction, thinking it fruitless to run away further to the Southward under the circumstances abovementioned, I shaped my course to the Northward for my intended port. –

Account 2. John Miers. *Edinburgh Philosophical Journal*, 1820, pp. 367–80:

Art XXI – *Account of the Discovery of New South Shetland, with observations on its importance in a Geographical, Commercial, and Political point of view: with two plates.*[1] By Mr. J Miers. Communicated by Mr Hodgskin.

During my last visit to Santiago, to convey A – and Lady C[2] to Valparaiso, I employed my first leisure hours in drawing up the following paper. I shall introduce the detail in regular order, previously hinting my opinion that a large Southern Continent is about to be discovered. The existence of this continent was believed many ages since; the ancient, and many modern philosophers being fully convinced that a vast tract of land must lie within the limits of the Antarctic Circle, to which they gave the name of Terra Australis Incognita. Many were the speculations of the ingenious on this subject, but perhaps none more highly pictured in imaginative colours than those of Maupertuis (in his

[1] [Miers's note:] See Plates XII and XIII [Plates 5 and 6].
[2] Admiral and Lady Cochrane.

Letter to the King of Prussia), who pourtrayed a continent far larger than any of those known to us, where the inhabitants, animals, vegetables, indeed the natural productions of every description, differed from all others yet known; and also where objects for commercial traffic might be found that would exceed all the treasures of the known world. Buffon, De Brosses, Campbell, and many others whose works, at this distance from the seats of knowledge, I am unable to consult, treated the subject in lively colours; some even went so far, as to calculate the superficies of this supposed continent at 8 or 10,000,000 square leagues; an extent of territory equal to the amount of all the continents and territorial possessions yet discovered. These speculations led to expeditions of diligent enterprise; but the attempts of the most celebrated navigators, at the head of whom Captain James Cook stands most eminently distinguished for his persevering and bold efforts to determine the question, entirely failed; and all hopes were long since given up of ever being able to ascertain the truth of the old favourite notion of a Southern Thule. Captain Cook, for many reasons, detailed particularly in his description of Sandwich Land, which he conceives might be part of this supposed large continent, says,[1] 'if anyone should have resolution and perseverance enough to clear up this point, by proceeding farther to the south than I have done, I shall not envy him the honour of the discovery, but I will be bold to say that the world will not be benefited by it.'[2]

He was led to form this conclusion from the intensity of the everlasting frost; the apparent absolute barrenness of Sandwich Land, which lies in latitude 58° south; the dangerous navigation, and the abundance of ice islands about it, erroneously concluding that all land placed in a similar southern latitude must be equally inclement and unapproachable. All hopes of discovery have therefore long since been abandoned, and it will excite no little surprise to hear that a large tract of *apparently habitable land* has been ascertained *to exist to the southward of Cape Horn*, by the captain of a British merchant brig, trading between the Rio de la Plata and Chili, who has displayed a spirit of enterprise that would do honour to a more enlightened navigator.

Independent of any national consideration, the result of this inquiry will clear up an important question in hydrographical and geographical science.

Mr William Smith, master of the brig Williams of Blythe, in a voyage from Buenos Ayres to Valparaiso, fancying that the passage round Cape Horn might be weathered better by preserving a more than usual southerly course, being on the 19th of February 1819 in Lat. 62°40' south, and Long. 60° W. imagined he saw land at the distance of 2 leagues; at that time he observed many fields of ice floating about, but so distinctly different was the appearance alluded to, that he was convinced it must be land. At this time, encountering hard gales of wind, accompanied by flying showers of snow, he thought it prudent to haul off to the northward during the night. Next day (February 20.) he again stood in for the supposed land; at noon his Latitude by observation was 62°17'S., Long. 60°12'W. by an excellent chronometer; the weather was moderate, and the atmosphere clear, when he again made the land. So fine was it, that he could not

---

[1] [Miers's note:] Cook's *Second Voyage*, [Vol II] p. 243.

[2] Cook, 1777, II, p. 243, reads: 'If any one should have resolution and perseverance to clear up this point by proceeding farther than I have done, I shall not envy him the honour of the discovery; but I will be bold to say, that the world will not be benefited by it.'

mistake the appearance. Fearing the return of blowing weather, he was deterred from approaching nearer, and being principal owner of the brig, he was unwilling to endanger the validity of his policy of insurance, in case of meeting with any accident in his research. He observed, however, to the westward more land, which he approached to the distance of 10 miles; this, as well as the former, appeared to be an island; both at this time offered the appearance of snow only in a very few places; and were almost wholly bare, barren and rocky. The air felt pleasant and temperate, with a fine clear atmosphere, and agreeable sunshine: he observed great abundance of whales and seals. In such a responsible situation with regard to his ship and cargo, he contented himself with this distant survey, and on his arrival at Valparaiso, he related everything that he had seen to the English there, who all ridiculed the poor man for his fanciful credulity and his deceptive vision; no one, in fact, gave the least credit to his tale, all endeavouring to persuade him that what he had seen was no more than ice-islands. Mr Smith was not, however, to be thus easily laughed out of his own observation; he is a native of Blythe in Northumberland, and had been brought up in the Greenland whale-fishery; and had learned to distinguish land from icebergs; though it must be confessed that the most experienced eye is often deceived by the striking similarity. If I mistake not, I informed you thus far of the discovery, in a letter I wrote you soon after my arrival in this country. What I then learned of it was from a young man, who took his passage during this voyage.[1] Mr Smith on his return to the River Plate in June following, was determined, if possible, to verify what he had seen: he steered in the latitude 62°12′S., but when he reached the longitude of 67°W. he became so beset with loose pack-ice, that he was alarmed for the safety of his ship and cargo; in a few hours he got clear, and stood off on his course, considering that all attempts in this situation, with the very short days and in the depth of winter, would be extremely indiscrete.

On his arrival at Monte Video, he was again ridiculed for his credulity: his confidence in the observations he had made was certainly shaken; but he could never be led entirely to renounce his former conclusions. On this occasion, Mr Smith conducted himself in a manner becoming an Englishman: His account reached the ears of some American merchants, who endeavoured to obtain from him the true situation of the land; they offered to charter his ship on a voyage of discovery, and to employ it in whaling, making that the apparent object of the enterprize. Copies of articles were drawn up. The Americans now endeavoured to ascertain from him the longitude and latitude of the land; but he, to his credit, refused to disclose it to any but a British born subject: he honourably offered to conduct the vessel there, and, if no land existed, to receive no freight; but that was not the object of the other party: Thus defeated in their manœuvre, the Americans withdrew their contract, and the honest Englishman determined to run the chance of waiting many months for employment of his vessel. At length, having obtained freight a second time to Chili, he set off on his voyage, and on the 15th of October last, at 6 P.M. being then about the same latitude and longitude as before, he discovered the same land, bearing S.E. by E. 3 leagues. The weather was hazy: he bore up for it, and approached within 4 miles of it, when he proved it to be an island, or rather a large barren rock, inhabited only by innumerable penguins: he sounded, and in

---

[1] This was probably Joseph Herring, whose account of his own voyage was published in the *Imperial Magazine*, July 1820, pp. 674–5, and is given at pp. 190–91.

40 fathoms found a bottom of fine black sand: he hauled in for the same island, till it bore E. by S.; having sounded when in 60 fathoms, he procured the same bottom of black sand. During the night, he hauled off for security to the northward, but at daylight next morning he again stood in for the island: he could now distinguish it perfectly at the distance of 3 leagues; he sounded in 95 fathoms, and brought up fine sand and ooze. At 8 A.M. the weather being very clear, he could plainly distinguish the mainland, bearing S.S.E., the island being distant from it about 3 leagues. The mainland presented itself as a cape, to which the coast tended in a N.E. direction, having peculiar marks, of which he took rough sketches: he stood in, and ran along the land as far as the point, to which he gave the name North Foreland, A, Pl. XII. Fig. 2. obtaining all the way regular soundings of sand and gravel, lessening gradually from 35 to 20 fathoms; the bottom was good and regular. He now hauled in for the cape, and proceeded, within 3 leagues, more easterly: the island now bearing N.W., distant 7 leagues, and observing the appearance of a good harbour, he sent a boat's crew and his first mate on shore, where they planted a board with the Union-jack, and an appropriate inscription, with three cheers, taking possession in the name of the King of Great Britain. To the mainland was given at first the name of New South Britain; but as that title, it was suggested, might lead to confusion with other places, Mr Smith changed its name to *New South Shetland*, on account of its lying in about the same latitude as the Shetland Islands. The coast here was barren and rocky, and from the description I could obtain from the mate, I should suspect it to be chlorite-slate or schistose hornblende. The land was high, disposed in strata, offering projecting knots, dipping westerly, the highest points being covered with snow, particularly the peak of a very lofty hill marked E.[1] in the chart, remarkable for a large black spot mid-way up the snowy height. At the place of landing the spot was barren, being stony, not of rounded pebbles, but of bluish-grey slaty pieces, varying in size from very large to very small. The harbour appeared to proceed inland as far as the eye could reach; and to afford a good anchorage. This place, I. in the chart, he called Shireff's Cove, in honour of the Commanding Officer in the Pacific. The day drawing to a close, the boat pushed off, the master, with the most prudent views, hauling off the shore with his ship. The harbour appeared to abound with the real spermaceti whale, Physeter macrocephalus, which he says exists there in greater abundance than he imagines has ever been elsewhere known: that it was the real spermaceti whale he is certain, having himself been brought up in the whale-fishery. Seals and sea-otters abounded, as also an animal differing from the sea-otter, which I imagine may prove to be a variety of ornithorynchus.[2] He continued to haul off during the

---

[1] The only lofty peak at the east end of King George Island, the name by which this island is now known, is Melville Peak, 564 m (1850 ft), which lies 8 miles south of North Foreland. The highest charted point on the island, 680 m (2228 ft) lies 30 miles WSW of North Foreland. A ridge between these two positions, but not connected to either, rises to heights of over 610 m (2000 ft). From the chart (Plate 5) it is possible that Melville Peak is here referred to, but it might equally well be another summit.

[2] Brian Roberts, who edited this article for *Polar Record*, 5, pp. 565–75, remarks (n. 8, p. 575) that it is most unlikely that William Smith really reported seing sea-otters and that the suggestion that the 'animal differing from the sea-otter' might be a variety of ornithorynchus (platypus) was probably added by Miers.

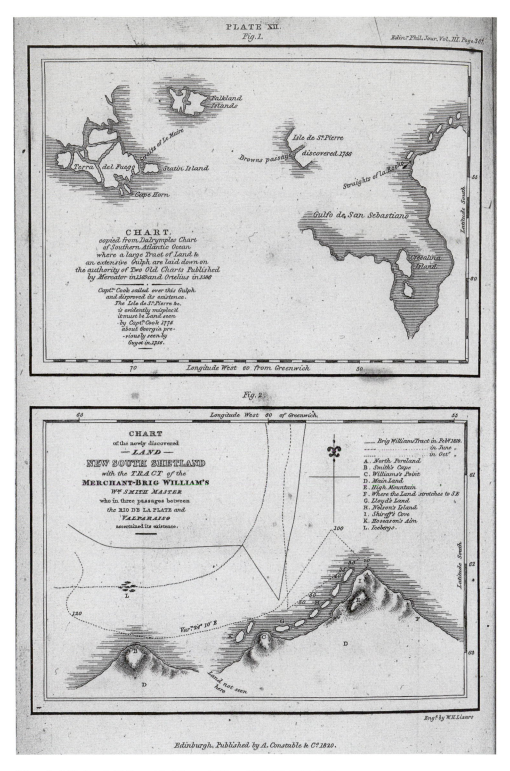

Plate 5. *Edinburgh Philosophical Journal*, Plate XII, BL 257 d.20.

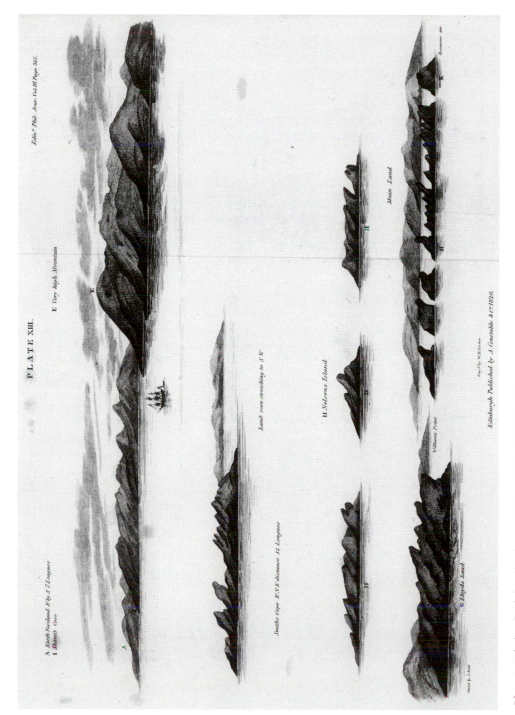

PLATE XIII.

Edin.ʳ Phil. Jour. Vol III Page 367.

A North Forland E.b.S 7 Leagues
I Birnets Cove

E Very high Mountain

Land even stretching to S W

II Nelcons Island

Main Land

Smiths Cape E.N.E distance 12 Leagues

Williams Point

G Lloyds Land

Engd by W.H.Lizars

Edinburgh Published by A Constable & Cº 1820.

Engd by J.Bald

Plate 6. *Edinburgh Philosophical Journal*, Plate XIII, BL 257 d.20.

53

night to the northward, to such a distance that he could just keep the cape in sight to the southward. Next morning at day-break, he could perceive the land marked F in the chart, trend in a S.E. direction. At 11 A.M. the Foreland bore S.E. by E. 5 leagues distant. Keeping his course to southward and westward, still preserving the mainland in view, the several other islands called Nelson's Islands, H, all appeared to be distant from it about 3 leagues. The islands were all alike barren and rocky. To one of the largest, marked G in the chart, he gave the names Lloyd's Island; the mainland, however, was very considerably higher. The wind changing to the eastward, attended with thick squalls of snow, he thought it prudent (always having the safety of his cargo as his primary consideration) to haul off. The weather moderating, he made the point of land which he called Cape Williams, C; at that time the atmosphere was quite clear, and with a telescope he could distinctly perceive trees, which bore the resemblance of Norway pine, and which seemed to grow to a tolerable height: Indeed, he describes the whole appearance of the land, the structure and shape of the hills, the quantity of snow, the appearance and quantity of ice about the coast, as being more like the Norwegian coast than any land he ever saw.[1] His course hence was S.W., but the weather becoming thick and squally, he began to abandon all thoughts of exploring the coast farther. He had now clearly ascertained the existence and situation of the land for the length of 150 miles in a W.S.W. direction so satisfactorily, as to remove the doubts of the most sceptical; and considering that no curiosity could justify his farther delay, consistently with his duty as master of the brig, he shaped his course westerly on his voyage.

The weather at daybreak next day becoming more settled, he was surprised at descrying another headland, B, far higher than any yet seen bearing E.N.E. distant 10 leagues. This point he named Smith's Cape: and the weather being remarkably clear and fine he proved it by observation to lie in 62°53′S.; longitude 63°40′W.[2] From Smith's Cape, the land appeared to extend in a south-westerly direction; but however eager he was to prosecute his search, he concluded that he had fully attained his object, having proved the existence of the coast for the distance of 250 miles. He therefore shaped his course to the northward; and in the month of November reached the port of Valparaiso, having delayed the vessel six weeks on the voyage, for the mere purpose of prosecuting this interesting object of pursuit. I have omitted to mention, that during a visit on shore in Shireff's Cove, independent of penguins and various sea-fowls, abundance of wild land fowls and fresh water ducks were observed, which were so little shy, that they could be approached very close before they would stir. The existence of these birds augurs well for the adaption of the place for the habitation of man. The harbour, too, offered an excellent anchorage: it was well protected in all points, but one very small angle, – the island affording a good shelter to the mouth; from this cause, there appeared very little surf, and the shore seemed very bold. One may judge of the sensation produced in the breast of an Englishman on hearing the relation of Mr Smith; every one became struck with the advantages which a British settlement would offer,

---

[1] Although Miers stated that Smith had been 'brought up in the Greenland whale-fishery' there is no indication that he had ever seen Norway so that it is possible this is an addition by Miers, with the report of 'Theodore Gerrards' in mind – see pp. 58–9 below (and pp. 17–18).

[2] The NE point of Smith Island (62°52′S, 62°18′W) is now known as Smith Cape.

not only to our whalefisheries, but to our commercial interests in this part of the globe. Until the political arrangements of these countries (the Spanish colonies) become in some degree settled, the consequences resulting from the animosities that may possibly arise between the many contending parties must necessarily be feared. Those who were here during the affair at Cancharayada,[1] well know the value of anything like a British settlement, however miserable, to retire to. On the arrival of the Williams in November last, there was a general and simultaneous feeling among the English merchants, who instantly set about taking up a vessel, which should be chartered on a voyage of discovery at their expense. Mr Smith, on his arrival, having transmitted his observations to the commanding officer in the Pacific, Captain Shireff of the Andromache, who was at that time in Santiago, conducting diplomatic arrangements with the Government, prior to his visit to the north-west coast of America, – this excellent officer, ever alive as well to British interests as to the pursuit of objects of science and utility, instantly chartered the same brig Williams on Government account, in order to make an accurate and regular survey of the coasts and harbours, and to ascertain the advantages it might offer to our whalefisheries. So prompt were his measures, that although the vessel was loading to convey my goods to Concan Bay, the moment of his arrival in the port the bargain was concluded. Every article of mine was again transhipped. The Williams was refitted completely with every necessary for the voyage, – and in one week put to sea, being placed under the charge of Mr Edward Bransfield, master of the Andromache, who had under his orders Mr Bone, Mr Blake, and Mr Poynter, three midshipmen of the Andromache, and Mr Young, assistant-surgeon of the Slaney sloop of war. Mr Bone, son of the celebrated enameller, is a good draughtsman. They were all ordered to observe, collect and preserve, every object of natural science, during the prosecution of the more important objects of the expedition. The Williams got under weigh and quitted Valparaiso on the 19th December, and the same day the Andromache left the port for Callao.

It was at first stated by many captains of vessels lying in this harbour, that the discovery of this land was not new; – that it was laid down in several old charts. These I examined, but found in all cases they were copied from Mr Dalrymple's chart, published in 1770,[2] (See Plate XII. Fig.1.) in which an extensive tract of country is placed between

---

[1] This probably refers to the occasion when the Spanish forces under General Osorio surprised the patriot forces, under Bernado O'Higgins, in their camp, and defeated them on 19th March 1818, at Cancha Rayada (p. 25, n. 2).

[2] *A Chart of the Ocean between South America and Africa. With the tracks of Dr Edmund Halley in 1770 and Monsr. Lozier Bouvet in 1738.* Published April 1769 (illustrated in David, 1992, p. xxxvii, Pl. 9). The chart was accompanied by a Memoir (Dalrymple, 1769) which explains the authority for the various features on the chart. P. 5 reads:

The extensive tract of land to the eastward of AMERICA was taken from ORTELIUS'S map, 1586; he calls the gulph *St. Sebastiano*: this map places the N.W. point in the same position LA ROCHE does in 1675, and the Lion in 1756.

BUACHE (Mem. de l'Acad. 1757, p. 201) says "MERCATOR's sea chart of the world, published in 1569, in eighteen sheets, marks in this situation a large gulph called St SEBAS-TIAN, and an island called CRESALINA ..." [also in Buache, 1763.]

BUACHE also mentions the land seen by the Lion in 1756, which he describes to be an island, and in a map lays down the ship's track to the eastward of this land; DANVILLE does not describe *it* directly as an island, but leaves the eastern side undelineated. I think a *hint* from

the latitudes of 54° and 58°S., and of longitude 40° and 53°W. having a large gulf, called Golfo de San Sebastiano. This land was first laid down in a chart published by Mercator in 1569,[1] and subsequently in another by Ortelius in 1586. Its existence was doubted by many, and Captain Furneaux (the coadjutor of the celebrated Captain Cook) visited in 1774, in the Adventure, that tract of the globe, for the purpose of verifying or disproving its existence. He passed over both the western and eastern shore of the Gulf laid down as above mentioned, his tract being,

61°45′S. Lat	89° W. Long
61 49	84 1′.. ..
61 20	71 50 .. ..
60 34	57 43 .. ..
60 20	53 20 .. ..
60 2	48 25 .. ..

But he could neither discover the least indication of land, nor could he obtain any bottom soundings.

'It was proved, therefore,' says Dr Forster in his account of the voyage, 'that this gulf (and of course the encircling land) does not exist, or that it is not rightly laid down in former charts, and the latter is much more probable, since it can hardly be conceived by what means such a discovery could obtain a place in the old charts.'[2]

M. DANVILLE is *better* authority than the most *positive assertion* of BUACHE, and the whole tribe of French Geographers.

Although neither LA ROCHE's *observations, nor those* of the Lion, prove the existence of such a continent as is laid down in the antient maps, yet their finding land in the situation described by those maps, is a very strong presumption, that the other parts do exist, though the memory of the discovery is lost: HALLEY had also signs of land in its neighbourhood. Isle de St Pierre is not shown on Dalrymple's chart. See note below on Mercator's World Map of 1569 and also p. 19 & n.2, and p. 20.

[1] Mercator's world map of 1569 shows an Antarctic Continent which encircles the globe. The continent appears to be based on that shown on the world map of Oronce Finé of 1531, which is on a much smaller scale and consequently shows far less detail. The Antarctic Continent is inscribed *Terra Australis recenter inventa sed non dum plene inventa*. It includes Tierra del Fuego, and all the land south of the Strait of Magellan. It passes well south of Africa in about 48°S, coming north again to about 15°S to the south of Java. To the east of South America it shows Golfo di Sebastiano and I. de Cressalina together with a coastline showing capes and rivers (e.g. R. Dolcissimo, C. de Crepusculo, C. della Yolette etc) leading to C. de Fuego opposite C. 11000 Virgines at the entrance to the Strait of Magellan.

This was followed by Ortelius in his World Atlas of 1570 of which over 40 editions had been issued by 1612. The map of *Americae sive novi orbis nova descriptio* in the 1587 edition shows Golfo de San Sebastiano, Cressalina and R. Dolcissiomo in the same way as on Mercator's World Map, Plate 2. The map which Edward Wright produced for Richard Hakluyt in 1600 leaves the Southern Ocean free from land, but in general Mercator and Ortelius were followed by most map makers in the seventeenth century and by a few in the eighteenth although by this time the concept of a vast Southern Continent had been seriously eroded. Guillaume de Lisle, in 1714, published his *Hemisphere meridional* which has only one remark in the Antarctic, just south of the *Cercle Polaire*, south of South America indicating land supposed to have been seen by Francis Drake, however Drake did not go beyond a little over 57°S (p. 16).

[2] Forster, 1777, II, p. 523, reads: 'It appears therefore that either this gulph does not exist, or that

Captain Cook, next year in the Resolution, sailed over the same tract with similar views, 'to ascertain the existence of San Sebastian's Gulf, and the extensive tract of coast laid down in Dalrymple's chart.'[1] Leaving Staten's land, he passed to

| 57°21'S. Lat | 57°45'W. Long |
| 58° 9'.. .. | 53°14' .. .. |

which is the point assigned by Dalrymple as the S.W. point of the Gulf; but fearing he might miss the land said to have been discovered by Duclos Gayat, in the ship Lion in 1756,[2] which Dalrymple places in 54°30' lat. S. and 45° long. W., yet laid down in D'Anville's chart 9° or 10° more to the westward,[3] he hauled to the north, and passed to

| 56° 4'S. Lat | 53°36'W. Long |

where he sounded in 130 fathoms, without finding any bottom; hence to

55° 4'S. Lat	51°45'W. Long
55 12	50 15 .. ..
54 35	47 56 .. ..
54 38	45 10 .. ..
54 28	42 8 .. ..

which is 3° to the eastward of the N.E. point of the Gulf, as assigned in the charts. His track then was to

| 55° 7'S. Lat | W. Long |
| 53°56' .. .. | 39°24' .. .. |

where he found a muddy bottom in 175 fathoms: hence he arrived at Willis's Island and Georgia.

In latitude 60°S. and in long. 31°W. Captain Cook met with a heavy swell from the westward, 'a strong indication,' says he, 'that there was no land in that direction; so that I think I may venture to assert, that the extensive coast laid down in Dalrymple's chart of the ocean between Africa and America, and the Gulf of San Sebastian, does not exist.'[4]

It is difficult to conceive how so extensive a tract could obtain a place in the old

---

it is not rightly laid down in former charts; and the latter is much more probable, since it can hardly be conceived by what means such a discovery could obtain a place in the old charts, without some authority to support it.'

[1] Cook, 1777, II, p. 207, reads: 'Our course was S.E., with a view of discovering that extensive coast, laid down by Mr. Dalrymple in his chart, in which is the Gulph of St. Sebastian.'

[2] This was South Georgia which was sighted 30 June 1756. It was located by Captain Cook (see p. 22), who named it Isle of Georgia: Cook, 1777, II, p. 218. The *León*, commanded by Gregorio Jerez, was a Spanish merchant vessel in the service of the French merchants returning home from Valparaíso. Nicolas-Pierre Guyot, Sieur Duclos was embarked and it was from his account that Dalrymple's was taken. The ship was carried east by bad weather. They believed land was sighted on 29 June and this was confirmed next day, but they did not land: Burney 1803–17, V (1817), pp. 138–9.

[3] Jean-Baptiste Bourguignon d'Anville, 1697–1782. This is his hemispherical world map of 1761 which places 'I. de S. Pierre' in 54° or 55°W of Greenwich.

[4] Cook, 1777, II, p. 223, reads:
We had now a long hollow swell from the West, a strong indication that there was no land in that direction; so that I think I may venture to assert that the extensive coast, laid down in Mr. Dalrymple's chart of the ocean between Africa and America, and the Gulph of Saint Sebastian, do not exist.

charts, unless some authority had been offered for it. We are, however, ignorant of the authority, though, from the name of the Golfo de San Sebastiano, it may be presumed to have originated in the accounts of the Spaniards. The particular formation of the land, – the existence of an island within the Gulf, called La Isla de Cressaline, – offer additional reasons for believing it had been seen. These considerations led Dr Forster, who in the Adventure had satisfactorily disproved its existence, as laid down in the charts, to draw a similar conclusion. He adds, 'I am inclined to believe that Sandwich Land has been discovered by those early navigators, who furnished the geographers with the Gulf of San Sebastian, and the Island of Cressalina,'[1] – an observation now more applicable to the land seen by Mr Smith. In support of this opinion, it is worthy of remark, that the shape of the land, as described by Smith, bears a striking resemblance to that tract of coast laid down in the old charts. The islands in the latter bearing the same situation in regard to the mainland as Smith's and Nelson's Isles, the direction of the coast of the mainland bearing as well a W.S.W. direction in both instances; the headlands, too, of the old charts, strongly resembling the North Foreland, Williams's and Smith's Capes. The existence of a gulf in New Shetland, similar to that of San Sebastian, is yet undetermined: it is, however, to be remarked, that Smith could not observe the land in the same relative situation, the weather being at that time extremely hazy, – indeed he had concluded that he had lost sight of the land altogether. Should a gulf be hereafter ascertained to exist there, it would place it beyond doubt that this newly discovered land has been before noticed by the earliest navigators of those parts, but incorrectly laid down in the old charts. However this may be, it would seem that this land was seen subsequently to the dates both of Mercator's and Ortelius's charts, by a Dutch Captain; but the exertions of our indefatigable circumnavigators, had taught us to place little reliance upon the accounts of old navigators. In the present instance, however, we have this circumstance in its favour, that it is stated to exist in the same latitude as laid down by Smith.[2]

'Theodore Gerrards, one of the first Dutch who attempted to voyage into the South Sea, after passing the Straits of Magalhaens, being carried by tempests into 64° of south latitude, says the country was mountainous, and covered with snow, looking like Norway, and seemed to extend to the islands of Salomon,'[3] – that is to the Cape of New Holland.

---

[1] Forster, 1777, II, p. 539 reads:
Captain Cook at first gave it the general name of Snowland, but afterwards honoured it with that of Sandwich Land. I am inclined to believe that this land has been discovered by those early navigators, who have furnished the geographers with the Gulph of St. Sebastian, and the isle of Cressalina.'

[2] [Miers's note:] See Dalrymple's Collection of Voyages to the Southern Atlantic and Pacific, vol i. I could not obtain the 2d volume, where I believe he has collected some other authorities in proof of land having been seen to the south.

[3] Dalrymple, 1770, I, p. 94, reads:
Theodore Gerards (one of the fleet in the voyage wherein W. Adams was pilot) being carried by tempests in 64 deg. S. in that height, the country was mountainous, and covered with snow, looking like Norway, and seemed to extend towards the islands of Salomon.
Purchas, IV, p. 1391, note, and Barlaeus's Collection, p. 193 are quoted as authorities.

It is also worthy of remark, that the observation of Mr Smith, of the great similarity in the appearance of the land to Norway, exactly coincides with the observation of Gerrards.

As yet it remains an interesting topic of conversation, whether New Shetland be an island of considerable size, or if it be part of a continent. It is by no means an improbable supposition that it is connected with Southern Thule, the most southerly point of Sandwich Land seen by Captain Cook in 1775, and situated in 59°30′ lat. S., and 27°30′ W. long. The observations of Captain Cook seem to favour this conclusion. He says: 'I conclude that Sandwich Land is either a group of islands, or else a point of a continent; for I firmly believe that there is a tract of land towards the Pole, which is the source of the ice spread over this vast ocean. I think it also probable, that it extends farther to the north, opposite to the Southern Atlantic and Indian Oceans, because ice was always found by us farther to the north in these oceans than any where else, which I judge could not be, if there were not land to the south; I mean land of a considerable extent.'[1] About the longitude of 27°W., Cape Montagio,[2] the most northerly point of Sandwich Land, lies in the latitude of 58°25′, and icebergs are found hereabout in the latitude of 48°. In the longitude of 57°30′, North Foreland, the most northerly point of New Shetland exists in the latitude of 62°; and in the longitude of 67°W. the same land appears to fall off to the latitude of 64°S. Fewer icebergs are met with still more to the westward; for noticing the Adventure's track in 1774, it was observed, that in longitude 106°54′ W. icebergs were not met with till the latitude of 71°10′S. In long. W. 142°54′, he was beset with icebergs in the latitude of 67°31′S., and in long. 172°W. he found them numerous in the latitude of 62°10′S. Cook remarks, that between the meridians of 40°W. and 60°E. ice is invariably encountered in the latitude of 51°S. Modern researches have proved that icebergs always derive their origin from adjacent land. Between the meridians of 40° and 60°W. icebergs are invariably encountered in a somewhat lower latitude, from which we may infer, that land exists along one continued tract to the southward within these meridians, and it is by no means unfair to conclude, that New South Shetland and Sandwich Land form two points of one large continent.

There exists, too, some similarity between the appearance of Sandwich Land and South Shetland. 'Approaching the former,' says Dr Forster, 'within half a mile, the rocks

---

See comments on this voyage at pp. 17–18, which discusses Barlaeus's translation of Herrera, 1622. Purchas, 1625, IV, p. 1391, has a marginal note to the *Observations of Sir Richard Hawkins, Knight, in his voyage into the South Sea. An. Dom. 1593.* at section 4 where he discusses the entrance to the South Sea, which is virtually identical to Barlaeus. It reads:

Voiage where in *W. Adams* was Pilot (whose voiage and *Seb. Werts* ye have in the former Tome) *Theodore Gerards* one of that fleet, was caried by Tempest, as they write to 64 degrees South, in which height the country was mountainous & covered with snow, looking like Norway. It seemed to extend towards the Islands of Salomon.

[1] Cook, 1777, II, p. 230.

[2] This is now known as Montagu Island. Cook sighted Southern Thule from HMS *Resolution* on 30 January 1775. He then turned north and sighted Bristol Island before reaching Montagu Island. The weather was bad and he was unable to examine them, and so thinking they might be promontories of a larger land mass he named it Sandwich Land after John Montagu, 4th Earl of Sandwich, and First Lord of the Admiralty. He subsequently continued northwards sighting Saunders Island (named for Admiral Sir Charles Saunders under whom Cook had served in the St

were black, cavernous, and perpendicular to a vast height; thick clouds veiled the upper parts of the mountains,'[1] &c. Hence, proceeding to Southern Thule, ' the mountains appeared to be of vast height, their summits being constantly wrapped in clouds, and the lower part covered with snow down to the water's edge, so that it would have been difficult to pronounce whether we saw land or ice, if some hollow rocks had not shown their black and naked caverns in several places.'[2] Precisely similar were the appearances of the mountains of the North Foreland in South Shetland, where the uninterrupted white surfaces of the higher hills were in parts broken by black spots: one very large one on the peak of land marked E in the chart,[3] was probably the effect of a cavern in the mountain, – an occurrence very common in mountains of hornblende-slate, of which I am inclined to believe the hills of both countries are chiefly composed.

The climate of New Shetland would seem to be very temperate, considering its latitude; and should the expedition now sent out bring assurances that the land is capable of supporting population, – an assumption which the presence of trees renders very probable, the place may become a colony of considerable importance. So little advanced as the season must be in October, the atmosphere was by no means cold: it was pleasantly temperate, like that felt in the north of Scotland at a similar season. Even in June, the very depth of winter, nothing like excessive cold was experienced.

The prompt measures adopted by the Naval Commander on the station merit the warmest praise, for having availed himself of every means he could attain for arranging the survey. Those who are aware of the extent to which the whale-fishery may be carried on in this hemisphere, must be immediately struck with the immense benefit which the acquisition of New Shetland might offer as a British settlement. We have only to call to view the chance we stand of being outrivalled by another maritime

---

Lawrence in 1759) and Candlemas Isles (it being then 3 February), which were seen to be islands. In his journal he added 'I concluded that what I had seen, which I named *Sandwich Land* was either a group of Islands or else a point of the Continent, for I firmly believe that there is a tract of land near the Pole.' Beaglehole, 1961, pp. 636–7.

[1] Forster, 1777, II, p. 536, referring to Southern Thule, the land discovered on 31st January, 1775, reads:

We ran towards it near an hour, when we were within half a mile of the rocks, which were black, cavernous, and perpendicular to a vast height, inhabited by flocks of shags, and beaten by dreadful breakers. Thick clouds veiled the upper parts of the mountains, but one immense peak appeared towering beyond them, covered with snow. It was agreed by all present, that the perpendicular height of this mountain could not be far short of two miles.

[2] Forster 1777, II, p. 537, reads:

The mountains appeared to be of vast height, their summits being constantly wrapped in clouds, and the lower part covered with snow down to the water's edge in such a manner, that we should have found it difficult to pronounce whether we saw land or ice, if some hollow rocks had not shewn their black and naked caverns in several places.'

[3] This may have been Ternych Needle, 364 m (1195 ft) which stands on a ridge in about the position indicated on the chart. It is a nunatak, a needle of bare rock, rising about 91 m (300 ft) above the ridge and the highest point for a considerable distance all round. It appears a distinct black spot above the ridge when seen from seaward.

nation, there being at this time upwards of 200 American whale-ships lucratively employed in the Pacific, when Great Britain cannot boast of more than 30 or 40.[1] We have only to state this fact, to exhibit the advantage of this settlement as connected with that branch of trade; but if we take into view the whole mercantile trade with Buenos Ayres, Chili, Peru, and the immensely extensive provinces of the interior, which is increasing with strides unknown, and establishing a demand for articles of British manufacture that must eventually prove the channel for the consumption of British produce, and the employment of British capital; if we consider, too, that these places must eventually become established as places of barter and entrepôt to our India and China trades, – then must the importance of the situation, if it can admit of a settlement, be strikingly apparent. Comparing this spot with the Cape of Good Hope and New Holland, it will be seen that these three places form equidistant depôts in the Southern Hemisphere, respectively situated so as to defend, if not to command, a superiority of trade with more extensive markets than were ever offered to any commercial nation at any former period of the world; and this, too, at a time when the late eventful circumstances in the history of Europe have turned in no small degree British commerce out of those channels in which it has flowed uninterruptedly for so many years.

No one can deny that the want of a British settlement contiguous to the coast of South America is seriously felt; for since the abandonment of the Falkland Islands,[2] we have no possession, – not even a watering-place, – nearer than the Cape of Good Hope or New Holland; and no one can calculate upon the absolute necessity Great Britain may one day feel for such a possession. Under every point of view, as well national, commercial, and scientific, must the discovery of New South Shetland be valued; and without doubt the results of the present expedition will be anxiously looked for by every wellwisher to his country★.

Valparaiso, *January* 1820

★ We understand that Captain Basil Hall, F.R.S., has been sent out for the purpose of exploring and surveying this new region. The highest expectations may be entertained from the known skill and enterprise of our eminent countrymen.[3] – Ed.

---

[1] Miers, 1826, II, pp. 287–9, records the fate of a whaling venture by Messrs Henderson and Wooster (an Englishman and a North American), who upon encouragement from the Chilean government invested the sum of 60,000 dollars in the enterprise. Vessels were chartered, equipped and sent to sea: the refining establishment was to have been set up at Coquimbo whither were sent all the barrel-staves and barrels that could be purchased. When the military expedition sailed from Valparaíso, shortly afterwards (August 1820), to liberate Peru it called at Coquimbo and requisitioned all the available hogsheads prepared for the whale-oil. When the company tried to build tanks ashore for the reception of the oil, they were halted by the Governor on the ground that it would injure the health of the inhabitants, despite being several miles from the town. On the arrival of the first vessel the Governor then claimed a right to levy duty, on the authority of an old Spanish law, of about one eighth share of the produce. The enterprise was abandoned with considerable loss.

[2] Port Egmont, the British settlement in West Falkland, was abandoned on 24 May 1774, a plaque being set up to retain the sovereignty of the islands for the British Crown.

[3] Captain Hall did indeed go out to South America, but he did not visit the South Shetland Islands.

Account 3. *Literary Gazette and Journal of Belles Lettres*, 14 October, 1820, p. 668:

THE NEW CONTINENT

We have been favoured with the following extract from the log-book of the brig Williams, by a vessel just arrived from Buenos Ayres. It states several particulars respecting the newly-discovered continent of New Shetland, or South Shetland; and as every thing relative to this matter is interesting, we lay it exactly as it reached us before our readers. There was a map with the packet, but it appears, (with the exception of Dalrymple's chart) to be similar to that in Brewster's Philosophical Journal,[1] which may be referred to.

Extract from the Brig William's Log Book, on a Voyage from Buenos Ayres to Valpariso. Feb. 19th 1819.

1st Track – Having sailed round to the eastward of the Falkland Islands, and keeping our reach to the southward and westward, winds variable from south to south west, in lat. 62°40′ south and long. 60°00′ west by chronometer. Land or ice was discovered ahead, bearing S.E. by S. distant about 2 leagues, blowing hard gales with flying showers of snow, the day breaking at 6 A.M. wore ship to the northward, at 9 A.M. more moderate and clear; a large field of ice was distant 10 miles; at noon moderate and fine weather; lat. observed, 62°17′ south, long. 60°12′ west; wore ship and made sail for land again at 2 P.M.; the large body of ice bore west distant 4 miles; at 4 P.M. tacked ship the land or islands bearing S.E. by E. to S.S.E. distant 10 miles; the weather fine and pleasant. It was discovered to be land a little covered with snow; down tacks and steered to N.W. at 6 P.M. the ice E.N.E. distant 1 mile floating about, and whales and seals observed in abundance; afterwards made all sail on our intended voyage.

From Valpariso to Mantinidio – May 12th.

2nd Track.– On my arrival at Valpariso, this land being doubtful from not having sounded, I determined on looking for it again, and steering in a parallel of 62°12′ south for the Islands, when in lat. 67°00′ west, on 15th June at 6 P.M. and in the above lat. found the vessel completely beset with broken ice, standing immediately to the north, under easy sail, and going at the rate of 1½ to 2 miles per hour; night very dark; it was found impossible to make further progress this season, in consequence thereof we abandoned the attempt, and stood on for our destined port. On arrival, notwithstanding all the precaution that was observed, the ice had torn off the vessel's bottom several sheets of copper.

From Mantinidio to Valpariso

3rd Track.– After departing from this place, we were favoured with fine weather and a fair wind which allowed us to pass Cape Horn in 14 days, the wind then favourable to go to the westward; however, as it was our intention to make the islands, we stood away

---

[1] There does not appear to have been a journal with this title published. However *The Edinburgh Philosophical Journal*, which carried John Miers's account with a 'Chart copied from Dalrymple's chart of the Southern Ocean &c.' and a 'Chart of the Newly Discovered Land New South Shetland', is stated on its title page to have been 'conducted by Dr Brewster and Professor Jameson'. It seems likely therefore that 'Brewster's Philosophical Journal' refers to *The Edinburgh Philosophical Journal*.

S.S.E. and on the 15th Oct. at 6 P.M. made them distant 3 leagues, in lat. 62°30′ south, and long. 60°00′ west; bore up and sailed towards them; at four miles distant sounded in 40 fathoms, fine black sand, islands bearing E. by S. at S.E. by S. sounded again in 60 fathoms, sand bottom. Hauled off during the night to north; at daylight stood in at three leagues distance from the islands; sounded and found 95 fathoms, fine sandy bottom, at 8 A.M. clear pleasant weather; saw the main land bearing S.S.E. distant from the islands about three leagues. Having now as far as the Cape found the land to run off N.E. coasting to the eastward, sounded and found it similar to the former.

The point which is called North Foreland, bearing E. by S we hauled in for it, and got the island to bear N.W. distant half a league, sounding regular from 20 to 35 fathoms; fine bottom, sand and gravel; finding the weather favourable, sent in the boat and succeeded in landing: it was found to be barren and covered with snow; seals were observed about the shore in abundance. Night coming on the boat returned, when we made sail off the shore for the night; in the morning altered the course so as to keep the land to the southward in view. At 11 A.M. the North Foreland bore E.S. by E. distant five leagues; the land then took a S.E. direction.

After this we hauled to the westward, and proceeded on our voyage.

I again from variable winds made Cape Williams, and perceived some trees on the land to the S.W. of the Cape, stretching in a S.W. direction; the weather became thick and squally; made sail to the westward, having sailed about 150 miles W.S.W. The weather became more settled, saw another headland bearing about E.N.E. distant about 10 leagues, very high; by observation in lat. 62°53′ south, and long. per chronom. 63°40′ west of Greenwich, named the Smith's Cape; found the land to extend at the Cape in a southerly direction. Finding it dangerous to proceed further to the southward and in an unknown coast, shaped my course for Valpariso, where I arrived on 23rd Nov. 1819.

It is to be remarked, that the land was taken possession of in the name of Our Sovereign Lord George III, King of Great Britain and Ireland, and in this name planted the Union, and left a board stating the discoverer, &c.

Account 4. *The Globe*, 2 November 1820: Copy of article in *Literary Gazette and Journal of Belles Lettres* of 14 October.

Account 5. William Smith's Memorial:

> To the Right Honorable the Lords Commissioners of His Majesty's Admiralty
> The Humble Memorial of William Smith, Master of the Ship Williams of Blyth –
> Sheweth,
> That your Memorialist on a voyage from Buenos Ayres to Valparaiso in Chili on the 19th. Feby. 1819 – when rounding to the Eastward of the Falkland Islands, the wind prevailing from the West North West to the West South West, and finding no chance of making a Passage round Cape Horn, without being in a high Southerly Latitude, Keeping a good look out for the Ice, when on the 19th. aforesaid at 7 A.M. Land or Ice was discovered bearing South East by South, distance two or three Leagues – Strong Gales from the South West accompanied with Snow or Sleet – Wore ship to the Northward at 10 A.M. more moderate & clear, wore ship to the Southward & made sail for the Land

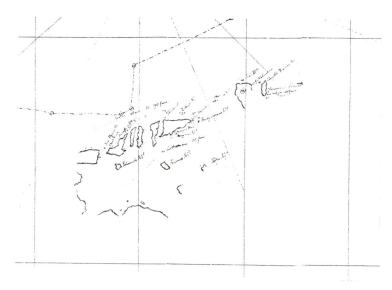

Plate 7. Portion of Chart accompanying the Memorial of William Smith. UK HO s.91, Ac1.

– at 11 rounded a large Ice Berg; at noon, fine & pleasant weather, – latitude by Observation 62^{dg}.15^m South – Longitude by Chronometer 60^d–01^m West – steering in a South South East direction – at 4 P.M. made the land bearing from S.S.E. to S.E. by E, distance about 10 miles – hove to, & having satisfied ourselves of Land hauled to the Westward & made sail on our Voyage to Valparaiso –

That your Memorialist on his arrival at the above named Port reported the Particulars of his Discovery to Captain Sherriff of His Majesty's Ship Andromache, when Captain Sheriff expressed his doubts as to the existence of the Land saying he probably mistook the Ice for Land –

That your Memorialist sailed on the 16th of May 1819 – from Valparaiso with a Cargo for Monte Video in the River Plate, being resolved to visit again the new discovered Land, that on this Voyage nothing particular Occurred untill the 15th of June 1819 – at 6 P.M. being in Latitude 62^d–12^m South & Longitude 67^d West, he found the Sea very Smooth with some small particles of Ice & Supposed it might be from a heavy fall of snow; in less than half an hour, we were completely hemmed in by loose Ice, hauled our Wind to the Northward & regulated sail, so as not to go more than from one to One & half Knots through the Ice for fear of damaging the Ship – at Midnight, clear Weather & it not being practicable to remain in so high a Latitude at that season of the Year proceeded on Voyage to Monte Video convinced that land must be near from the forming of Ice –

That on Memorialist's arrival at Monte Video the Report of his Discovery got into Circulation, that the Americans at that Port & Buenos Ayres offered your Memorialist large Sums of Money to make Known unto them the Discovery he had made; But your memorialist having the Good of his Country at heart (if any should be derived from such Discovery) & as he had not taken possession of the land in the name of his Sovereign Lord the King resisted all the offers from the said Americans, determined again to revisit the new discovered Land –

That your Memorialist sailed from Monte Video on a voyage to Valparaso, with the intention of again looking for land in an high Southern Latitude – That on the 15th. of October at 4 – P.M. your Memorialist discovered Land bearing S.E. by E distance 3 Leagues – Weather hazy Sounding at 65 Fathoms with fine sand and ouze – Wore ship to the Northward for the Ensuing night – 16th. in the Morng. made sail for the land at Noon fine & pleasant Weather observed a large tract of land laying in a W.S.W. & NNE. direction, very high & covered with Snow, vast quantities of Seals, Whales, Penguins &c about the Ship –

That on the 17th. day of October, 1819 – your memorialist landed & took formal possession of the new discovered land in the Name of his Majesty George the Third & named the said land New South Britain, & after making every possible discovery, made sail for Valparaiso –

That on your Memorialist's arrival at the said Port, he immediately reported a second time his discovery & taking possession of the said Land in his Majesty's name to Captain Sherriff of His Majesty's Ship Andromache, with the different Soundings & all the observations your memorialist had made, upon which Captain Sherriff was pleased to send the Ship Williams, with a sufficient number of Officers & seamen for the purpose of visiting the new discovered land named by your memorialist New South Britain – On the return of the Ship Williams to Valparaiso from her said voyage she was discharged from the service by Captain Searle of HMS Hyperion & the name of New South Shetland was given to the new discovered land –

That your Memorialist sailed from Valparaiso for the Coast of New South Shetland for the purpose of fishing for Whales & Seals with a Crew of 43 men – on your Memorialist's arrival on the said Coast, he found several Bays & Harbours which are pointed out in the Chart (Submitted to your Lordships with this Memorial) that shortly after to your Memorialist's Surprize, there arrived from 15 to 20 British Ships, together with about 30 sail of Americans, & during the fishing season, it was with great difficulty your Memorialist maintained Peace, between the Crews of the two Nations, who were on shore – There are many mineral productions on different parts of the Coast – The Fishing trade has been followed up with great perseverance & has already employed about 1200 British Seamen – The End of the Coast has not yet been ascertained –

Your Memorialist therefore humbly craves your Lordships will be pleased to take into your Consideration the anxious Solicitude with which your Memorialist followed up his attempts to discover & ultimately by his perseverance discovering the Land named by him New South Britain, his having taken possession of the Same in his Majesty's name & through his information to Captain Sherriff of HMS Andromache the same discovery having been fully proved to be true & correct & that your Lordships will be pleased in consequence to grant to your Memorialist such remuneration as in your Judgement may seem meet –

And Your Memorialist as in duty bound will ever Pray

W. Smith

No 5 Griffin Street
Shadwell

The Memorial is inscribed, on the second page, in the hand of J. W. Croker,[1] Secretary to the Admiralty: 'Dec 29. Send copy to the Treasury – acqtg them that tho this department has no means of rewarding this person my Lords think it right to communicate it to the Treasury. Acqt the party.'

And in a different hand: 'The Chart herein referred to has been sent to the Hydrographer'.

Accounts 6, 7, 8: see Appendix 1: Accounts by Purdy, 1822; Weddell, 1825; Norie, 1825; Blunt 1827.

★ ★ ★

Comparison of the different versions and assessment of the origin of the various texts of the *Williams* log book

Captain Shirreff's account [1], Miers's account [2], and Smith's Memorial [5], would all appear to be independantly based on the original, see pp. 42–3 above. The *Literary Gazette* article [3] bears a strong resemblance to [1] although it is not identical with it. In [3] it is stated that the *Williams* was on passage to and from Mantinidio and not Monte Video; there is an additional final paragraph stating that the land was claimed for King George III in [3], and the distance the ship was from the island when the boat was sent ashore is given as half a league while [1] (and [2]) has 7 leagues. From the map and text it seems certain the island in question is that which was subsequently named Ridleys Island. If this is correct 7 leagues would have put the landing well east of North Foreland, where there is no land, while half a league would have put it in what is now known as Venus Bay with the landing itself in Esther Harbour on the west side of the bay.[2] There are other minor differences. It would appear, from the reference to 'Brewster's Philosophical Journal' in the rubric (p. 62 & n. 1 above), that the article in the *Edinburgh Philosophical Journal* was available to the editor of the *Literary Gazette* before this article was published, so that it is possible it was based on it but the differences are such that this seems highly unlikely. The impression is that the article is based on the same original as Captain Shirreff's and John Miers's, i.e. Smith's Journal, or a copy of it sent home as stated.

---

[1] John Wilson Croker, 1780–1857, was born in Galway, 10 August 1780. His father was Surveyor General of Customs and Excise in Ireland. He was brought up in Cork and attended Trinity College in Dublin. In 1800 he became a student of Lincoln's Inn, but was more interested in literary pursuits. In 1802 he returned to Ireland and made his way at the Irish bar. He married Miss Rosamond Pennell in 1806, whose father later became British Consul in South America. He was a member of Parliament from 1806 to 1832 representing various constituencies in Ireland and England. He was Secretary of the Admiralty between 1809 and 1830. *DNB*, s.v.

[2] Esther Harbour is described in the *Antarctic Pilot*, 1974, p. 160, as one of the best anchorages for a small vessel on the north side of the South Shetland Islands.

Purdy's account [6] (pp. 193–6), which includes only brief remarks on the first and second voyages but gives the third in detail, is very similar to that in the *Literary Gazette* although there are a number of significant differences. Mantinidio has reverted to Monte-Video; the nature of the sea bed at the second sounding on 15 October (60 fathoms) has 'same bottom' while the *Gazette* has 'sand bottom'. In 95 fathoms Purdy has 'fine sand and oaze' the *Literary Gazette* 'Fine sandy bottom.' Purdy agrees with Captain Shirreff's text in both cases. Again Purdy says 'Having ran as far as the cape, we found the land trend off to the N.E.', the *Literary Gazette* has 'Having now as far as the cape found the land to run off to the N.E.' but Captain Shirreff has 'having run as far as the Cape we found the land tend off to the N^d and E^d.', which is much closer to Purdy. The reason for leaving the coast 'having a merchant's cargo on board, and perhaps deviating from the insurance' is given in Captain Shirreff's account and appears slightly altered in Purdy but is not mentioned in the *Literary Gazette* (it is given by Miers as the reason for terminating the first investigation in February, 1820, and on the 3rd track he says 'always having the safety of his cargo as his primary consideration'). There are points where Purdy does not agree with Captain Shirreff, such as the order in which the soundings are given approaching the island were they landed (20 to 35 fathoms, for 35 to 20 fathoms) and the distance to the island, when the boat was lowered (the latter appears to be a mistake on Captain Shirreff's part).

There are, as one would expect, far more similarities than differences, but the latter do not appear to perpetuate themselves from the *Literary Gazette* to Purdy's text which tends to indicate that both are based independently on the original. It is interesting to note that subsequent editions of Purdy alter the initial longitude to 62°W, and avoid mentioning the names of North Foreland and Cape Williams.

Weddell [7] (pp. 193–6) also has 'same bottom', 'having ran as far as the Cape, etc.', the order of soundings reversed to '20 to 35 fathoms', a statement on 'deviating from the insurance' and like Purdy gives the date of arrival in Valparaíso as 24 November (the *Literary Gazette* has 23 November – probably a confusion resulting from the journal having been kept in nautical time). However he follows the *Literary Gazette* with 'fine sand' in 95 fathoms. The principal differences are in the matter of the names, Cape Millan and South Cape for Cape Williams and Smith's Cape which are probably due to type setting errors reading Weddell's manuscript which were not picked up at the proof reading stage.[1] Having dealt

---

[1] The latter is named Smiths Cape on Weddell's chart of South Shetland etc. Cape Williams is not named – it is not named on Bransfield's or Norie's charts either. Weddell, first edition 1825, included an erratum slip, all the entries on which were corrected, together with some minor punctuation errors, in the 1827 edition. These names remained unaltered.

with Smith's journal Weddell goes on to mention the voyage of Bransfield who is twice referred to as 'Mr. Edward Barnsfield', (although the chart of South Shetland has Bransfields Strait while that of the tracks of the *Jane* and *Beaufoy* has Branfields Strait) Purdy uses 'Mr. Edw. Barnsfield'. From this it would appear that Weddell probably used Purdy's text for his book, which, if correct, would tend to confirm that Weddell's statement that the *Literary Gazette* was the origin of the first accounts of the discovery refers to the article on 5 August, 1820.

Since Norie [8] (pp. 193–6) has changed the text from the first to the third person, it is more difficult to form an opinion. He does not give any nature of the sea bed in 60 fathoms where the other texts discussed have 'same bottom', in 95 fathoms he has 'sand and ouze' as in Captain Shirreff's account, he gives the reason for naming North Foreland, which is not in any of the other accounts, he gives the soundings approaching land as 35 to 20 fathoms, he makes no mention of the insurance as the reason for leaving the coast and does not give the date of arrival in Valparaíso. It would seem possible, but no more than that, that this is another independent account based directly on the original, but it would seem more likely that it too is based on Purdy.

Two other points deserve mention. Captain Shirreff, John Miers and the *Literary Gazette* all mention trees in the vicinity of Cape Williams. Smith, who had spent a season sealing before his return home, knew this was incorrect and makes no mention of them in his Memorial. Furthermore by 1822 it would have been well known in England and it is therefore no surprise that they are not mentioned in the later accounts. William Smith's claiming the new land for his sovereign is mentioned in his Memorial, John Miers's account, and as an afterthought in the *Literary Gazette*, possibly added from Miers's account. It is not in Captain Shirreff's, Purdy's or the later accounts and it would seem possible therefore that it may not have been mentioned in the original journal.

To sum up the accounts of Captain Shirreff [1], and John Miers [2], and William Smith's Memorial [5] are apparently taken directly from the original log. Accounts in the *Literary Gazette* [3] and Purdy's memoir [6] appear to be based on the original, the former via an intermediary; *The Globe* [4] is a reprint of the *Literary Gazette* [3], and Weddell [7] and Norie [8] appear to be based on Purdy [6].

CHAPTER 5

VOYAGE OF EDWARD BRANSFIELD

Captain Shirreff was in Santiago concluding diplomatic arrangements with the Chilean government[1] when William Smith arrived in Valparaíso on 24 November 1819,[2] with confirmation of his discovery. The British merchants in the port immediately set about chartering a vessel to proceed on a voyage of discovery on their own account. However as soon as Captain Shirreff heard the news he chartered the *Williams*[3] (see pp. 199–200 for the charter agreement), retaining William Smith to act under the orders of the master of HMS *Andromache*, Edward Bransfield.[4] John Miers's machinery, which he had contracted with William Smith to carry the short trip to Concón was disembarked; additional stores and live animals were embarked; the master, Edward Bransfield, together with the master's mate, Midshipman Poynter

---

[1] Captain Shirreff's Merchant's Letter Book, NMM, SHI/2, has a letter to C. Delegal Esq. dated 11 December from Santiago, so presumably he remained there until at least that date.

[2] Recorded in HMS *Andromache*'s log PRO ADM 51/2131.

[3] The actual charter started on 19 December, although a working party was sent on board the *Williams* on 14, 15, 16, 17 and 18 December to get the vessel ready for the voyage: HMS *Andromache*'s log, PRO ADM 51/2131.

[4] It is not entirely clear what the respective positions of Edward Bransfield and William Smith were. In the charter agreement William Smith is instructed to receive on board 'such Officers and Men … and to proceed on such service as he shall be directed to perform by the Senior Officer' which could be taken to mean that the naval contingent were travelling as passengers. John Miers says: 'The Williams … put to sea … under the charge of Mr Edward Bransfield.' The orders given to Bransfield start, as if addressed to a commanding officer, 'You are to proceed to about the Latitude 62 S…'; Dr Young says 'The command of the expedition was given to Mr Edward Barnsfield [*sic*]' (p. 79), however, there is no appointment in command. It is possible that this was done verbally or by a separate document which was not copied for the Admiralty.

The vessel is referred to by Poynter as His Majesty's Hired Brig, and a pendant (used by HM ships in commission for the Commanding Officer) was hoisted 'which ceremony was accompanied with a Gun', and on their return to Valparaíso, on 16th April the pendant was struck. Furthermore Poynter states that he was himself in charge of one of the watches on deck, which would appear to indicate that the naval officers were fully integrated in the company.

It is also worth noting that when Smith was acting on his own it was his mate who was sent in shore in the boat to Shireff's Cove (*sic*) to take possession of the new land in the name of the sovereign (according to Miers in the *Edinburgh Philosophical Journal* (p. 51), who also quotes the mate for his

and Midshipmen Bone and Blake, from HMS *Andromache*,[1] and the assistant surgeon, Dr Young of HMS *Slaney*[2] joined and the brig put to sea on 19 December 1819.

A copy of the orders given to Bransfield by Captain Shirreff was forwarded to the Admiralty,[3] they read:

By William Henry Shirreff Esq.
Captain of HMS Andromache and
Senior Officer of H.M. Ships and Vessels
on the Western Coast of South America

You are to proceed to about the Latitude of 62 S and Longitude 62 W to discover and ascertain the extent of the tract of Land there seen by Mr Smith Master of the Brig Williams in October last, and whether it be merely an Island or part of a Continent, if the latter as would appear, not improbable, you will explore the Coast to the Eastward, and determine if possible if it be connected with the Southern Thule and Sandwich Land. If however you should find great difficulty in performing this, you will explore the Coast to the Southwd and Westwd of that part seen by Mr. Smith, the Climate from the observation of former Navigators being more temperate, and the Sea more free of Ice.

---

description of the shore; the *Literary Gazette*, Purdy and Weddell do not say who landed, and Smith says 'your memorialist landed and took possession' which does not necessarily mean that he did it in person but that he ordered it to be done). However, with Bransfield embarked, there is no doubt he went himself in the boat to look for an anchorage, leaving the brig in a very dangerous situation, on 16 January, and subsequently took the boat sealing while the brig remained under way, both actions he is unlikely to have taken if he was in command and responsible for the safety of the vessel.

Finally, and perhaps more positively when the Brig returned to Valparaíso Bransfield wrote to Captain Searle of HMS *Hyperion,* the senior officer present: 'Herewith you will receive the Log Book of the Hired Armed Brig Williams of Blyth, under my Command on a Voyage of Discovery...': Appendix 3, PRO ADM 1/2548.

For these reasons it would seem that Bransfield was in fact in command of the *Williams* although his relationship with William Smith may well have been more similar to that between an admiral and his flag captain, than the nineteenth century one between the captain and the master of a naval ship.

[1] The log records for 19 December 'Chartered the Williams and sent the Master and three Midshipmen on board her to survey the new land' (PRO ADM 51/2131). The master, Edward Bransfield, and Midshipmen Back, Bone and Poynter are shown in the Muster Book of HMS *Andromache* (PRO ADM 37/6074) and against each name during the period 19 December 1819 to 27 May 1820 they are marked as being absent in the *Williams*. They are the only members of the ship's company so marked and therefore it can be safely accepted that no one else from HMS *Andromache* accompanied the party. A similar check of the muster list of HMS *Slaney* (PRO ADM 37/6471) indicates that only Dr Young from that ship sailed in the *Williams*. Poynter's remark in his journal for 17 and 18 December (p. 97) That 'an extra number of hands were shipped' must either refer to William Smith embarking extra hands (see p. 102, n. 1), or to an enlargement of the working party getting the *Williams* ready for sea.

[2] O'Brien, 1839, p. 316, records: 'When our surgeon, Mr. Burnside and his assistant, Mr. Young, administered to them [the local population] medical relief, so thankful were they, that every morning we had canoes alongside, – a very unusual thing, – with poultry, eggs and vegetables, ...'. No doubt Dr Young was pleased by the prospect of a change in this routine.

[3] PRO ADM 1/2548. See Appendix 2 for covering letter and charter agreement.

You will explore every harbour that you may discover, making correct Charts thereof and noting the soundings therein, and whether they are secure for Ships to Ride and refit in, and you will ascertain the truth of the account brought here of the uncommon abundance of the Sperm Whale, Otters Seals &c upon the Coast and in the Harbours.

You will ascertain the natural resources of the Land for supporting a Colony and Maintaining a population, and if it should already be Inhabited you will minutely observe the Character, habits, dress, customs and state of civilization of the Inhabitants to whom you will display every friendly disposition.

You will note minutely the appearance of the Land, the face of the Country, its natural productions, discription thereof, and depth of Soil, and you will collect specimens of each particular Kind of Rock, noting the Inclination and dip of the Strata, and mark upon each sample the order of their superposition and locality and ascertain as nearly as possible the height of the Mountains, and particularly note the existance or appearance of Rivers, Streams and Lakes of fresh and Salt Water, their breadth and depth, whether Navigable, and by what discription of fish or Animal inhabited.

You will collect and preserve specimens of each plant or Vegitable, the flower and leaves of Trees, and specimens of each kind of Wood, taking care that Mr. Bone make drawings of each, as well as of every species of Land and Amphibious Animal, Bird, fish, Insect and Reptile, specimens of which you will also preserve, but of such as cannot be preserved, you will carefully Keep the Skins, Bones, Teeth and Claws.

You will Keep a Meteorological journal noting therein the Variation of the Barometer, Thermometer and Weather every two hours, and you will carefully observe and note The Variation of the Magnetic Needle both on shore & on Board.

You will take every means in your power of ascertaining correctly the Latitudes and Longitudes of the different Head Lands, Harbours &c that no doubt may hereafter exist as to the correctness of your observations you will carefully note down all the data whence the result of your observations are deduced and you will most minutely remark in your journal every trifling occurance of however little importance it may appear to you, and this the Gentlemen under your orders will also do, each Keeping a separate and secret journal, which they are on no account to compare, but to deliver to me on their return sealed up.

In case of your meeting with any foreign Vessel upon the Coast, which may be about to make settlements there, you will inform the Captains or Masters that the Country has already been taken possession of, but more strongly to insure the Right to Great Britain, you will yourself on each separate Quarter of the Land, take possession of it in the Name and behalf of His Majesty King George the Third his Heirs and successors, planting a board with an Union Jack painted on it, and words written under to the above purpose.

As it is impossible to tell what Weather or resources you may meet with upon the Coast, you must be entirely guided by your own discretion, as to the length of time you remain upon this Service, should you discover however that the Land presents facilities for Wintering there, and that its productions are likely to be advantageous to the trade of Great Britain, you will then remain there in pursuit of your object as long as your provisions will admit, or until you have finished your Survey.

Should your time exceed six Months, instead of returning to this Port in quest of me, you will make the best of your way to England, touching at any Port you may find necessary on your passages, and immediately upon your arrival give notice to the Lords Commissioners of the Admiralty of your proceedings.

You will be most careful should you touch in any foreign Port, to conceal every discovery that you may have made during your Voyages, and for which reason you will have as little communication with other vessels as possible.

Altho' I have thought it necessary to point out in these instructions, many things which may be of great utility to Natural History, you will remember that the great and leading object which you are to attend to, and which is on no account to be delayed for the other objects of minor importance, is the Survey of the Coast and Harbours.

> Given under my hand on board HMS
> Andromache Valparaiso this 19th. day of
> Decr. 1819.
>
> W. H. Shirreff

To/
Mr. Edwd. Bransfield
Master of HMS Andromache

The *Williams* weighed anchor at 1700 on 19 December 1819, and at the same time HMS *Andromache* put to sea for Callao.[1] The *Williams* had to anchor again due to the lack of wind and finally got away the next day.

Initially they had light and baffling winds and were carried north by the current, so that it was not until 30 December that they actually got south of Valparaíso, and not until 16 January 1820 that they were in soundings off the South Shetlands. The first landfall was in the bay now known as Barclay Bay; the weather was poor and the visibility got worse. Having had trouble with their water casks leaking, the first thought was to water ship and for this an anchorage was sought. William Smith set out in the whale boat to find it. Although the anchorage he found was a possibility, it was definitely not recommended and they put to sea again. Rocks were sighted and the weather closing in forced them to anchor. After a very anxious few hours listening to waves breaking under their lee in the fog, the weather cleared and the wind veered so that they could get clear. The anchor was lost in weighing.

They then proceeded along the north coast of the Islands, generally in poor visibility, charting the coast as best they could, as they went along; rounded the North Foreland, which was the limit of William Smith's earlier exploration, and approached the south side of the islands (Plates 8 and 9). On 22 January an island was sighted and then a bay, which they entered, sounding carefully as they went, until a safe anchorage was found. Here Bransfield went ashore and with due ceremony claimed the land for King George III, his Heirs and Successors, in accordance with his orders, naming it New South Britain. Observations were taken for latitude

---

[1] PRO ADM 51/2131.

on board and longitude ashore and the bay was surveyed and named George's Bay in honour of the King (now King George Bay). They watered ship, and relieved of this very real problem (which is still a source of anxiety to mariners today, although with the ability to produce fresh water from salt, considerably less so than it used to be) put to sea again on 27 January. The weather remained thick with short periods of improved visibility. The *Williams* sailed slowly westward along the south coast of the islands, noting inlets, which were not investigated due to the weather.

On 29 January, in poor visibility with a falling glass and rising sea, they stood away south to get clear of the land. Early next morning they fell in with a group of small islands and then sighted what must have been Deception Island to the westward. They continued southward to get away from the land and in the afternoon were amazed, during a clear spell, to find themselves 'half encompassed with islands' with a 'high rude range running in a NE and SW direction' beyond. This was the first sighting of the Antarctic land mass.[1]

---

[1] It has been argued by, among others, Lebedev, in *Antarktika, Doklady komissii*, 1960 (the following quotations are taken from the 1966 Jerusalem translation, pp. 8–19), that Bellingshausen, in the naval sloops *Vostok* and *Mirnyi*, was in fact the first to sight the continent. Lazarev, captain of the *Mirnyi*, described the first encounter with the continent in 1820 as follows: 'On 16 January (28 January on the Gregorian Calendar – V. Lebedev) [since Bellingshausen was keeping nautical time, and this was after noon the civil date should be 27 January], having reached the latitude 69°25′ and longitude 2°10′, we met with continuous ice, at whose edge were pieces piled one on another, with ice mountains seen at different places in a southerly direction': *M. P. Lazarev, Dokumenty*, ed. A. A. Samarov, Moscow, 1952–6, I, p. 147. Lazarev [in a letter to A. A. Shestakov, dated 24 September 1821] described the first encounter with the continent which occurred on 27 January (16 January Julian Calendar), 1820, as follows:

On January 16 we reached latitude 60°23′S. where we encountered an ice shore of extreme height, and that evening, which was very fine, as we watched from the crosstrees, it stretched before us as far as the eye could see. But we did not enjoy this wonderful view for long, because it became cloudy again and as usual it began snowing. This was in longitude 2°35′W. from Greenwich. From here we continued our course eastward, bearing south at every opportunity, but we kept encountering the ice continent each time we approached 70° (p. 14).

At this time the expedition was about twenty miles from the currently charted coastline.

In a letter to the Marquis de Traversey, dated 8 April 1820, Bellingshausen wrote:

after midnight between February 5 and 6 we reached latitude 69°7′30″S. and longitude 16°15′E. There, behind small ice flows and islands, the continent of ice was seen. It had edges broken perpendicularly and stretched beyond the limit of our vision, sloping up towards the south like a shore. (pp. 16–17).

In his report to the Minister of the Navy, Bellingshausen made a special mention of the fact that he had not seen 'land' and that it could not be distinguished because it was possibly covered by ice both on top and on the sea side. He wrote towards the end of his journal (II, 250) for 12 January 1821 [24 January 1821]:

I designate as continental the huge ice which, on approaching the South Pole, rises into sloping mountains, as I believe that when it is four degrees of frost on the best summer day, then further to the south the frost does not, of course, become any milder, and therefore I can

They were in a perilous position off an unknown coast abounding in rocks and islands, with poor and variable visibility; in the event of accident there was no possibility of succour and the information so far obtained would be lost with them. It is not therefore surprising that, 'fearfull of a change of wind', they wore and hauled off to the northward while they were able to do so. Next day they set course east north east to try and follow the coast of the mainland and in due course raised Hope Island, which they named 'from the hope we entertained that the range might continue to stretch Easterly untill joined by the Thule'. Behind, and to the south south west they saw mountains of considerable height, now known as Mount Bransfield. The weather closed in again and again they stood off to the northward.

On 2 February, shortly before seven in the evening, with a fresh gale and heavy squalls, the sea was seen to be breaking violently over three very large rocks (probably Simpson Rock, seven miles east of King George Island). All hands were stood to. Then the wind fell and they were driven towards the shore. 'At midnight with foggy weather and a very heavy swell from the northward it fell calm... about 15 minutes after midnight a breeze springing up from the SW caused a degree of pleasure not easily to be described'; they steered clear to the eastward and all those off watch retired.

The vessel passed north of the O'Brien Islands, named for the captain of Dr Young's ship, HMS *Slaney*, north of Elephant Island and north and east of Clarence Island, on the southern extremity of which Bransfield landed to plant another flag and claim it for King George. From there Bransfield decided to steer east until they should reach 50°W and then go south so that they could determine if there was any connection with Sandwich Land, discovered by Captain Cook in 1775, in order to clear up that particular point in his orders. This plan was frustrated by thick fog and they returned to the land they had recently left.

The weather continued thick so that it was not practicable to achieve very much. They sailed back north round Clarence and Elephant Islands and William Smith landed on Seal Island to collect as many skins as he could. There were occasional breaks in the poor visibility when high mountains were seen, so that although they knew Clarence Island was indeed an island they thought Elephant Island might be connected to the mainland south of Hope Island.

On 22 February, in clear weather, Bransfield decided to make another attempt

---

conclude that the ice spreads over the Pole and must be immovable, touching the ground or islands in some places similar to Peter I Island. (p. 17).

From the above it would seem probable that Bellingshausen and his people were the first to sight the fast ice with the continental ice front behind it. It is also clear that, although he did not see solid rock, he appreciated what he had seen.

to get south, and see if there was a connection to Sandwich Land. Initially the sea was clear but before evening several pieces of ice were encountered and they had to heave to during the hours of darkness. Next day they continued southward but at noon encountering a range of field ice, with thirty-eight large bergs around them, they gave up and turned north again having reached nearly 65°S. Back round the east and north sides of Clarence and Elephant Islands, with no improvement in the visibility and the season now far advanced it was decided that they would attempt to land at Cape Shirreff and plant another flag there before returning to Valparaíso. They came up with Ridley Island (Ridleys Island) at the north east end of King George Island but were driven eastward by storms and it was not until 16 March that they recovered their position. They worked their way westward along the coast well off shore and on 19 March closed Greenwich Island but were unable to land and so turned back north westward bringing the season to a close.

The brig called at Cumberland Bay, (Bahía Cumberland, Isla Robinson Crusoe, Archipiélago de Juan Fernández) which proved a very welcome relief after such an arduous cruise and finally reached Valparaíso on 14 April where Bransfield reported to Captain Searle, HMS *Hyperion*, the senior officer present who instructed him to render all charts and journals to him and forbade communication with the shore.[1] The brig was paid off on 16 April.[2] Bransfield and his party rejoined HMS *Andromache* on her return to Valparaíso on 27 May, 1820[3] and HMS *Hyperion* put to sea on 31 May.[4]

The resulting British Admiralty Chart was published In 1822, titled *New or South Shetland, seen in 1819 by Willm Smith, Master of the Brig WILLIAMS, Surveyed by E. Brans field Master R.N. in 1820.* It also states *NB This Land was known to the Old Navigators and said to be first discovered by Theodore Gerrards in 1599.* (Plate 31)

Looking at this chart, and comparing it with the track chart (Plate 9a) based on the modern chart, the most striking point is that the line of the South Shetland Islands is shown as a peninsula with two possible channels through it. They were

---

[1] See p. 202, for letter covering charts and journals, and p. 207, report in *The Times* of 10 August forbidding contact with the shore.

[2] It is possible that Bransfield and his party moved on board HMS *Hyperion* when the *Williams* was paid off, however there is no mention of this in the log or muster book of HMS *Hyperion* (PRO ADM 51/3214 and 37/6088) and the latter includes a list of supernumeries borne for victuals which does not mention them. Furthermore if they had moved on board HMS *Hyperion*, to ensure secrecy, communication between her and the shore would also have had to have been forbidden. It would seem, therefore, that they remained on board the *Williams*.

[3] PRO ADM 51/3012, Log of HMS *Andromache*.

[4] PRO ADM 51/3214.

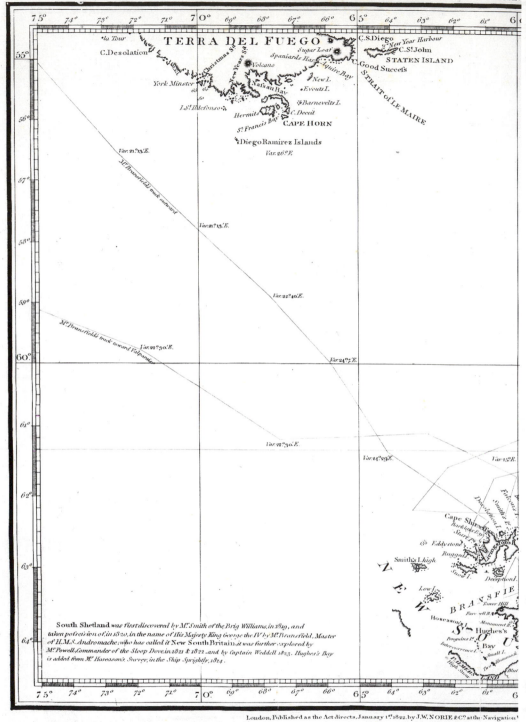

London, Published as the Act directs, January 1st 1822, by J.W. NORIE & Co at the Navigation

Plate 8. Chart of New South Shetland, J. W. Norie, 1822. UK HO L.9945 Tw.

LAND

Var. 23°.30'.E.

55°

56°

57°

58°

59°

60°

Var. 25°.E.

Bellsham

Seal I. *Cornwallis I.*

Lloyd's Promontory

West Reef *Clarence Island,* *visible 100 miles in clear weather.*

Cruisers

O. Brien's I. *Elephant I.* *C. Bowles*

C. Lookout

Narrow I. *Var. 20°.56'.E.*

Aspland I.

61°

Ridley's I. *Mobille*

North Foreland

Rownd Pt *Bridgeman's I. Volcano*

Falcons *Penguin's I.*

Baker's I. *Martin's Head*

62°

Cape Shirreff *George's Bay*

Barkleys Bay *Var. 23°.57'.E.*

Starr I. *Prickly Str.*

Eddystone *English Str.*

Ruggedd *Mac.Farlane Str.*

Snow I. *Deception I.* *Middle I.* **SOUND** *Hope I.*

63°

BRANSFIELD'S

S O U T H   **S H E T L A N D**

High Mountain covered with Snow

Tower Hill **Trinity Land**

Farewell R.

Hoscason's *Monument R.* **Hoscason's Harbour**

S. **Hughes's** *Charles*

Penguins Pt **Bay**

Intercurrence I. *Small I.*

64°

Explored by M.ᵣ Hoscason, 1824.

Var. 19°.56'.E.

Bluff Point

LAND

. NORIE & C.ᵒ at the Navigation Warehouse and Naval Academy, N.ᵒ 157, Leadenhall Street.

Fields of Ic.

well aware that it might be a group of islands, but the almost continual fogs and poor weather had made a detailed examination of any of the inlets sighted impracticable so that this was much the safest way to show it. The accuracy, considering that neither Bransfield nor any of his people had experience in hydrographic work, is remarkable (see Chapter 7).

To understand the difficulties of this voyage and hence appreciate their achievement, it is first necessary to visualise forgoing the facilities available today – the ability to direct the course and speed at will, accurate charts, satellite navigation, radar, echo-sounders, weather forecasts and so on, and to consider operating in an area beyond the edge of the known world. Not only was the extent and location of the land unknown, but from what could be seen of it, it was all too evidently iron-bound and unforgiving, covered in snow and ice; underwater hazards were unknown – they might be revealed by the lead or breakers, or indicated by the configuration of the waves over them or grounded ice bergs, but were just as likely to be found by the keel; large pieces of ice were floating about which were quite capable of crushing the vessel; the weather was unpredictable and frequently violent, the visibility was poor with long periods of thick fog; movement was dependant on the wind and unknown tides; position was dependant on seeing the sun or stars (and the horizon) and the going of the chronometer; and being in a single vessel, there was the certain knowledge that in the event of difficulties only the Lord would hear a cry for help.

It is always easy, with hindsight, to feel it should have been possible to do more (they did after all spend a great deal of time north of Elephant and Clarence Islands), but one of the hardest things in life, and in exploration in particular, is knowing when to turn back. They achieved what they set out to do, and returned to tell the story. Furthermore they did it remarkably well, and without loss of life; more no one could ask. Although they could not be certain, they believed they had seen the fabled Antarctic continent, and subsequent exploration was to show that they were right.

Documentation

Until Poynter's journal came to light there was no known manuscript account of Bransfield's voyage in the brig *Williams*. There were, however, two different published accounts, the first of which was reprinted in other works:

1. Dr Young, Surgeon of HMS *Slaney*; brief account in *Edinburgh Philosophical Journal*, April 1821 (pp. 345–8).
2. *Literary Gazette and Journal of Belles Lettres*, 7 April, 1821, p. 218, reprint of Dr Young's account [1].
3. Purdy, J. *Memoir Descriptive and Explanatory, to accompany the New Chart of the*

Ethiopic or Southern Atlantic Ocean etc. R. H. Laurie, London, 1822, pp. 194–5, reprint of Dr Young's account [1].

4. *Literary Gazette and Journal of Belles Lettres*, in three parts on 3, 10 and 24 November 1821, pp. 691–2, 712–13 and 746–7 (pp. 82–90). This account was first attributed to Midshipman Bone, from internal evidence, by R. T. Gould,[1] but it is composed largely of extracts from Poynter's journal. The majority of the statements not in Poynter are prefixed by such remarks as 'Mr Bone… observed …', 'Mr Bone … states his opinion…', indicating that the original was augmented from Bone's journal or from oral statements made by him to Mr William Jerdan, the *Literary Gazette's* editor.

Account 1. Dr. A. Young. *Edinburgh Philosophical Journal*, 1821, pp. 345–8:

Art XVII – *Notice of the Voyage of EDWARD BARNSFIELD [sic], Master of his Majesty's Ship Andromache, to New South Shetland.*[2]

About a twelvemonth ago, an English merchant brig, in performing a voyage to this port, made what they supposed to be land, several degrees to the southward of Cape Horn, and in a situation in which it is positively asserted that no land *can* exist. From the difference in opinion of those on board the vessel, and, from some other circumstances, little credit was attached to it at the time; but the master being fully convinced that what had been seen was actually land, determined to put it beyond doubt, should he come round again. He accordingly made the land last October, and having sailed along it for some considerable distance, he returned about the beginning of December to this port, and laid before the Naval Commander in Chief here, such charts and views, as induced him to hire the brig on account of the Government, to complete the discovery. The command of the expedition was given to Mr Edward Barnsfield, master of HMS Andromache, with three midshipmen from the same ship, to assist him in his nautical researches; and as it was deemed necessary to send a medical officer, I went as a volunteer on the occasion. We sailed from Valparaiso on the 20th of December 1819, but did not arrive on cruising ground till the 16th of January 1820, having been almost constantly harassed with baffling winds and calms till we arrived in a high southern latitude. On that day, however, we had the good fortune to discover the land to the south-eastward, extending on both bows as far as the eye could reach. At a distance, its limits could scarcely be distinguished from the light white clouds which floated on the tops of the mountains. Upon a nearer approach, however, every object became distinct. The whole line of coast appeared high bold and rugged; rising abruptly from the sea in perpendicular snowy cliffs, except here and there where the naked face of a barren black rock shewed itself amongst them. In the interior, the land, or rather the snow, sloped gradually and gently upwards into high hills, which appeared to be situated some miles from the sea. No attempt was made to land here, as the weather became rather

---

[1] *Geographical Journal*, 65, 1925, pp. 220–25.
[2] [note in original] See this *Journal,* III, p. 367, particularly p. 374, and Plate XII of that volume. [This is a reference to John Mier's account given at pp. 48–61.]

threatening, and a dense fog came on, which soon shut every thing from our view at more than a hundred yards distance. A boat had been sent away in the mean time to try for anchorage; but they found the coast completely surrounded by dangerous sunken rocks, and the bottom so foul, and the water so deep, that it was not thought prudent to go nearer the shore in the brig, especially as it was exposed to almost every wind. The boat brought off some seals and penguins which had been shot among the rocks; but they reported them to be the only animated objects they had discovered. The latitude of this part of the coast was found to be 62°26′S and its longitude 60°54′W. (See Vol III. of this Journal, Plate XII. Fig. 2.) [Plate 5]

Three days after this, we discovered and anchored in an extensive bay, about two degrees farther to the eastward, where we were enabled to land, and examine the country. Words can scarcely be found to describe its barrenness and sterility. Only one small spot of land was discovered on which a landing could be effected upon the Main, every other part of the bay being bounded by the same inaccessible cliffs which we had met before. We landed on a shingle beach, on which there was a heavy surf beating, and from which a small stream of fresh-water ran into the sea. Nothing was to be seen but the rugged surface of barren rocks, upon which myriads of sea-fowls had laid their eggs, and which they were then hatching. These birds were so little accustomed to the sight of any other animal, that, so far from being intimidated by our approach, they even disputed our landing, and we were obliged forcibly to open a passage for ourselves through them. They consisted principally of four species of penguin; with albatrosses, gulls, pintadoes, shags, sea-swallows, and a bird about the size and shape of the common pigeon, and of a milk white plumage, the only species we met with that was not web-footed. We also fell in with a number of the animals described in Lord Anson's voyage as the Sea-Lion, and said by him to be so plentiful at Juan Fernandez, many of which we killed. Seals were also pretty numerous; but though we walked some distance into the country, we could observe no trace either of inhabitants, or of any terrestrial animal. It would be impossible, indeed, for any but beasts of prey to subsist here, as we met with no sort of vegetation except here and there small patches of stunted grass growing upon the surface of the thick coat of dung which the sea-fowls left in the crevices of the rocks, and a species of moss, which occasionally we met with adhering to the rocks themselves. In short, we traced the land nine or ten degrees east and west, and about three degrees north and south, and found its general appearance always the same, high, mountainous, barren, and universally covered with snow, except where the rugged summits of a black rock appeared through it, resembling a small island in the midst of the ocean; but from the lateness of the season, and the almost constant fogs in which we were enveloped, we could not ascertain whether it formed part of a continent, or was only a group of islands. If it is insular, there must be *some* of an immense extent, as we found a gulf nearly 150 miles in depth, out of which we had some difficulty in finding our way back again.

The discovery of this land must be of great interest in a geographical point of view, and its importance to the commercial interests of our country, must be evident from the very great numbers of whales with which we were daily surrounded; and the multitudes of the finest fur-seals and sea-lions which we met both at sea and on every point of the coast, or adjacent rocky islands, on which we were able to land. The fur of the former is the finest and longest I have ever seen; and from their having now become scarce in every other part of these seas, and the great demand for them both in Europe and India, they will, I have no doubt, become, as soon as discovery is made public, a favourite speculation amongst our merchants. The oil procured from the sea-lion is, I am told, nearly equal in value to that of the spermaceti whale. And the great number of whales we saw every where near the land, must also be an important thing to our merchants, as they have lately been said to be very scarce to the north-ward.

We left the coast on the 21st of March, and arrived at this place on the 14th of April, having touched at Juan Fernandez for refreshment.

HMS Slaney }

Valparaiso, 26*th May* 1820 }

The reproduction of Dr Young's account in the *Literary Gazette* omits the original introductory remarks and substitutes a new introduction, (in which Bransfield is referred to as 'Barnfield' and not 'Barnsfield' as in the *Edinburgh Philosophical Journal*) and at the end leaves off 'HMS Slaney, Valparaiso, 26*th May* 1820'. It starts at 'We sailed from Valparaiso on the 20th of December 1819 …'. That by John Purdy in the *Memoir Descriptive etc.* reads 'With respect to the latter [South Shetland Islands], it may be added that, about twelve months after its first discovery, the British naval commander-in-chief, on the South-American station, directed a farther exploration; and for this purpose a hired brig, the *Slaney,* was sent, under the command of Mr. Edw. Barnsfield.' 'We sailed,' says the reporter, 'from Valparaiso …', as in the *Literary Gazette* account, but concludes well before the end at '… we could not ascertain whether it formed part of a continent, or was only a group of islands. If it be insular, there must be some of immense extent, as we found a gulf nearly 150 miles in depth, out of which we had some difficulty in finding our way back again'. It is interesting to see that the *Notes on South-Shetland printed to accompany the chart of the Newly Discovered Lands &c* by George Powell, printed for R. H. Laurie, 1822, p. 3, which state that particulars of the discovery of South-Shetland are given in this Memoir also states that 'the results of an exploration by Mr Edward Bransfield, (not Barnsfield)' are given. (Subsequent editions of Purdy correct Barnsfield to read Bransfield and omit the last sentence 'If it be insular … etc.'). It is thus probable that Purdy took his text direct from the *Edinburgh Philosophical Journal* and not from the *Literary Gazette*. Norie, in *Piloting Directions for the East and West Coasts of South America …. also for the South Shetland, Falkland, Galapagos and other islands etc.*, London, 1825, p. 11, includes what appears to be a brief précis of Young's account following the section covering William Smith's voyages. Purdy's account is also reproduced by Edmund Blunt in *The American Coast Pilot,* eleventh edition, 1827, pp. 521–3, (see remarks at end of Appendix 1).

Account 2. *Literary Gazette and Journal of Belles Lettres*, 3 November, 1821, pp. 691–2:

NEW SHETLAND

The lands discovered in the Antarctic regions, by Captain Smith, of Blythe, in the brig Williams, have been the subject of various papers in the different periodical works which pay attention to such subjects. The *Literary Gazette* furnished the first notice of this discovery,[1] and, not long after, one of the Edinburgh Magazines[2] supplied some farther particulars, which we copied into our pages. There has not yet, however, appeared any full and regular history of the *new land*, of which maps and charts are now selling in all the principal shops in London. We have reason to believe that no official account is meant to be promulgated from that high branch of our government to which such matters belong; and as events of this kind, though the lands be barren and frost-bound, are always curious, as well as to a certain extent important, we have procured for our Paper an authentic copy of the Journal kept on board the brig Williams during her second voyage to New Shetland, when employed by authority to examine and survey the coasts to which she had in the first instance been accidentally driven. Without going too minutely into details, we shall lay the prominent facts of this *Journal* before our readers; only premising that since the English expedition took place, the two Russian frigates[3] on a voyage in the same quarter, have (we understand) circumnavigated the *New Shetland Islands*, for so they turn out to be, and also the *Sandwich Land* of Captain Cook, thus proved to be another island. From the whole of these remarkable geographical discoveries it results that a very lucrative trade in seals may be carried on, as the sea absolutely swarms with these creatures, of great size, full of oil, and with the

---

[1] The article of 5 August 1820 (pp. 204–6) was the first to appear in *The Literary Gazette* but the first newspaper anouncement of the discovery was that in *The Courier*, 2 May 1820 (p. 203).

The Imperial Magazine, 3, November 1821, col. 1214, states under a heading OBSERVATIONS ON SOUTH SHETLAND:

> It was our good fortune to be possessed of all the leading facts which related to them long before their existance was announced to the public; but at the particular desire of our correspondent, who was in the first vessel that ever touched on these inhospitable shores, we omitted giving it publicity until several weeks had elapsed; and it was not until some reports had found their way into the world, that our embago was taken off. This circumstance enabled the conductor of a weekly journal to announce the existance of these distant lands to the public, just before the day of publication with us. Of this incident he has readily availed himself; and in a recent number, has claimed the exclusive honour of having furnished the first public notice of his discovery.

This would appear to refer to the account of Mr Herring's voyage which appeared in the *Imperial Magazine*, August 1820, cols 674–6, and is dated 3 July 1820 (pp. 190–91).

[2] Presumably this refers to *The Edinburgh Philosophical Journal* article by Dr Young in the April 1821 edition, which was copied by *The Literary Gazette* on 7 April 1821, since the earlier article by John Miers on William Smith's voyages, published in October 1820, had not been copied.

[3] The *Vostok* and *Mirnyi*, under the command of Captain Bellingshausen. A report on his voyage appeared in the *Literary Gazette*, by Alexander von Humboldt, January 1824, p. 26. See also p. 73, n. 1 above.

finest furs. In other respects animal existence is limited in variety, though not in the numbers of particular species. The shores are covered with penguins, which even disputed possession with the human visitors. There are gulls, albitrosses, and one land bird about the size of a pigeon. The sea-elephant also inhabits these dreary parts, and whales are very numerous, but excessively lean and poor. No fish were caught or seen, and the conchological products on the shore were the empty shells of limpets.

JOURNAL[1]

The brig Williams was taken up on the part of the British government, and fitted out by Captain Shireff, of HMS Andromache. Every exertion was used to equip her; provisions for twelve months were put on board, and water for 90 days, besides four bullocks, and a large supply of live stock. On the 19th of December, 1819, the master of the Andromache, an assistant surgeon, three midshipmen, and a crew amounting altogether to twenty-six, hoisted the British pendant, weighed, and stood off. On the 20th they took their departure from Valparaiso. The men were divided into three watches, and put on an allowance of three quarts of water per man daily.

On Christmas-day an extra allowance of grog, and a dance to a fiddle, *rigged* for the occasion, made all hands merry. "On the 30th (we quote the Journal) our latitude was 33°9'S. six miles to the southward of Valparaiso, which we had been nine days in obtaining. Soon after, in longitude 84°8'15W., we first got the S.W. breezes, which were only partial until the 3rd of January, when we got a breeze from the westward, which sent us to the southward. On the 8th we were in latitude 49°24' and longitude 79°18'. All this evening, and more particularly the next morning, great quantities of albatrosses and grey petul,[2] or sperm birds, were around us. When the former are seen to settle on the water, it is said to indicate the approach of strong winds. Whether this be correct or not I am unable to affirm, but true it is, in the afternoon we were suddenly caught in a heavy squall, which split our square main-sail, fore-top-gallant-sail, top-mast studding-sail, and sprung the boom. On the moderation of the weather, the latter entirely left us. These are seldom seen in great numbers, except where the sperm whale are to be found; hence the derivation of their name.

"On the 11th our latitude was 56°30'S. longitude 72°30'30"W. and variation, by an amplitude taken the preceding evening, 21°13'6"S.[3] which had been increasing gradually since we left Valparaiso. It is generally said that penguins are never seen far from land, nor indeed ever leave their native place. To prove this supposition erroneous, in the forenoon we passed close by two, the island of Diego Ramuez, (the nearest land,) above one hundred miles distant.

At noon we threw a bottle overboard, containing a paper bearing the following inscription: 'This bottle was hove overboard from the Williams, an English brig, on a voyage of discovery, to the southward, on the 12th of January, 1820, in latitude 57°48' and longitude 69°55'W. Should any vessel pick this up at sea, it is requested the master will note the latitude and longitude, putting it overboard again; or should it be found on any coast or harbour, the person so finding it will, I hope, inclose this paper to the

---

[1] Notes on that part of the voyage taken from Poynter's journal are given in Chapter 6.
[2] The journal has 'Grey Petrells'.
[3] The journal has 'Easterly'.

Board of Longitude, in London, stating when, where, and how he came by it; signed Edward Bransfield, master of HMS Andromache."

The water-casks having leaked, the allowance was reduced to half a gallon daily. On the 15th the latitude was 61°23′S. and longitude 63°59′15″W.

"Several shoals of seals and a few penguins being seen, we tried for soundings about eight o'clock, but obtained no bottom with 120 fathoms. During the night we kept the lead going[1] two hours, but unsuccessfully, still passing through and by large shoals of seals and penguins. So great a sign of land being in the neighbourhood, made it necessary to keep a very vigilant look-out, when about eight o'clock in the morning, land was discovered making in a moderate height, and partly covered with snow. At nine we hove too, and sounded with 55 fathoms brown sand and ooze, the extremes of the land bearing from east to S.S.E.; filled and bore up E.b.S. for a supposed entrance to a spacious bay or at least where we thought we might bring up and water. In standing in, an unconnected chain of rocks, detached from the main, presented themselves, forming in very remarkable shapes. When within a mile or a mile and a half of the land, we hove too and hoisted the whale boat out, put leads and lines, and armed her, when Mr Smith took her to go in search of an anchorage where we might lie in security."

A thick fog came on and caused some danger. On the 17th, however, the latitude and longitude of a headland was determined to be 62°42′S. and 61°27′W., which was named *The Start*, not only from its similarity, but from its being the first part of the land where operations were commenced. Hence the land takes a northerly direction. The point received the name of Cape Shireff; it is a most remarkable headland, and resembles a mass of ruined fortifications. A tremendous sea broke on every part of the coast; after noticing which the Journal proceeds –

"The breakers in smooth water are scarcely perceptible, except at intervals when the sea breaks. A short distance to the eastward of the cape is a small island pierced through, resembling the arch of a bridge. After determining the latitude of Cape Shireff, we ran to the eastward until abreast of an island, which, from its barren, uncomfortable appearance, was named the Island of Desolation. Its latitude is 62°27′S. and longitude 60°35′ and ten miles due east of the last cape. Previous to the going down of the sun, we determined the variation, by an excellent azimuth, to be 23°52′ east, and an amplitude soon after 22°30′ east. During the time we were prosecuting our pursuits, we were surrounded by shoals of seals and penguins. From Desolation Island we ran in a N.E. direction for a cluster we perceived, which, when abreast of, were supposed to be the same seen by Mr. Smith in the month of February, 1819. The whole of these islands, along the part of the coast which we had already seen, were composed of black rock, and above the reach of the water patches of snow made but a dismal aspect. The main entirely capped which gave us but very faint hopes of ever being able to speak well of its fertility."

On the 19th, they saw a great number of whales, which deserted them as they closed the shore. For several days observed rocky and barren islands, at which the fogs prevented the vessel touching till the 22nd, when "At 1 30, an island was observed nearly

---

[1] The journal has 'every two hours'.

clear of snow, bearing W.S.W.; at four, the bluff bow[1] N.E. At five, observing the land to the S.W. of the island appear like a bay, we made sail, steering W.S.W. with a moderate breeze. The necessary precautions were taken by keeping the lead going and a hand forward to look out for foul ground, and ice being taken, we rounded the island, and at 7 30 brought up with the chain cable in sixteen fathoms, coarse sand, with black gravel. the eastern point of the island bearing N.E.b.E.; a small island near the bottom of the bay W.b.N. and the southern point of the bay S.W. While rounding the island we observed its shore covered with penguins, whose awkward movement had the most strange appearance, and at the same time the most intolerable stench assailed our noses that I ever smelt, arising from these gentry. As soon as every thing was secure, we hoisted the boats out, manned and armed the whale-boat, and after breakfast Mr. Bransfield proceeded in her to effect a landing, where he might plant the Jack, and take possession of it by the name of New South Britain, in the name and behalf of H.M. George IV.[2] his heirs, and successors. At eight o'clock, observed the boat land on a shingle beach, which bore from the brig N.N.W.; observed soon after, with the aid of our glasses, the Jack planted; we hoisted on board the brig our ensign and pendant, and fired a gun; he likewise buried a bottle, containing several coins of the realm, given by different people for that purpose."

(We have been thus particular in noting the bearings, &c. of the new land, so attached to the British empire, and shall hereafter condense the most curious facts connected with it into a short compass, for more amusing, if less important reading.)

★★By an accidental arrangement of our matter, *this* Original Paper which should have come under another head, has been placed among our Reviews.

Ibid., 10 November 1821, pp. 712–13

NEW SHETLAND
(Second paper)

We resume from last week the accounts of this *new country*, of the occupation of which in the name of the British monarch, and of its actual situation and condition, we have been enabled to give the first authentic details.:–

We sent in the afternoon, says our journalist, the boats in search of water. It would be impossible to describe the manner in which the penguins disputed our landing, both on the main and island; it was not until great slaughter was made, and a lane cut through them, that we could proceed. It is well known that every animal, however timid at other times, will defend its young with the most determined courage, and this being the breeding season with these birds will account for the decided opposition we met with. Before we had been long on shore we discovered several streams of water, but as they passed through the filth of these animals, they were unfit for use. To remedy this, a well was constructed and surrounded by stones to prevent its pollution.

---

[1] The journal has 'bore N½E at 5'.

[2] King George III was still alive when the land was claimed; he died on 29 January, 1820 (the news of his death did not reach Valparaíso until 11 May 1820: log of HMS *Hyperion*, PRO ADM 51/3214) and according to the journal it was in his name that the land was claimed. This must therefore have been 'corrected' by the editor.

The island lies N.E. and S.W., is nearly a mile long and the same in width. It is, without doubt, an exhausted volcano, the east side being composed of ashes and cinders. On the top was found the crater, with water trickling through the ashes, which formed the various streams we had previously seen. Some of the people, during their stay on shore, contrived to kill an elephant and two or three seals; while we were thus employed, the whale-boat pulled over to the main shore, likewise in search of water. There, as one of the men was attacking an elephant, he had the misfortune to receive a very severe bite on the hand from the animal, which threw itself back, and surprised its assailant behind, would certainly have bit his hand off had it been less exhausted. The streams on the main land were very fine-tasted water and conveniently situated for completing even a large squadron in a short time. This suiting our purpose, though more distant from the brig than the island, we pitched on the point where we were to commence operations in the morning, and in the mean time amused ourselves with walking about; and before we had marched far fell in with an immense shoal of elephants asleep. On waking, they were evidently so unaccustomed to the sight of man, that they eyed us with the utmost indifference, but when we attacked them with our lances, &c., they betrayed their astonishment in a stifled bellow. Several were killed and fletched of their blubber, which was casked up. Some seals and penguins were also killed.

Next day the watering was successfully carried on; the streams flowed from three lakes about a mile or more up the country, the banks of which were nearly a mile in circumference, and lined with penguins and their young. Several irregular-shaped stones and some mosses were found and taken on board. The latitude of the anchorage was ascertained to be 62°6′S. at the S.E. end of the island, which was named Penguin Island; the longitude, where the jack was planted, 58°7′W.; latitude 62°4′S.; variation of the needle 23°59′ easterly.

On the 24th (January, 1820,) the boats could not pursue their operations on shore, being entirely encompassed with ice, occasioned by the N.W. wind. By 11 o'clock, however, a change enabled them to land without difficulty, and the brig was fully watered in the course of the day. A box of earth was brought from the Lakes as a specimen of the soil, and the bay (which is generally deep, and with a bad holding bottom of black gravel, sometimes mixed with coarse sand,) having been surveyed by the master, (Mr. Bransfield,) was named "George's Bay," in honour of his Majesty, on account of its being the first part on which the British flag was hoisted. Appropriate names were also given to high lands, capes, &c.

On the night of the 25th there was a heavy fall of snow and a swell from the eastward, and an immense iceberg was drifted nearly upon the vessel. Next day the snow and a thick fog prevented them from moving, but they sailed on the following morning.

Previous to leaving this bay, the journal contains some general observations, the substance of which is, that the tides rise pretty regularly from 14 to 16 feet, and appear to be entirely influenced by the winds; and that there is a channel between the island and the main in which a vessel of small draught might find shelter. The coast at the bottom of the bay consists of high snow cliffs, from which, owing to thaws, prodigious masses are continually falling with a noise like distant thunder, but of a shorter duration; these form into bergs and drive to sea with the wind, increasing to such a degree from the snows as soon to warrant the name of islands. Notwithstanding the sterility of the land, there was a light soil at the back of the watering-place, a mixture of sand and mould, by digging into which, not more than a foot in depth, water was found.

The swampy land, the lowest of all, was covered with a sort of grass and moss, nourished by the dung of the several oceanic birds; this moss and grass abounds in great quantities, and is all that deserves to be called vegetation. The little rocky ridges, at the foot of the snow, seemed to be the haunt of the albatrosses; their nests are of small pieces of broken stones scraped together, in which their eggs are deposited. So unused were they to the sight of man, that they would not stir from their nests till forced off with sticks, which they bit with the most savage determination. There was also a large brown bird, with a few white feathers in the upper part of the wing, a sharp bill and web-footed. It builds a nest of moss, and lays a brownish, spotted egg; this bird is frequently found among the albatrosses. The other marine birds were Cape-pigeons, petterel, and several species of the gull, besides a shag, which has a singular mud nest on the rocks, close to the water. No land animal and no other bird were seen, except a sort of pigeon, which build in the crevices of rocks with grass from the swamp; these were so tame that they allowed the people to approach and knock them down with sticks, though sufficiently on their guard not to be captured by the hand. Of penguins there were five different kinds, all equally troublesome. What these creature subsist upon it is difficult to divine, as no fish was seen but the limpet, which came up with the ship's anchor when she weighed. Only a few seals were seen, but they produced a very fine fur. The sea elephants seemed to reign the undisputed monsters of the whole bay." On the shore, Mr. Bone, the young and able draughtsman, to whose talents the expedition owes so much, observed several mounds of stones thrown up by means of which it is impossible to form any idea. Some were from ten to twelve feet in height, and entirely surrounded by snow. *Snow of a reddish tint* was seen here as in the Arctic regions; when thawed it became darker, but was not of the same colour as that described by Captain Ross.[1] Upon this subject Mr Bone curiously remarks:– 'The cause of this colour I and all of us were at a loss to account for, as it evidently could not be occasioned by soil,

[1] Ross, 1819, p. 138, for 17 August 1818 in position latitude 75°54′N, longitude 67°15′W, in the vicinity of Cape York, Baffins Bay, states:

We now discovered that the snow, on the face of the cliffs, presented an appearance both novel and interesting, being apparently stained, or covered, by some substance, which gave it a deep crimson colour. Many conjectures were afloat concerning the cause of this appearance; it was at once determined it could not be the dung of birds, for thousands of these, of various descriptions, were seen repeatedly sitting on the ice, and on the snow, but without producing such effects.

This colour is caused by unicellular red snow algae (cryoalgae). It is a biological phenomenon which occurs from mid to late summer in alpine, low Arctic and the northern Antarctic regions. It occurs on 'rotting' or firn snow when it becomes highly crystalline and very wet. Within the surface ice, single-celled algae of several species are scattered. During the winter and spring they are called resting cells and are colourless. When conditions are suitable they develop a red pigment in their cell. As the wet firn snow melts these cells are washed down and form aggregations of very dense cells in patches on the ice fields and glaciers, giving rise to what is termed 'red snow'. Where these aggregations are very dense they can be blood red and occasionally cover quite large areas. There are also other species of similar single celled algae which develop green or yellow pigments, giving rise to the less common 'green snow' and 'yellow snow'.

since under the chief place where the snow was found there ran a very rapid stream of considerable depth, and at this time we were passing over valleys filled with snow.' "[1] Having finished the scanty enumeration of the products of this dreary land, the journal adds, that the stones and rocks consist principally of white and brown granite and lime-stone, together with some varieties, of which specimens were preserved.

(Having brought the narrative to the close of our mariners' first position, we seize the opportunity to conclude this paper, reserving what further appears to be interesting for another insertion)

Ibid., 24 November 1821, pp. 746–7

NEW SHETLAND
(Third and last Paper)

From the bay (George's Bay) in which our countrymen first hauled up, and took pos-session of New Shetland, or, as they christened it, "*New South Britain*," in the name of his Majesty, the Brig Williams sailed on 27th of January.[2] Their course was W.S.W. On the 28th, several whales and shoals of seals were seen; and the whole day they were sur-rounded by penguins, snow-birds, pintadoes, and albatrosses. The land, wherever seen, appeared to be immense mountains, rude crags, and barren ridges covered with snow, close to the water's edge, presenting a most dreary and dismal aspect. Thick fogs occurred now and throughout the voyage so often as to render observation uncertain and naviga-tion difficult. On the 29th, a glimpse was caught of a very high mountain due north; and on the 30th, a small group of islands, extending S.E. to E. by S. was discovered, part of a range stretching E. by N. to S.W. "The winds at this time," we quote the Journal, "were strong, and the horizon very hazy, which opened and shut occasionally, offering to our view an unknown coast, evidently abounding with rocks and small islands. At noon, our latitude by meridian altitude was 63°16′, and longitude by chronometer, 60°28′W." They now, in consequence of the weather, steered southward, and seemed to be running from the land; but at three o'clock in the afternoon, after having their attention attracted by three immense icebergs, the haze clearing, they very unexpectedly saw land to the S.W.; and at four o'clock were encompassed by islands, spreading from N.E. to E. The whole of these formed a prospect the most gloomy that can be imagined, and the only cheer the sight afforded was in the idea that this might be the long-sought Southern Continent, as land was undoubtedly seen in latitude 64°, and trending to the eastward. In this bay or gulph there was a multitude of whales, and a quantity of sea-weed, apparently fresh from the rocks. A round island was called Tower Island, latitude 63°29′, longitude 60°34′, and the land Trinity Land, in complement to the Trinity Board.

About this period sheet-ice abounded a-head, and not fewer than 31 icebergs were counted at once. The weather was very stormy, and the fatigue of officers and men

---

[1] A note appeared in the *Imperial Magazine*, 4, 1822, col. 192: '*Red Snow* – Snow of a reddish tint has been found in New South Shetland. It appears to owe its colour to some cryptogamic veg-etable.' See note above for explanation.

[2] [note in original] On sailing, the land ran in a S.W. direction as far as the eye extended; but a little distance to the southward of a headland, named Martin's head, it abruptly trended to the W.N.W. forming to the view a spacious sound.

excessive. Land and islands were observed in latitude 61°30', and longitude 56°54'. This land was of a moderate height, and chiefly covered with snow. On the 4th of February they hauled up, 6 or 7 miles off the centre of an immensely high mountain. The master here went on shore, and planted in a small cove, at the foot of a most tremendous precipice, a board with an inscription similar to that which was left on the coast of George's Bay. The shingle beach swarmed with seals and penguins; and several streams fell in cascades from the hills. The above-mentioned precipice, in latitude 61°19'S., longitude 54°16'W., was named Cape Bowles: it seemed to be an abrupt termination of the land to the southward, as, after leaving it and steering due east, no more was seen till the brig was in the longitude of nearly 50°.

On the 5th they passed a very large sea-lion, who amused himself by looking at them most attentively: several whales were about at the same time. Till the 12th, the Journal relates various tacks, &c. among islands; on that day they went through shoals of grampusses, the first they had seen. On the 13th Mr. Smith landed on some uncouth crags, which run about four miles from the main. They, like all other places, were covered with seals. Several shags flew so near the brig, that the men struck them down with pieces of wood which they flung at them. Their plumage is white on the breast, black on the head and wings, the beak long, narrow and sharp. Among a flock of penguins, some were seen entirely white, the only variety of that colour observed during the voyage. Latitude 61°2', longitude 55°32'. The largest island was named Seal Island: on this the boat collected 90 fine fur skins, and several pieces of rock resembling canal coal.

A small sandy beach where Mr. Smith effected a landing, he reported to be so covered with seals, as to render it almost dangerous to go among them: he described them as being *stowed in bulk*. Of these he destroyed 300 and upwards; and the boat not being large enough to contain them, they were skinned, and a load brought on board. Several sea-elephants and marine birds were seen. The latter were so voracious, that while the men were skinning the seals, they were absolutely obliged to beat them off with their clubs, to prevent interruption. Next day the sea had washed away many of the seal carcasses left by the boat, and the birds so mangled the rest as to render them useless.

When in W. longitude 52°23'45", and S. latitude 61°30', on the 22nd of February the brig made a dash to the southward, determined to enter the Antarctic Regions, no ice being visible on the eastern coast, or that which they had just quitted. After a run of 40 miles, however, with a fine N.E. breeze, icebergs were encountered in immense numbers, and towards evening loose pieces of sheet-ice stopped their progress. The attempt was persevered in on the 23rd; but the accumulation of ice rendered it altogether abortive, and the ship's head was turned once more towards Cape Bowles. Running along their old coast, other islands were seen, and other prominent lands named. The sea breaks with dreadful force on the islands which line the coast. The whole line, from the Start Point, latitude 62°42', longitude 61°27', to Cape Bowles, latitude 61°19', longitude 54°10', a distance of 7°17', is of the same wild and dismal aspect; and from Cape Melville latitude 62°1', longitude 57°44', to Desolation Island, lat. 62°27', long. 60°35', the shore is so defended by innumerable rocks, breakers, and small islands, as to render landing impracticable.

On the 18th of March the crew took their last look at this dreary and inhospitable coast, which seems to afford nothing beyond an excellent seal-fishing, from which, however, much commercial benefit may be derived.

Mr. Bone, with perfect accuracy, (as has since been proved by the Russian Expedition),[1] states his opinion, that "the whole which was seen was a group of Islands, very narrow and of considerable magnitude." He conjectures, that passages may be found between them and across the chain early in the season, the William being there very late, as she remained till the sun crossed the equator. The whales, are (as already noticed) very thin, even if they are of the right sort, which does not appear to have been ascertained; but the elephants are exceedingly fat, and yield a great deal of oil. The sea-lions are peculiarly fine.

Our gallant tars reached Valparaiso on the 15th of April, having touched on their route at the island of Juan Fernandez, where they found the fruits, the vegetables, the climate, and every thing else, a thousand times more exquisite than ever they were before, though the place is in reality a sort of terrestrial paradise. On landing, their charts, journals, &c. were, agreeably to the rules of the service, given up; and it is owing to the kindness of a friend, one of the officers, not disapproved by the authority to which such matters belong, that we have been enabled to give, in three short papers in the *Literary Gazette*, the sum and substance of this remarkable voyage.

The cold was never severe; the lowest point of the thermometer being 30.

We cannot conclude, without adverting to the steadiness, prudence, zeal, and courage of the officers and men to whom this task was assigned. The combination of intelligence, perseverance and ardour which they displayed, reflects honour on the profession, and is truly characteristic of British seamen.

---

[1] Expedition of Thaddeus Bellingshausen (Faddei Faddeevich Bellinsgauzen), 1819–21, in *Vostok* and *Mirnyi*. The ships were in the South Shetland Islands in January 1821. See F. Debenham, *The Voyage of Captain Bellingshausen to the Antarctic Seas 1819–1821*, London, Hakluyt Society, 1945, and p. 73, n. 1, and p. 82, n. 3.

CHAPTER 6

JOURNAL OF MIDSHIPMAN
CHARLES WITTIT POYNTER

Poynter's journal has been transcribed using his spelling and punctuation as far as practicable, and where it is not discernible, modern spelling. Contractions, with a few currently standard exceptions, have been expanded in italics. The journal is written in ink with a few, apparently contemporary, amendments in ink which have been taken into the text without comment. It is in a legible hand and, in view of the small number of corrections, may well be a fair copy produced on board the *Williams* either as the voyage progressed or on her return to Valparaíso.[1] There is also a number of pencil amendments, which appear to be in Poynter's hand, as if he had been trying to polish his text at a later date. Minor additions which add to the sense of the existing text are included in square brackets, but the majority and all the more lengthy remarks are given in the notes. These amendments would not appear to have been used in the printed version in the *Literary Gazette*.

The journal contains seventy three pages of text; a drawing entitled 'Killing Sea Elephants – N.S.B.';[2] one small-scale chart of the area entitled 'New South Britain, as surveyed by Officers from Andromache in the Hired Brig Williams', covering the area 60° to 64° South and 51° to 62° West, on a Mercatorial projection; two plans, one of Georges Bay (now King George Bay) and the other the bay south of Cape Shirreff (shown as Shirreff's Cape on the plan); a sheet of three views entitled 'Trinity Land and Islands' (in pencil across the top), the top view untitled, but it may be to this that the line above refers, then 'Hope Island' (showing Trinity Peninsula in the background) and 'O'Brien's Islands'; outline drawings

---

[1] See p. 174, n. 1.

[2] 'N.S.B' presumably means New South Britain, the name for the South Shetland Islands first used by William Smith and used in Poynter's journal. This sketch is initialled at the left lower corner 'TMB' in a hand similar to that with which Midshipman Thomas Mein Bone's passing certificate for lieutenant is signed, indicating that it was drawn by Bone.

Plate 9a. Chart of South Shetland Islands showing track of His Majesty's Hired Brig *Williams*: January–April 1820.

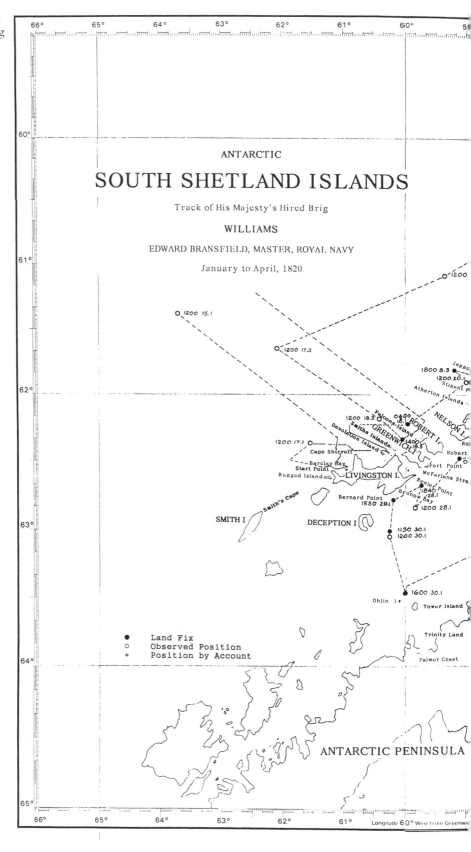

ANTARCTIC

SOUTH SHETLAND ISLANDS

Track of His Majesty's Hired Brig

WILLIAMS

EDWARD BRANSFIELD, MASTER, ROYAL NAVY

January to April, 1820

● Land Fix
○ Observed Position
+ Position by Account

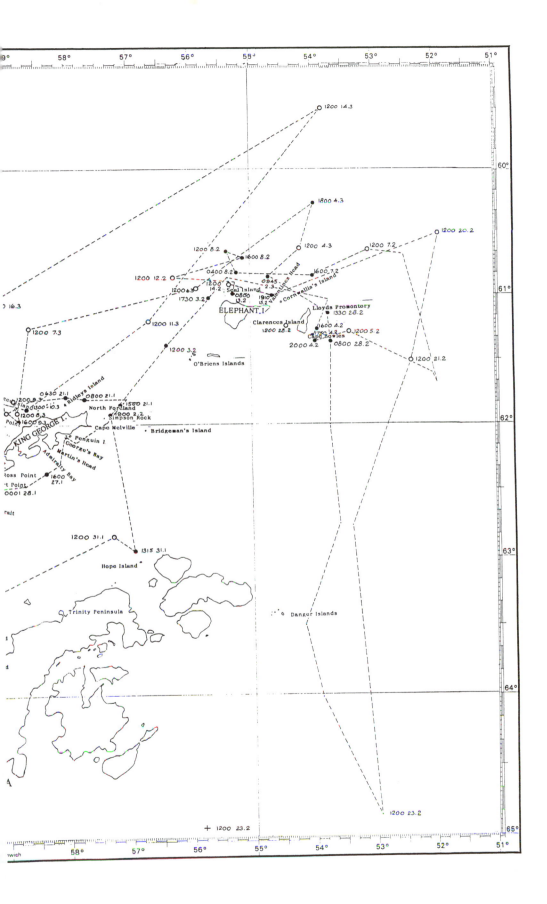

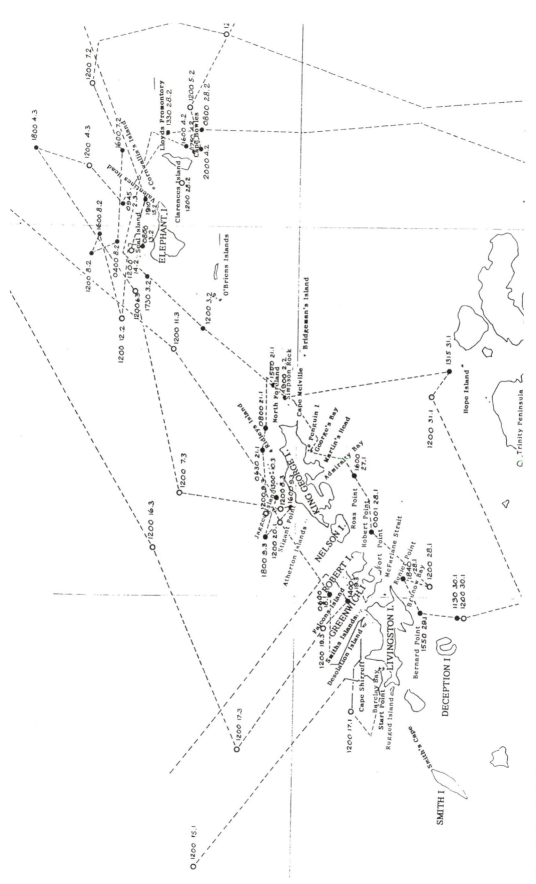

Plate 9b. Detail of Chart at 9a.

of 'Seal Islands & rocks Westerly' in three lines; untitled sheet of views showing two sets of islands; Plates 10, 11, 14, 22 and 30.

There is also a printed page of diagrams marked 'Astronomy Pl: X',[1] and four pages of genealogical information on the Clouston family from 1790s to 1890s, which are at the back and were added at a later date. These are not included below. There are ninety-three other pages (which include the family information but are otherwise blank) and the whole is in a well-worn binding of half red leather with marbled boards. Its dimensions are 26 by 21 cms. It was purchased by the Alexander Turnbull Library from the Clouston estate.

---

[1] This page appears to come from *The Elements of Navigation*, by John Robertson. All copies of Robertson, up to and including the 7th edition, 1805, have this plate as Plate V in volume 1, so it may have come from a pirated edition. It may or may not have been inserted after the voyage.

His Majestys Hired Brig Williams
on Discovery towards the South Pole.

December 1819
Thursday 16th.

Friday = 17th.
Saturday = 18th.

I received an Order from Captain Shirreff of His Majestys Ship Andromache, Senior in command in the South Pacific to join the Brig Williams chartered by him on the part of Government to proceed on Discovery of unknown land made by the Master of the said[1] brig on his late and preceding passages from the River Plate to Valparaiso – On the two following days every exertion was made with the assistance of a party from the Andromache towards her necessary equipment and for this important service an extra number of hands were shipped – Provisions got on board for Twelve Months, Ninety days Water, Four Bullocks – besides a great

[1] Text amended to read: 'an unknown land which had been fallen in with by the Master of the Williams'.

Plate 10. Drawing from Poynter's Journal. 'Killing Sea Elephants N.S.B.'

Sunday – 19th.

quantity of different kinds of live stock, One heavy boat and Two lighter ones – On Sunday the 19th. at 8 (AM) The Master of the Andromache Edward Bransfield, Messrs. Blake and Bone Midshipmen besides Myself came on board and hoisted the Pendant which ceremony was accompanied with a Gun – His Majestys Ship Slaney contributed her portion by supplying us with a Surgeon (M^r. Young) who joined us in the course of the forenoon – At 5 (PM) We weighed and continued standing off and on waiting for our Master until 10 oClock, when light and baffling Easterly airs set us in among the shipping and obliged us to drop an Anchor under

Monday 20th.

foot[1] – At daylight on the following Morning we again hove it to the Bows and towed out in the fair way, but Calms prevailing we despatched our Whale boat to the Slaney to fill an empty Water cask –

December 1819

Soon after 10 oClock a Moderate breeze sprung up from the SW which as soon as the boat returned and was hoisted in we took advantage of,[2] but this as the Sun went down died away – At 8 I took my departure from Valparayso point bearing SSE about 8 Leagues[3] – Light airs having prevailed during the Night, little progress was made [during the night] and on

Tuesday = 21st.

the following Morning the land was still in sight astern – At Noon we found ourselves to the Northward of Valparayso occasioned by a heavy Southerly Swell with constant light airs – and on the following Noon we were 29 Miles to the

Wednesday – 22nd.

Northward – However unfortunate we were in being driven Northerly our progress to the Westward proved more successful and Sights taken this Forenoon for the Chronometers gave us 73°.32′W – We could not avoid but observing with[4] regret this continuance of unfavorable Winds, every hour proving a dead loss: having a passage of at least Three or Four Weeks to accomplish and the Season rapidly advancing against us – This afternoon ~~we~~ placed our People in Three

---

[1] 'Under foot': directly under the bows with no additional cable.

[2] Text amended to read: 'of which as soon as the boat returned and was hoisted in we took advantage'.

[3] 'League': 3 nautical miles.

[4] Text amended to read: 'observe without'.

Watches one of which I was appointed to take charge of, and likewise put them on a daily allowance of 3 quarts of Water each – Before leaving Valparayso we obtained the loan of a Barometer and Thermometer from the Merchant Ship Thais – Some of the quicksilver having been accidentally spilt, Captain Robson before delivery

December 1819

admitted more in doing which a portion of air had crept into the Tube – After its being fixed we observed it constantly stood at 28⁷⁄₁₀ and upon examination discovered it required a greater supply of Silver – At first we were puzzled how to effect this, the air contained in the Tube preventing the entrance of the Mercury – After some time, at the suggestion of D^r. Young,[1] by immersing the Tube in scalding hot Water and then in the Fire, whereby the air became Totally expelled, the Silver was seen rushing in and thereby[2] the Tube presently filled – The heating of the Glass must be done by degrees or it is liable to fly and much patience [is] required to keep the instrument in an upright position, the aperture for the admittance of the Mercury being so very confined. This operation was taken in hand by D^r. Young himself who dis-

Saturday 25th.

played no common share of precision – The following being Christmas day and having fair Weather without the least appearance of a change, our People were indulged with Two Gallons of Liquor extra and in the evening we managed to muster a Fiddler among the crew who proved himself a very tolerable scraper – For the first and in all probability the last time in my life I witnessed the refusal of Grog by our crew en masse – In the course of the afternoon their

December 1819

becoming noisy and quarrelsome induced us to mix an extra

---

[1] Text amended to read:

… it had been fixed we observed that it constantly stood at 28⁷⁄₁₀ upon examination discovered it required a greater supply of Silver – At first we were puzzled how to effect this, the air contained in the Tube preventing the entrance of the Mercury –, at the suggestion of D^r. Young….

[2] Text amended to read:

the Tube was immersed in scalding hot Water and then set in the Fire, by which means the air became Totally expelled, and as soon as this was accomplished the Silver was seen rushing in and….

Jorum as a <u>Night cap</u> – When offered [to them] they all to a
Man refused it, [and] said [that] the Officers wished to make
them drunk and they would "be damned if they would be
so" – Soon however they changed their Minds and the result

Thursday 30th. wound up the <u>pleasures</u> of the day – On the 30th. at Noon
the Sun gave our Latitude 33°–9'S six Miles to the South-
ward of Valparayso which we had been nine days in attaining[1]
– Soon after, in Long*itude* 84°.8'W we first caught the SW
breezes which however were only partial until 3rd. January
when the NW and SW quarters shared the <u>honor</u> of con-

January 1820 ducting us to the Southward – On the 8th. we were in Lat*i-
tude* 49°–24'S and Longitude 79°–19'W abreast of Cape
Corzo[2] on the Coast of Patagonia and about 213 Miles dis-

Saturday = 8th. tant – All this Evening and more particularly the following
Morning great numbers of Albatrosses,[3] and the Grey Petrells
or Sperm bird[4] were around us – When the former are seen
to settle on the water it is said to be an indication of winds.
whether this is correct or not I cannot possibly affirm but

Sunday 9th. true it is [that] in the afternoon, we were suddenly caught in
a heavy Squall which split our Square Mainsail,[5] Fore Top-

[1] Text amended to 'reaching'.

[2] This would appear to be the extremity of Península Corso on the north side of the entrance to Canal Trinidad.

[3] Albatrosses: there are several species of albatross found in the waters off Patagonia. These include the two great albatrosses, wandering (*Diomedea exulans*) and royal (*Diomedea epomophora*) the former being the commoner. Of the smaller mollymawkes the commonest species are the black-browed albatross (*Diomedea melanophris*) and the grey-headed albatross (*Diomedea chrysostoma*), both of which breed in large numbers on Diego Ramírez. The light-mantled sooty albatross (*Phoebetria palpebrata)* also occurs, but in smaller numbers. It is however strikingly different in size, colour and behaviour from typical albatrosses and likely to have been readily distinguished. Two giant petrels (*Macronectes giganteus* and *Macronectes halli*) are similar to albatrosses and may be mistaken for them.

[4] 'Sperm birds': many species of smaller seabirds are often found associated with marine mammals, most notably prions or whale-birds (*Pachyptila* species). If these were not prions they may well have been southern fulmars, also called silver-grey petrels (*Fulmarus glacialoides*). In this part of the Southern Ocean it is very unlikely that the birds were the true grey petrel (*Procellaria cinerea*), which is a species of more northerly regions.

[5] 'Square Mainsail': elsewhere in this journal the 'boom mainsail' is referred to. A brig is a two-masted vessel with the mainsail secured to the main mast by hoops attached to the fore edge of the sail which slide up and down the mast when the sail is hoisted and lowered; it is spread by a gaff above and a boom below. However it was not uncommon for a brig to carry a square mainsail set from the mainyard in addition (known in French as a *langard*) and this is presumably the sail referred to in this case.

Gallant Sail[1] Topmast Studdingsail[2] and sprung[3] the boom – On the Weather moderating the latter entirely left us – These are seldom seen in

January 1820
Tuesday = 11th.

in numbers except where the Sperm Whale are [is] found – hence the derivation of their Name – On the 11th. our Latitude was 56°.30′S Longitude 72°.30′W and the Variation by an Amplitude[4] taken the preceding Evening 21°.13′ Easterly which had been encreasing gradually since our Departure – It is commonly advanced the Penguin is never seen at Sea far from Land or indeed[5] seldom ever leaves the shores of its birthplace – To prove this supposition erroneous, in the morning we passed several, the Island of Diego Ramirez (the

Monday = 12th.

nearest land) above an hundred miles distant[6] – At Noon we set a bottle adrift well corked up, containing a Paper bearing the following inscription "This bottle was hove overboard from the Williams, an English Brig on a voyage of Discovery to the Southward on the 12th. January 1820 – in Latitude 57°.48′S Longitude 69°.55′W – Should any Vessel pick this up at Sea, it is requested the Master will note the Latitude and Longitude putting it overboard again, or should it be found on any Coast or Harbour, the Person so finding will I hope

[1] 'Fore Topgallant Sail': the fore mast carries three square sails set from yards at right angles to the keel. From the bottom these are the course or foresail, the fore topsail and the fore topgallant sail.

[2] 'Studding-sails': fine weather sails set outside the square yards. Their heads are spread from yards which are hoisted to the yardarms and they are secured at the foot to yards which slide out along the lower yards.

[3] 'Spring': a crack running obliquely through any part of a mast or yard, which renders it unfit to carry the usual sail thereon, and the spar is then said to be sprung: Smyth, 1867, p. 645.

[4] See p. 32.

[5] Text amended to read: 'It is commonly asserted that the Penguin is never seen at Sea far from Land or indeed but it seldom ever leaves the shores of its birthplace – What proves this supposition erroneous, is that in the morning we passed several, altho the Island of Diego Ramirez (which is the nearest land) was above an hundred miles distant –'.

[6] The commonest species of penguin off southern Patagonia are the rockhopper (*Eudyptes chrysocome*) and the macaroni (*Eudyptes chrysolophus*) both of which breed on Diego Ramírez. Gentoo (*Pygoscelis papua*) and magellanic (*Spheniscus magellanicus*) could also occur and in the 1800s the king penguin (*Aptenodytes patagonicus*) may well have been breeding on southern Patagonia. Rockhopper, macaroni and king penguins are relatively pelagic species and commonly seen up to 100 miles (200 km) from land. Gentoo seldom venture more than 5 miles (10 km) from land while the magellanic is intermediate while breeding and leaves the region in the austral winter.

enclose this Paper to the Board of Longitude in London, stating When, Where and How he came by it" (Signed) Edward Bransfield, Master of HMS Andromache – On examining the Water casks in the forenoon we found every one of them had leaked more or less – and some very considerably; this necessarily obliged us to decrease our allowance to ½ a Gallon, fixing the daily expenditure

January <u>1820</u>
Thursday – 13th.

at 20½ Gallons, including 5½ for the use of the stock[1] – At noon on 13th. we were abreast of Cape Horn in Lat*itu*de 57°.54'S Long*itu*de 67°.44'W[2] the Variation of the Needle by an Amplitude taken the preceding Evening 22°.1' East-

Saturday = 15th.

*erl*y An Azimuth[3] at the same time 23°.27'E – From the preceding day to the 15th. we experienced a continual series of light Weather interrupted only by occasional and very light showers – The temperature was as mild as in the finest Season in England, the Barometer standing as high as 29°–2½' – On the 15th. at Noon we were in Latitude 61°.23'S Long*itu*de 63°.53'W and 65 Miles distant from the Ground we intended to start from – Soon after Noon we became enveloped in a thick damp fog which we continued to pass through until the following Morning experiencing but occasional reliefs and those but of very short duration – Several shoals of Seals having been seen about 8 oClock, besides previously a few Penguins,[4] induced us to try for Soundings but we found no bottom with 120 *fath*oms of line

[1] From this there were fifteen gallons per day for the ship's company, i.e. a total complement of 30 men; made up of Edward Bransfield, three midshipmen and the surgeon, together with William Smith and 24 men. This figure agrees with the 'twenty-five men and officers' required by the charter agreement (p. 200). (*The Literary Gazette*, 3 November 1821, p. 691, states that the total was 26 men – p. 83.)

On his first voyage to Valparaíso William Smith had a crew of 22 men, (his arrival in Valparaíso on 11 March, was reported in *Gazeta ministerial de Chile*, 27 March 1819, from Buenos Aires, after a passage of 45 days, with details of the crew). On his fifth voyage, sealing in the South Shetlands, he had a crew of 43 (Smith's Memorial to the Admiralty, p. 65, PRO ADM 1/5029). This considerable increase was presumably to enable him to land as many men as practicable to take seals.

[2] Cape Horn (Cabo de Hornos) is in position 55°59'S, 67°16'W.

[3] See p. 32.

[4] Text amended to read: 'intermissions and those of short duration – Several shoals of Seals having been seen about 8 oClock, EG:AM and previously a few Penguins'.

Sunday = 16th.

– During the night we continued sounding every Two hours but without Success and were constantly passing[1] by and thro immense shoals of Seals[2] and Penguins – So great an indication of the vicinity of land made it necessary to keep a most strict and active look out when about 8 oClock [e.g.:PM] we descried it of a moderate height and partially covered with Snow – At 9 We hove too[3] and got soundings in 55 *fathoms* – Brown sand and Ooze, The extremes of the Land bearing

[1] Text amended to read: 'either among or close to immense shoals of Seals and Penguins – So strong…'.

[2] In these waters, at this date, these were almost certainly fur seals (*Arctocephalus gazella*).

[3] 'Heave to': to put a vessel in the position of 'lying-to' (i.e. with her head steady), by adjusting her sails so as to counteract each other, and thereby check her way, or keep her perfectly still. In a gale, it implies to set merely enough sail to steady the ship; the aim being to keep the sea on the weather bow whilst the rudder has but little influence, the sail is chiefly set on the main and mizzen-mast; as hove-to under a close-reefed main-topsail, or main-trysail, or driver. It is customary in a foul wind gale, and a last resource in a fair one: Smyth, 1867, p. 377.

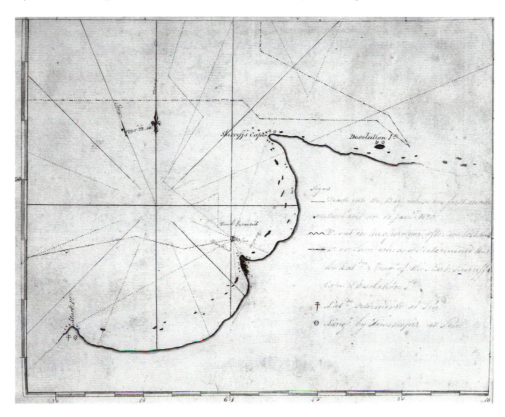

Plate 11. Poynter's Journal. Chart of bay south of Cape Shirreff (Shirreff's Cape).

from East to SSE. On filling we bore up E^{b}S for a break having

January <u>1820</u>

the appearance of affording an Anchorage – While standing in, an unconnected chain of rocks detached evidently[1] from the Main displayed themselves, forming in [themselves] very remarkable shapes and breaking off with peculiar abruptness – When within about a Mile and a half from the opening we hove too and hoisted out the Whale boat – A lead and line having been provided M^r. Smith went in quest of an Anchorage where we might lie in Security while filling up our Water casks a supply of which we had no doubt but in[2] obtaining here – Soon after he shoved off a thick fog came on which entirely precluded[3] the land from our view – this gave us some uneasiness on account of the much broken water we could hear under our lee[4] at no considerable distance At 1(PM) the fog clearing away the extremes of the land bore from SW^{b}S to North, the centre of low land at the bottom of the bay E^{b}S. At half past one the Whale boat returned when M^r. Smith reported [that] there <u>was</u> Anchorage in shore, and although a vessel might run in, in a case of emergency still the passage was narrow and the roadstead insecure[5] – From this report we deemed it imprudent to

[1] Text amended to read: 'evidently detached'.
[2] Text amended to read: 'no doubt of obtaining'.
[3] Text amended to read: 'hid'.
[4] Text amended to read: 'water heard under our lee'.
[5] The track shown on the plan of what came to be known as Barclay Bay, between Start Point and Cape Shirreff (Shirreff's Cape), shows that the *Williams* passed through the position where the 55 fathom sounding is placed on the main chart (off Shirreff's Cape) and proceeded to a position in the middle of the Bay whence the boat went inshore to look for an anchorage off Rowe Point. The *Antarctic Pilot*, 1974, p. 168, says Barclay Bay is 'reported to be encumbered with rocks and very dangerous' and that 'Rowe Point is situated 9 miles SSW of Cape Shirreff and is fronted by ledges and reefs up to two miles offshore. Frederick Rocks (62°33'S, 60°56'W) lie 3 miles N of Rowe Point and two above water rocks are charted 2 miles farther N'. The latter are probably the 'unconnected chain of rocks' mentioned by Poynter. Subsequently the *Williams* appears to have anchored where the anchorage symbol is shown on the plan. Plate 11.

New Plymouth is shown on Bransfield's chart west of Start Point. It actually lies between Start Point and Rugged Island (which is not shown on the chart). It has also been known as Rugged Harbour, Ragged Harbour and President's Harbor. It would appear to have been the harbour used by the American Brig *Hersilia* when she arrived to take seals on Sunday 23 January, to find another vessel already at anchor (p. 190). This vessel is thought to have been the *Espírito Santo*, with Mr Herring on board who stated that his vessel anchored on 25 December 1819, and would therefore

attempt an Anchorage – We had made sail but little more than 20 minutes after hoisting in the Whale boat, the Weather thickening fast, when breakers were sighted close under our Bows

January <u>1820</u>

to clear which the Brig was instantly put about – Almost immediately after this the fog becoming exceeding thick we lost sight of the land ~~we~~ and discovered a reef running athwart our bows which by an instantaneous exertion we managed to clear by Wearing – The [Brig] was scarcely round when others were descried on the lee bow and these also we providentially weathered at about ½ a Cables length by cracking on every stitch the [Brig] could stand under – Finding she drifted fast in shore we let go the Chain Cable in 24 *fathoms* on a bottom of small black stones – On sounding a second time after veering 70 *fathoms* of Chain we found it foul and rocky – Here we remained in great suspense until ½ past 5 when the fog clearing away we perceived ourselves at about One Mile and a half from the Main[land] and just out of the wash of a reef lying off it – At this time the wind which had been very scant,[1] freshening and veering favorably withal, we began to heave up, when just as the Anchor became up and down,[2] the Chain parted occasioned by a sudden and heavy jerk ~~the brig gave while~~ in the act of breaking it out of the Ground – The sails being trimmed we were soon out of danger and obtained soundings in 17 *fathoms* on a hard rocky bottom – the extremes of the land bearing from NE^bN to SSW a headland resembling the Start Point SSE½E. the breeze continuing to freshen, we hauled our wind[3] seaward to avoid being hemmed in on a lee shore.

have been at anchor while Bransfield was in Barclay Bay. The two vessels must have passed within about 5 miles of each other.

[1] 'Scant': a term applied to the wind when it heads a ship off, so that she will barely lay her course when the yards are very sharp up: Smyth, 1867, p. 595.

[2] 'Up and down': the cable vertical in the water between the ship's bow and the anchor.

[3] 'Haul her wind': said of a vessel when she comes close upon the wind. 'Haul your wind' or 'haul to the wind', signifies that the ship's head is to be brought closer to the wind – a very usual phrase when she has been running free: Smyth, 1867, p. 371.

January <u>1820</u>

Monday = 17th.

It proved fortunate [that] we did so for towards Midnight we had heavy Squalls with sleet and a topping confused sea – We remained with our head off until 4 oClock on the following morning when we tacked and bore up NE^bN to regain the Coast we had left on the evening before – While running in, myriads of Seals, together with Whales[1] both sperm and humpback[2] were constantly around us besides a large concourse of Oceanic birds attracted by the bodys of the Seals brought on board yesterday and which our people were skinning – At Noon Our Latitude by a Meridian Alt*itude* was 62°.22′S Long*itude* 61°.44′W At this time we discovered the land veiled in haze and soon recognized it as the point left last Evening – At 1 We determined the Latitude and Longitude of a headland to be 62°.42′S Long*itude*

Start Point

61°.27′W[3] which we named the "Start point" – not merely because it resembled that of the same name in the British Channel but its being from Whence we commenced operations[4] – From here the Coast takes a Northerly direction and the bearing from the Start to the Northernmost point in sight, which breaks off abruptly trending Easterly, is about North, distant between 5 and 6 Leagues – This [latter] point

---

[1] Text amended to read:

Whales both of the sperm and humpback species were constantly around us besides a large concourse of Oceanic birds the latter ~~which had been~~ attracted by the bodies of some Seals that had been brought on board yesterday and which our people were now in the act skinning –.

[2] Sperm whale (*Physeter macrocephalus*) and humpback whale (*Megaptera novaeangliae*): in addition to these, in the nineteenth century, these waters would almost certainly have harboured southern right whales (*Eubalaena australis*), blue whales (*Balaenoptera musculus*), fin whales (*Balaenoptera physalus*), sei whales (*Balaenoptera borealis*) and minke whales (*Balaenoptera acutorostrata*).

Robert Fildes, who was the master of the Brig *Cora*, which was wrecked in Blythe Bay (south side of Desolation Island) on 6th January 1821, wrote in his log:

The Whales are all of the Fin-back tribe and very large. A dead one drove on shore near Elephant Point that measured with a tape 85 feet in length, he was very thin of blubber, neither the sperm or the right whale I believe have been seen here, tho the fin-backers are in swarms. From the hills you may sometimes see a hundred spouts at a time.: PRO ADM 55/143.

[3] Present position 62°35′S, 61°13′W.

[4] Text amended to read: 'but on account of it being the point from Whence we commenced our operations as connected with the object of the Expedition – From the Start the coast takes …'.

Cape Shirreff

[which] received the name of Cape Shirreff and lies in Latitude 62°.26′S Longitude 60°.54′W[1] – It is the most remarkable headland I ever saw forming like extensive and well constructed

January = <u>1820</u>

Fortifications, one rock in particular on the pitch of the Cape taken in any point of view appearing[2] like a Martello Tower[3] – It was here we intended to have planted the Union Jack with the usual ceremonies but a heavy Sea tumbling in, which caused a most tremendous surf made us relinquish this design. We could not but avoid being struck with astonishment at the violente manner in which the Sea broke over the Reefs we had so closely hugged the Evening before and remark what an interposition of Divine Providence had been afforded us in so easily extricating ourselves from such a perilous situation[4] – These in smooth Water are barely perceptible, the surface breaking only at intervals – When Eastward of Cape Shirreff an Islet abreast, affords[5] to the Eye an Arch resembling that of a Bridge, the archway runs thro' all and appears as correctly delineated as if executed by the most experienced Artist – On determining the situation of the Cape we coasted along to the Eastward until abreast of a small island which from its inhospitable and dreary appear

Desolation
Island

ance we named "Desolation Island" Its Latitude is 62°.27′S Longitude 60°.35′W[6] Ten Miles due East from the Cape. The Variation of the needle by a good Amplitude 22°30′E – an Azimuth 23°.52′ Easterly

January 1820

From Desolation Island we bore away NE for a cluster we perceived in that direction which when abreast of were

---

[1] Present position 62°27′S, 60°47′W, 14 miles 057° (NNE¾E Magnetic in 1820) from Start Point.

[2] Text amended to read: 'appears'.

[3] 'Martello Tower': a small circular fort, usually on the coast to prevent hostile landing. Called after such a tower on Cape Mortella in Corsica which proved difficult to capture in 1794.

[4] Text amended to read: at the violent with which in which the Sea broke over the Reefs we had so closely hugged the Evening before and did not fail to remark was an evident interposition of Divine Providence that in having so easily extricated ourselves from such a perilous situation –.

[5] Text amended to read: 'presents'.

[6] Present position 62°27′S, 60°23′W (north point), 12 miles east from Cape Shirreff.

ascertained to be the same as made by Mr. Smith in February 1819 – The whole of these Islets along the Coast we had already run, composed of black rock and displaying above the reach of the Water patches of Snow presented but a dreary aspect – against the~~m~~ the Western Ocean broke with unceasing violence – The Main[land] in the back ground, entirely capt with Snow added much to the Wintry Land-scape[1] – after Sunset we stood off until 10 o'Clock and then hove too with our head to the NW for the night – Soon after Midnight there came on a wet fog which was ~~soon~~ shortly accompanied by a heavy ground swell from the Westward –

Tuesday – 18th.   At 6 It partially clearing away we discerned a small but high Island SE^{b}E about 5 or 6 Miles[2] – but the fog still hovering

---

[1] Opinions of newcomers on first sighting the islands differ. An officer on the *George* wrote to his sister from New Plymouth on 3 January 1821, 'We left the Falkland Islands on 25th of Nove-meber, and made this detestable place on 1st of December; *detestable*, I say, because I am certain it was the last place that ever God Almighty made.' *Imperial Magazine*, 1821, 3, col. 454.

Robert Fildes in the log of the Brig *Cora*, after her loss, wrote *Remarks made during a Voyage to New South Shetland* and in this he records his impression of his first sight of this coast:

having nearly run to the spot where the new discovered land was supposed, or said, to lay, got the lead line passed along to try for soundings. While hauling the Foresail up the Fog cleared up a little and I was not a little gratified by hearing the Man who had the lead in is hand ready to lett go, sing out Land Ho! And land indeed there was, bearing SE 7 or 8 miles, but it had a most forbidding appearance, it displayed the most horrid picture I ever beheld. great high ragged rocks with every cleft in them full of snow behind which was seen what appeared like an impenetrable Ice Barrier, perhaps all nature never produced such a dreary, solitary and des-olate tract of Snow, Ice, Breakers, and Rocks of all shapes to the sight of man, before this dreary region was discovered. I said to myself, sure Madam Nature had been drinking too much Gin when she formed this place.

In the log itself, on approaching Cora Island, (Desolation Island) searching for an anchorage, he was more sensitive to the incredible beauty of the scenery, and wrote:

The Main being Mountains of a vast height and covered entirely with snow, the Base of them terminating in perpendicular Ice Cliffs. the whole having an awfully grand though teriffic & desolate appearance. the snowy mountains showing themselves one over another far above the Clouds, and striking in the mind a devotional reverence at the wonders of the Almighty; and though in a vessel surrounded on all sides with Rocks & Breakers, on an unknown Coast, the mind is forced into a pious contemplation of the Grandeur of the Scene.: PRO ADM 55/143.

It will come as no surprise that the *Remarks on approaching South-Shetland from the Northward, by Captain Fildes,* in the Sailing Directions of John Purdy, 1837, p. 134, are the latter and not the former.

[2] This was probably Table Island (62°21'S, 59°49'W) which is 182 m (595 ft) high. It was sub-sequently named Falcons Island and is shown as such on Bransfield's chart (Plate 31), see entry for 19 March, p. 159.

with a degree of uncertainty as to its clearance we did not stand in, on the contrary the Swell setting us in shore we made sail to secure an offing[1] – During this period we occasionally got soundings from 45 to 75 *fathoms*; outside we could not obtain bottom with 100 *fathoms* of line – On the edge of these soundings we had Fine brown sand but at some little distance further inshore Brown sand and Ooze – In the afternoon the fog partially dispersing enabled us to distinguish 5 or 6 Miles around, this we immediately took advantage off by bearing up SE for the land but just as the Supposed loom of it was seen it thickened worse than before which made

January <u>1820</u>

Wednesday= 19th.

it necessary to again[2] haul off – At 6 Sounding and not reaching bottom with 100 *fathoms* we hove too for the night – On the following Morning the fog preventing our nearing the Shore we Filled and Hove too occa*siona*lly for the purpose of ascertaining the soundings on the edge of the Bank which we found to extend between 4 and 5 Leagues off shore, the greatest depth we obtained soundings in was 145 *fathoms* – Brown sand and Ooze and here we saw an immense number of Whales which however deserted us as we drew inshore – The remainder of the day and the following forenoon the Weather continued thick accompanied with either a falling mist or small rain – during this time we saw several Whales, Penguins innumerable and a few Seals[3] –

Thursday – 20th.

At noon our Lat*itude* was 61°.54′S Long*itude* 59°.10′W. In the Evening we perceived through the haze a large rock bearing SE^bE about 5 Miles distant which at first had so much the appearance of a Vessel under TopG*allan*t Sails that the Colours were brought from below and already bent before we had ascertained our mistake – Judging ourselves too near the land we Wore and Sounded in 52 *fathoms*. Dark sand and Mud – Soon after we saw Breakers E^bN and a small

---

[1] 'Offing': implies to seaward; beyond anchoring ground. 'To keep a good offing' is to keep well off the land while under sail: Smyth, 1867, p. 505.

[2] Text amended to read: 'again to'.

[3] Text amended to read: 'a few Seals & Penguins innumerable –'.

Island S½E – In an hour more the extremes of the Main bore from S^bE to E^bN –

January <u>1820</u>
Friday = 21st.

On the following Morning we had Moderate breezes and cloudy Weather with a swell from the Westward – About One we bore up SSE for the Land which we descried about three bearing E½S. On making it we altered our Course to ENE and at a quarter after Four discerned a high and remarkable rock SSE 5 or 6 Miles distant[1] – At 5 Seeing land ahead we altered our Course to NE½N and at ½ past 6 passed a high craggy Island[2] partially covered with Snow bearing SSE 3 Miles distant – Having passed it we altered our Course to ENE and at 8 the Eastern extremity forming in a Bluff SSE½E 5 or 6 Miles[3] – At 9 We lost sight of the Island WSW and bore up SSE the Eastern bluff bearing SW^bS – In a little time we had the mortification of seeing the fog come on again which obliged us to haul our wind on the Larboard tack Sounding in 90 *fathoms* Coarse black sand with small stones At 1 We sounded in 130 *fathoms* with the same bottom as before At 3 the Weather clearing up we perceived the Land SWbS and a small round but high Island ESE[4] A

---

[1] Possibly Jagged Island (61°54'S, 58°27'W).

[2] This island was later to be named Ridleys Island, see entry for 8 March, p. 156. This position is about 15 miles from that off Jagged Island which would indicate a speed of nearly 7 knots. This would have been possible, however subsequent reports indicate that a tide setting eastwards was experienced off the north coast of the islands throughout the survey, which would tend to reduce this speed, and make the identification more certain.

[3] North Foreland (61°53'S, 57°42'W) is described as a plateau 30 m (100 feet) high projecting north from higher ice-capped land behind. This feature was named by William Smith and appears on the Foster chart, UK HO, s 90/3 Shelf Ae1, and that published in the *Edinburgh Philosophical Journal*, 3, p. 367, Plate XXII (Plate 5). See pp. 46, 51 and 63.

[4] This was Bridgeman Island (62°03'S, 56°45'W) a volcanic island, 240 m (785 ft) high (Plate 12), which is shown on Bransfield's chart as Bridgeman's Island in position 62°01'S, 57°04'W. It is one of the names on the chart which are not explained in the text but presumably it refers to Captain Bridgeman who was serving on the station and had been a member of the boards which had passed both Midshipmen Blake and Bone for promotion to lieutenant.

The Hon. Charles Orlando Bridgeman was captain of HMS *Icarus*, 10, and a friend of Captains Shirreff (HMS *Andromache*) and O'Brien (HMS *Slaney*), whose ships were together on the South American Station. The latter records in *My Adventures during the Late War &c.,* p. 311: 'Captain Shirreff, Captain Bridgeman, and myself visited Santiago, the capital of Chili; and, of course, we paid our respects to the supreme director, Don Bernado O'Higgins'. It is thus possible that this name was added subsequently at the request of Captain Shirreff. Bridgeman was born 5 February

Light breeze soon after springing up from the Northward we Made sail and Bore up S^{b}W for a Headland[1] which had the appearance of affording shelter – At 8 The outer and Western rocks bore NW The Bluff or headland SW^{b}W The round Island N^{b}E½E – At Sunset the Variation by an Amplitude was 23°.14′E – Having sent a hand to the Mast head to look round an Island was reported S^{b}E[2]

January <u>1820</u>

Saturday 22nd.

Just before midnight we tacked to clear an Iceberg and at Midnight again went about, the Bluff NNW 6 or 7 Miles. At 1.30 We observed an Island[3] nearly clear of Snow WSW at 4 The Bluff bore N½E at 5 Perceiving the Coast to the SW of the Island to form in a bight, we made sail with Moderate breezes – The necessary precautions of keeping the lead going and a hand forward to look out for broken Water being taken we rounded the Eastern point and at 7.30 (AM) Came too with the Chain Cable in 16 fathoms – Coarse sand with black gravel – The Eastern point of the Island NE^{b}E a small Island near the bottom of the Bay W^{b}N and the Southern point of the Bay SW. While rounding the Island we perceived the shore covered with Penguins[4] whose awkward

1791, the second son of Orlando, 2nd Baron and 1st Earl Bradford, and the Hon Lucy Elizabeth Byng, daughter of 4th Viscount Torrington and a descendant of Admiral Sir George Byng, 1st Viscount Torrington, whose fifth son Admiral John Byng, was shot in HMS *Monarque* 'pour encourager les autres'. He entered the Navy on 18 June 1804 as a first-class volunteer on HMS *Repulse*, 74, Captain Hon. A. K. Legge, became a midshipman in 1805 and after two more appointments was promoted lieutenant, 10 September, 1810. He served in HMS *Revenge*, 74, as flag lieutenant to Rear Admiral A. K. Legge. He was promoted commander 16 May 1814 and commanded HMS *Badger*, 10, on the West Indies Station until August 1816. He commanded HMS *Icarus*, 10, on the South America Station, from 24 June 1817 and was posted 2 September 1819. His last ship was HMS *Rattlesnake*, 28, in the Mediterranean which he commanded from September 1827 until May 1830. He retired October 1846 and became a rear admiral on the reserved half pay list 19 January 1852, and vice admiral 10 September 1857. He married Eliza Caroline, eldest daughter of Sir Henry Chamberlain, British Consul at Rio de Janeiro, in January 1819, and had three daughters. He died on 13 April 1860: Burke, *Peerage*; O'Byrne, 1849, p. 123; *Navy Lists*.

[1] Subsequently named Cape Melville (62°01′S, 57°34′W).

[2] No island exists in this direction – it may have been an iceberg.

[3] Subsequently named Penguin Island, 166 m (544 ft) high.

[4] The chinstrap (*Pygoscelis antarctica*) and Adélie Penguin (*Pygoscelis adeliae*) are the commonest species in this area today. In the South Shetlands gentoo (*Pygoscelis papua*) are also common and macaroni (*Eudyptes chrysolophus*) are widespread in small numbers.

Plate 12. Bridgeman's Island bearing NW distant one mile (1952). UK HO, *Antarctic Pilot*.

motions made the most ridiculous appearance – while our Noses were assailed with the most intolerable stench I ever smelt[1] – As soon as every thing was secured we tossed out the Whale and long boats, the former of which was armed – After breakfast M[r]. Bransfield proceeded in her to effect a landing where he might plant the British Union, taking possession of this Land in the Name and on the behalf of HM George the 3rd. his Heirs and Successors and Naming it <u>New South Britain</u> "New South Britain" – At ½ past 8 we observed the Boat land on a shingle beach bearing NNW of us and perceiving soon after with the aid of our Glasses the Jack planted – we hoisted on board the Ensign and Pendant, Fired

<u>January 1820</u> a Gun and concluded the Ceremony by serving to each Man a Glass of Grog to drink His Majestys Health – Besides

---

[1] Text amended to read: 'and at the same time our Noses were assailed with the most intolerable stench –'.

planting the "proud old British Union" he had but a few yards from it buried a Bottle containing several Coins of the Realm given him by the Officers of the Andromache and several of the English residents in Valparayso for that purpose – At Noon the Wind blowing in Fresh breezes with heavy Squalls from the NW we veered the whole of the Chain Cables – About ½ past Two, the breeze having moderated, I was ordered to proceed with the Long boat in quest of Water – M[r]. Blake at the same time taking the Whale boat on the same Service – For this purpose I landed on the Island, abreast of us, deeming it the most convenient for getting on board a supply should it produce a sufficiency – It would appear incredible was I even to give a rough calculation of the Multitude of Penguins I met on landing,[1] however

[1] Penguin Island today (1997) has 7500 pairs of chinstrap (*Pygoscelis antarctica*) and 3000 pairs of Adélie penguins (*Pygoscelis adeliae*) on it.

Plate 13. George's Bay. View from Penguin Island looking north to Turret Point (1994). Photograph Dr J. L. Smellie.

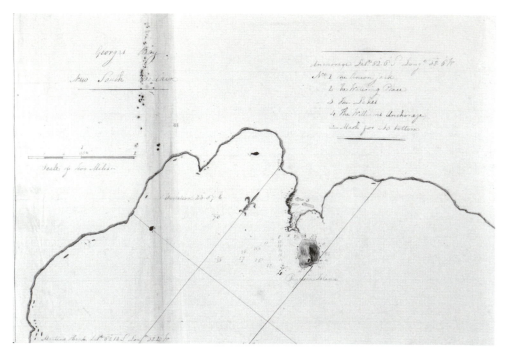

Plate 14. Poynter's Journal. Plan of George's Bay.

within bounds I might be induced to curb my opinion; suffice it to add[1] our progress was completely arrested by these Gentlemen who with the most determined obstinacy disputed our right to proceed and it was not until great slaughter had been committed and an opening forced through them with Lances, Seal clubs &c we were enabled to further[2] our research –

January <u>1820</u>

It is well known that every Animal however timid at other times will with the most determined courage defend its young and <u>this</u> being the breeding Season <u>here</u> may account for the decided opposition we met with – Before long we discovered several small Streams running down the side of the hill to the Water's edge but the whole of these flowed thro' the filth of the amphibious <u>Islanders</u> – In the event

[1] Text amended to read: 'were I to give a calculation of the Multitude of Penguins I met with on landing, however cautiously my opinion must be guarded in expression the Numbers; suffice it to say …'.

[2] Text amended to read: 'to proceed in'.

however of not finding a <u>better place</u> we constructed a well by the Water side, surrounding it with Stones – This Island lying NE and SW about a Mile in length we found to be very nearly as broad as long; the Eastern extremity rising to a considerable height while the Western decreased gradually to a point from which a Bar extends to the Main – It bears evident marks of Volcanic fire, the Eastern part in particular being entirely composed of Ashes – On the top of the rise was found the Crater, at the bottom of which Water was discernable, which trickling thro' the ashes formed the several Streams we had perceived. Having reimbarked we pulled alongshore to the Western end when seeing some Seals on the rocks we landed and easily dispatched them – While engaged in this business and fighting our way thro' the <u>Islanders</u> we perceived the Whale boat pulling towards us from the Main who on joining detailed the unfortunate particulars of one of the Crew having had his hand

January <u>1820</u>

dreadfully lacerated by a Sea Elephant,[1] who while attacked, by throwing himself over backwards, contrived to seize the poor fellow,[2] and it was not until three very severe blows were given [that] he relinquished his hold – Had the Animal been less exhausted he must have taken it off – The long boat having conveyed him on board and the Whalers informing me of a Stream they had seen on the Main I was induced to go there for the purpose of ascertaining the most advantageous method of commencing work on the following Morning – On being conducted to it, it proved a most capacious run of exceeding clear and fine tasted Water, conveniently situated just over the rise of the beach and capable of completing us with great expedition – While proceeding along shore we fell in with a Shoal of Sea Elephants asleep – who on waking were evidently so unused to the sight of Man as to eye us with an air of indifference, but on being attacked with Lances &c[3] betrayed their astonishment in a

[1] This is the southern elephant seal (*Mirounga leonina*).

[2] Text amended to read: 'contrived to seize the poor fellow by throwing himself over backwards'.

[3] Text amended to read: 'on being attacked they betrayed …'.

most audible bellow – Several being killed, were stripped of their blubber, which being junked up,[1] together with a few Seals and Penguins which had been picked up was taken on board – At half past seven we returned on board, and got ready for commencing operations at daylight –

January 1820

Sunday 23rd.

On the following Morning we had clear Weather with Fresh breezes from WSW when about ½ past 6 it becoming more Moderate I proceeded in Company with the Whale boat to the Stream with the water casks – We landed in a small bight round a rock bearing NNW from the Anchorage – The boat being too heavy for lying on shore was anchored clear of the rocks abreast of the Stream and by means of a hauling line the small casks being filled were taken on board and started[2] into the larger ones – While the people were employed in filling Mr. Smith and Myself proceeded to discover the rise of the Stream which we found to fall in various branches from the Mountains and running under the Snow had formed several excavations from whence they issued with a gentle rush until the mingling of the whole formed in one – We collected from the run various irregular stones and mosses from the swamp land which were afterwards boxed up as Specimens – After walking as far as the Snow would allow us which did not exceed a Mile & a half we returned to the Party who had filled Two Casks and with these we proceeded on board leaving the empty ones on shore,

January 1820

We found Mr. Bransfield had determined the Latitude of our Anchorage by an Observation taken on a Stage over the Brigs side at about 6 feet above the level of the Sea to be 62°.6′S.[3] the SE end of the Island which from its Natives was

---

[1] 'Junk up': to cut up. Junk is a term applied to pieces of cable cut into small portions for making points, mats etc and for reducing to oakum for caulking the seams (it was also applied to pieces of salt beef as tough to the teeth as bits of rope): Smyth, 1867, p. 415.

[2] 'To start' (applied to liquids): to empty: Smyth, 1867, p. 651.

[3] Astronomical sights taken in poor visibility were (and still are) taken from as low as practicable to obtain a clear horizon for use as the horizontal reference, care being taken not to get so low that the waves intrude. Assuming the brig was anchored in the position shown on Bransfield's chart this latitude is almost identical with the modern determination.

Plate 15. Penguin Island looking east across George's Bay (1975).
Photograph Dr J. L. Smellie.

Penguin Island
named "Penguin Island" NE½E. After dinner I again accompanied the Watering party to the Stream Mr. Bransfield employing the Whale boat in Surveying the Bay – After setting the people to work the Surgeon, Second Mate and Myself visited the discovered haunt of the Elephants Twenty One of whom we dispatched in less than half an hour – It was really astonishing to see the immense quantity of blood that flowed from them and never in my life have I witnessed[1] any two Animals produce as much as One of these – After this D[r]. Young and Myself proceeded in an inland and Northerly direction – During our ramble we picked up several different mosses and at a distance of not more than three quarters of a Mile from the Watering place stumbled on three Lagoons, One of them as large as the other two combined and the whole contained within the circuit of a Mile –

[1] Text amended to read: 'did I witness'.

January 1820

The whole of these were productive of Fresh water and on their banks were encamped thousands of Penguins with their Young – After noticing several things which I shall relate in a general way hereafter we rejoined the Waterers and at ½ past 9 returned on board – While away M^r. Bransfield had ascertained by the means of an Artificial Horizon the Long*itude*

Union Jack

of the spot he had planted the Jack on, which he found to be 58°.6′.30″W having previously settled the Lat*itude* by the Log 62°.4′S[1] – At Sunset we found the Variation of the Needle by a good Amplitude 23°.59′ Easterly – On the fol-

Monday – 24th.

lowing Morn*ing* – we had Cloudy Weather with Moderate Breezes from the WNW – At 4 The boats shoved off for the shore with the remainder of the empty casks – As we drew in we became completely encompassed with Ice occasioned by the North West*er*ly Winds and finally found it utterly impossible to land in the bight without great risk to the boats – Not judgeing myself authorized (especially on the Service we were) to run the slightest chance[2] I pulled round the spit to another Stream seen by M^r. Smith on the preceding day with an intention to complete <u>there</u> if possible although the Water was not so clear as at the one we left – but it unfortunately being low water and the rocks extending a great distance

January 1820

out I was not able to approach it within ½ a Cables length – Thus foiled in both attempts I resolved (that we might not remain idle) to land on the shingle beach and by setting half a dozen hands to work, junk up the Elephants we had killed the day before, the blubber of which being taken on board

---

[1] The artificial horizon is used for reflecting an image of the heavenly body observed. It may be a surface of mercury, oil or other suitable liquid, but, since it will only lie still on a steady base, it is generally only practicable to use it on shore. This can present problems with timing since it was not customary to move the chronometer on board, let alone take it ashore. Normally a 'hack' watch was used which was checked against the chronometer before landing and on return on board. The latitude 'by log' will have been adjusted from the anchorage position obtained on 23 January using a bearing, probably from the compass, and distance measured by a log in the boat. The present position of Turret Point, where the Union Jack was hoisted, is 62°05′S, 57°57′W.

[2] Text amended to read: 'hazard'.

and casked up, might on our arrival at Valparayso be produced as a sample – Had our Water casks been grummetted[1] I might easily have completed by rolling them to the
Stream but without being so it was running the risk of bilgeing[2] them, a loss we could but very ill afford – In the
space of a short time a quantity of blubber being obtained
and stowed away we returned on board to our breakfasts – a
Breeze off shore forcing the Ice to Seaward assisted by a
strong tide gave us reason to suppose a landing might be
effected, at all events on the beach – Grummets having
been fitted at 11 oClock we left the Brig and experienced
no difficulty in conveying them to the Stream from which
each with a Funnel were filled in a little less than a quarter
of an hour – Having no other object in view but in obtaining this supply we proceeded on board – In the afternoon
with the remaining empty casks I again made for the Shore
for the purpose of completing up – On landing I was
joined

January <u>1820</u>
by M[r]. Bransfield who in the Whale boat had been sounding
– As he had evinced a desire of seeing the Lagoons we set out
for them in Company with D[r]. Young and Bone – On our
way back we filled a box with the best earth we could find as
a Specimen of the soil of New South Britain – Soon after
Seven we returned on board with a completion of 27 Butts

Tuesday – 25th.
and 2 Puncheons[3]– On the following Morning we had dark
cloudy Weather with moderate breezes from the Westward
which assisted great quantities of Ice in driving to Seaward –
The Survey of the Bay being completed M[r]. Bransfield inti-

George's Bay
mated his intention of naming it "George's Bay" in Honor
of His Majesty and its being the first spot on which we had
been able to display the British Colours,[4] A high, bold and
projecting Cape bearing NE½E from the Union post he

Cape Melville
named "Cape Melville" in complement to the First Lord of

---

[1] 'Grummetted': bound about with a rope band.

[2] 'Bilgeing': the widest part of a barrel is called the bilge – bilgeing is to damage the bilge.

[3] 'Butt': wine measure of 126 gallons. 'Puncheon': cask of 72 to 120 gallons.

[4] King George III died four days later on 29 January, 1820 and was succeeded by his eldest son, the Prince of Wales, as King George IV.

Plate 16. Cape Melville looking north (1996). Photograph Dr J. L. Smellie.

Plate 17. Martin's Head looking north (1996). Photograph Dr J. L. Smellie.

the Admiralty,[1] the Lat*itude* of which is 62°.1'S Long*itude* ~~58°.20'W~~ 57°.44'W[2] – The SW Bluff of the Bay is in Lat*itude* 62°.12'S Long*itude* 58°.20'W[3] and was named

Martin's Head

"Martin's Head" in complement to the Comptroller of the Navy[4] – In the afternoon the Weather moderating M[r]. Bransfield sent the boats to sound, after which the Long boat procured three breakers[5] of Water which had been expended since our last supply – In the Evening we had Moderate Breezes with much Snow

January <u>1820</u>

and a heavy Swell from the Eastward and soon after 8

[1] Robert Saunders Dundas, 2nd Viscount Melville, 1771–1851. Born on 14 March he entered Parliament in 1794, at the age of 23, as MP for Hastings and became private secretary to his father, the First Viscount Melville who was Secretary of State for War and the Colonies, and President of the Board of Control for the Affairs of India. In 1801 he became MP for Midlothian and in 1807 entered the Cabinet of the Duke of Portland. He was Irish Secretary from April to October in 1809 and became First Lord of the Admiralty in 1812 a post he retained until 1827 when he resigned as he was unwilling to serve under Canning. He was reappointed when the Duke of Wellington came to power in 1828 and remained in post until 1830 when he retired to live at Castle Melville near Edinburgh where he died on 10 June 1851 aged 80. Melville's time at the Admiralty was marked, among other things, by a resurgence of interest in Arctic affairs. This resulted in the voyages of Captain John Ross to Baffin Bay in 1818, followed by those of Captain Parry, 1819–20, through Lancaster Sound (during which Melville Island and Viscount Melville Sound were discovered and named) and his two subsequent voyages in 1821–23 and 1824–25; Captain Franklin's expeditions overland to the North Canadian coast, 1819–22 and 1825–27, and a number of others: *DNB*, s.v.

[2] The present position is 62°01'S, 57°34'W. The point is 183 m (600 ft) high.

[3] The present position is 62°12'S, 58°15'W. The head is 277 m (908 ft) high.

[4] The Comptroller of the Navy was Admiral Sir Thomas Byam Martin, 1773–1854. His name was borne on the books of HMS *Canada*, 74, Captain William Cornwallis, in 1780 and HMS *Foudroyant* 80, Captain John Jarvis, in 1782. He entered the Royal Naval Academy in August 1785 going to sea in April 1786 as captain's servant in HMS *Pegasus*, 28, commanded by HRH Prince William Henry (third son of King George III and subsequently King William IV, see also p. 152, n. 1) with whom he continued to serve in HMS *Andromeda*, 32, as midshipman until 1789. After service in various ships, mainly on the home station, he was promoted lieutenant on 22 October 1790, and commander in May 1793 in HMS *Tisiphone*, 12, and post captain on 5 November the same year in HMS *Modeste*, 64. He continued in command at sea taking part in a number of actions and capturing a number of vessels until his promotion to rear admiral, 1 August 1811. He hoisted his flag in HMS *Aboukir*, 74, the following year in the Baltic, and subsequently served as second in command at Plymouth until 1815 when he became Deputy Controller of the Navy, and succeeded Sir T. B. Thompson as Controller the following year. He sat as MP for Plymouth from 1818 until 1831. He was knighted in 1814, KCB in 1815 and GCB in 1830, promoted Vice Admiral 12 August 1819, Admiral 22 July 1830 and Admiral of the Fleet 13 October 1849. He became Vice Admiral of the United Kingdom in 1847. He also became an Elder Brother of Trinity House, Director of Greenwich Hospital and a Commissioner of the Board of Longitude: O'Byrne, 1849, pp. 735–6; *DNB*.

[5] 'Breaker': small cask of less than 32 gallons.

oClock an Iceberg was so near driving on board us, that we were obliged to rouse the hands out to boom it off – Having nothing more to detain us at this Anchorage, it was M^r. Bransfield's intention to have put to Sea on the morrow but with it we were attended nearly the whole day with heavy

Wednesday – 26th. Snow and an exceeding thick fog – This necessarily obliged us to remain, and during this period I shall make my Remarks on the Bay and its Environs but as our stay was very short my description in consequence must be but limited – Although capacious it extends to no considerable depth and the Angles which were taken tended to lower the first impression – It is open to exactly half the Compass,[1] the two points, the outer end of Penguin Island and Martin's Head, forming the Entrance, bearing NE and SW – We had little opportunity of noticing the tides but from what I am able to judge, they appeared strongly influenced by the winds: on the 24th. in particular with the NW breeze it ran at about the rate of 2½ knots in a S E*asterly*. direction, but notwithstanding this I remarked it once setting to windward – The rise and fall seemed regular and about 12 – 14 or 16 feet[2] – I have great reason to believe our Anchorage in 16 *fathoms* about a

January <u>1820</u> Mile SW of Penguin Island to have been the best in the Bay and principally for this reason, that from whatever point the Wind might have blown we still had a corner to creep out of, had any accident have happened to our ground tackle – it was on a Bank which appeared to encompass the whole Island, and on this the safest and most Sheltered birth is to be obtained – Our soundings generally speaking, gave us no very favorable opinion of the bottom as holding ground, the greater part being black Gravel, in some places mixed with coarse sand – Inshore and towards the midship portion we found it rocky, and in the Middle was not able to reach

---

[1] Text amended to read: 'half the Compass exactly'.

[2] The *Admiralty Tide Tables*, 1997, do not quote figures for King George Bay (George's Bay), but Admiralty Bay, ten miles west is given where the Mean Higher High Water is 1·5 m (4·9 ft) and Mean Lower Low Water 0·4 m (1·3 ft), range 1·1 m (3·6 ft). The tides in the South Shetland Islands are diurnal (i.e. with two unequal high waters each day) and nowhere is the range between MHHW and MLLW greater than 1·5 m (4·9 ft). The largest predicted range in the vicinity is 2·2 m (7·2 ft).

bottom with 70 *fathoms* of line – Towards the fall of the Island however we had fine Brown sand in 8 *fathoms* but this was too near for an Anchorage – Between Penguin Island and the Main is a Channel through which a small Vessel might attempt in a case of emergency – Extending across from the low spit of the Island runs a bar with 2½ *fathoms* on it at the top of high Water – This being nothing more than a ridge, can only be struck with one heave of the lead – and on each side is 3½ *fathoms* – Should necessity ever force a Vessel to attempt it, the Island must be kept close on board and great attention paid

January 1820

in rounding the spit to avoid the rocks running some distance from it and only perceptible at low Water – The Coast at the bottom of the Bay forms in a high cliff of Snow, masses of which, by their constantly falling from the precipices occasion a confused rumbling noise, resembling that of distant thunder but of a much shorter duration – These masses, drive to Sea with the Northerly winds and being frequently reinforced by Snow showers, encrease to such a size as entitles them to the name of "an Island" – Notwithstanding the general sterility we had as hitherto witnessed – a kind of light soil was perceptible on the low land at the back of the Watering place resembling a mixture of sand and good mould, but invariably where it was tried, a foot in depth from the surface touched on Water[1] – The swamp land, the lowest of all, was partially covered with Moss and a bastard or dwarf grass[2] nourished by the fæces[3] of the several oceanic birds and on the little rocky ridges at the margin of the Snow appeared the favorite haunt of the Albatross – This Moss and grass the former abounding in Variety were the only appearance of Vegetation we saw – On each

---

[1] Text amended to read: 'water was found at a foot in depth from the surface –'.

[2] The only form of grass that grows in this area is antarctic hair grass (*Deschampsia antarctica*), one of only two native flowering plants in the Antarctic (the other is antarctic pearlwort, *Colobanthus quitensis*, which is nothing like grass). The moss cannot be identified with certainty, but *Drepanocladus uncinatus* is common in this area and grows in association with the grass in swampy situations near seabird colonies, and therefore seems the most likely form.

[3] Text amended to read: 'excrement'.

little ridge Albatrosses had formed their nests,[1] composed of nothing more than small stones regularly and neatly placed on which their Eggs were deposited – So unaccustomed were they to the sight of Man that we were eyed, with great indifference and to obtain

January <u>1820</u>

an Egg or Young one were obliged to force them away with sticks which they bit with the most savage determination – They consisted of Four different Species the White, Spotted, Brown and common Grey: ~~and~~ the whole of the~~se~~m whenever approached vomit their food cased in an oily substance at their intruder – Besides there was a large bird of a dusky brown [colour] with a few white feathers on the upper part of the wing; web-footed with a sharp and pointed beak[2] – these construct a comfortable nest of Moss & situated among the Albatross[3] – They seem~~ed~~ particularly savage and with loud schreeches ~~would~~ pounce down and frequently strike with the wing – a Dog we had was completely covered with blood by being attacked in this manner; we however were more fortunate being able to defend ourselves with sticks ~~&c~~ – The other Marine birds were the Cape Pigeon or Pintado,[4] Petrell, Snow bird,[5] several species of the Gull[6] and one of the Shag,[7] who build a singular mud nest resembling a chimney pot on the rocks – We saw no land Animal or bird of any

[1] Albatrosses do not normally build nests like this nor do they nest so far south. The probability, both from the description of the nests and the area, is that these birds were the southern giant petrel (*Macronectes giganteus*). The four species subsequently referred to are probably no more than the different plumage morphs shown by this highly variable species.

[2] This is the brown skua (*Catharacta lönnbergi* or *Catharacta antarctica* depending on the view taken of species limits). Its colouration and aggressive behaviour are well described. The species is very similar to the great skua or bonxie of the northern hemisphere, and there are several closely related species or subspecies in the southern hemisphere. The other species in the Antarctic Peninsula is the southern polar skua (*Catharacta maccormicki*) which is widespread on the continent and, until recently, confined to areas further south than the *Williams* sailed. Since 1965 it has expanded its breeding range (in small numbers) north to the South Orkney Islands.

[3] Text amended to read: 'The nests of these were found comfortably constructed of moss, among the ruder abodes of the Albatross –'.

[4] Cape pigeon or pintado petrel is now known as cape petrel (*Daption capense*).

[5] This is almost certainly the snow petrel (*Pagodroma nivea*).

[6] This is probably the kelp gull, also known as the dominican gull (*Larus dominicanus*).

[7] The taxonomy of the birds in the blue-eyed shag (*Phalacrocorax atriceps*) group is complicated and controversial. The form on the Antarctic Peninsula (*Phalacrocorax bransfieldensis*), referred to

Plate 18. Shag (*Phalocrocorax bransfieldensis*) on Hope Island (Snowy sheathbill (*Chionis alba*) in front) (1970). Photograph Capt. R. J. Campbell.

kind excepting a White Pigeon[1] who build, in the crevices of the rocks with grass conveyed from the Swamp – these were so tame as to allow themselves to be knocked down with clubs stones &c and many were obtained in this manner although they were too much on their guard to be taken by hand – The most singular in appearance however were is the Penguins[2] whose awkward and tottering motions resemble a child just learning to walk, their

January 1820

its fins extended as a balance instead of Arms – they are amphibious but possesse more of the properties of the fish than bird – have a false stomach from whose contents they

here, has recently been regarded as a different species from similar birds (king shag, *Phalacrocorax atriceps albiventer*) found in South America and the Falkland Islands and the endemic form found in South Georgia (*Phalacrocorax georgianus*) (Plate 18).

[1] This is the snowy sheathbill (*Chionis alba*) which is decidedly pigeon-like in appearance and behaviour (Plate 18).

[2] Apart from the colonies on Penguin Island mentioned above (p. 113, n. 1) there are currently (1997) about 16,000 pairs of chinstrap penguins (*Pygoscelis antarctica*) on Cape Melville.

nourish their Young – One distinguished Five different Species[1] but not equally troublesome for our almost sole and principal Enemies were adorned with black crests which they rose when wrangling; several of them from a body would proceed to the charge and although severely wounded would maintain their Ground with obstinate determination – Although their bite was not severe it nevertheless caused an unpleasant twitch which we conceive much better dispensed with[2] – What they live on I know not but I think in all probability on the carcases of Seals, Birds &c and not excepting

[1] Today (1997) at these latitudes the three commonest types of penguin are the gentoo (*Pygoscelis papua*), chinstrap (*Pygoscelis antarctica*), and Adélie (*Pygoscelis adeliae*). Macaroni penguins (*Eudyptes chrysolophus*) are widespread in small numbers, particularly in the South Shetland Islands. Neither magellanic (*Spheniscus magellanicus*) nor rockhopper (*Eudyptes chrysocome*) penguins are found this far south, and emperor (*Aptenodytes forsteri*) and king (*Aptenodytes patagonicus*) penguins are only rare visitors, although the latter breed in South Georgia. However James Eights (1798–1882), the naturalist and surgeon who accompanied Captains Palmer and Pendleton (*Annawan* and *Seraph*) to the South Shetland Islands in 1829–1831 states in his description of those islands 'of penguins there are five species. The *Aptenodytes patagonica* [*sic*], (King penguin) is the largest and by far the most beautiful of the species, and may be seen in great numbers covering the shores for some considerable extent': Eights, 1833. Although Murphy, 1936, I, p. 344, accepted this, Calman, 1937, p. 178, thought it possible he was mistaken and had in fact seen king penguins on Staten Island, where they were formerly plentiful. However, Robert Fildes states in his *Remarks made during a Voyage to New South Shetland*, in the log of the Brig *Cora*, 1820–21, describing the penguins in the South Shetland Islands: '... the other which is very scarce is the King Penguin they are much larger than the others, and have a beautiful neck. these are only found when well to the Eastward. they are the same kind as those found in the Isle of Georgia': PRO ADM 55/143. There would thus appear to be no doubt that the fifth kind were indeed king penguins.

The crew of the *Cora* lived ashore awaiting a ship to take them home and during this time 'a tent was constructed with sails & other materials the ground part of which consisted of 4 lines of Puncheons in form of a square. the heads of the inside ends being taken out so that two men could stow in an sleep, both warm and dry. one of these which was to spare was taken possession of by the Cat. and two Penguins one day come up out of the water and took up their station alongside of her in the cask, they neither minding the people in the tent or the Cat, nor the Cat them. poor shipwreckd puss used to sit purring alongside them apparently comfortable and pleasd with their company. These penguins used to go to sea for hours and as soon as landed again would make direct for the tent and get into the cask. the crew would sometimes to plague them endeavour to keep them out by keeping the tent shutt but they always found away to get in by getting under the Canvass, in this manner did they stop with us untill we left the coast.': PRO ADM 55/143.

[2] Text amended to read:

it is amphibious but possesse more of the properties of the fish the bird – ~~They~~ It have a false stomach from the contents of which its Young is nourished – One distinguished Five different Species of Penguin but not equally troublesome for our almost only and principal Enemies of that Race were adorned with black crests which they erected when angry; several of these in a body would proceed to the charge and although severely wounded would maintain

their own Species[1] for Several that had been killed were afterwards found very cleanly anatomized nothing being left but the bare skeleton – We saw very few Seals, but those few were productive of very beautiful skins, well clothed in fur[2] – but the Sea Elephant seemed to reign the undisputed Master of the range of the Bay and I have no doubt but a Ship might with great expedition procure a full cargo of Oil, they might either remain[3] at the Anchorage

January <u>1820</u>

or if disposed to make the very most of their time, by leaving a boat behind cruize[4] off the Mouth of the Bay which we found well sprinkled with Whales many of which if some of our Men can be relied on who have been employed on the fishery are of the right sort – by acting thus it would render their stay on the Coast of very short duration, especially if disposed to try down at the Falkland Islands which for many reasons I should conceive advisable – Having mentioned the few productions that came under my Notice of this dreary Land I shall conclude any further relation by remarking that the Rock and Stone appeared principally to consist of White and brown Granite and Limestone – specimens of each were carefully boxed up for Inspection on our return –

In the afternoon the fog clearing away we perceived the Coast had resumed its wonted wintry appearance by the late fall and presenting a uniform surface of Snow was not easily to be recognized as the same land – This fall backed by an Easterly wind proved severe and when over our Sails and rigging bore testimony of its power – At two oClock on the following morning with Calm and cloudy Weather we hove into a stay a peak[5] and at Four a Light air springing up the Anchor was weighed –

---

their Ground with obstinate determination – Although their bite was not severe it neverthe-less caused an unpleasant twitch which we conceive much better avoided.

[1] No penguin species are scavengers. They eat mainly crustaceans and fish.

[2] Text amended to read: 'furred'.

[3] Text amended to read: 'either remaining'.

[4] Text amended to read: 'cruizing'.

[5] 'Apeek': means with the anchor on the seabed under foot, i.e. with the cable up and down (see p. 105, n. 2), and 'a stay' means in line with the ships stays; 'long stay' in line with the main-stay; and 'short stay' in line with the fore-stay: Smyth, 1867, p. 46.

January <u>1820</u>   All sail being set, produced but little effect, so light and baffling were the airs and the boats being tossed out were sent ahead to assist – At 8 We tried for Soundings, but did not strike bottom with 70 *fathoms* of line – the small Island at the bottom of the bay – NW½N of us – distant about a Mile and a half – 10 The airs inclining N E*aster*ly the boats were recalled, the Brig gently moving out of the Bay – On opening Cape Melville with the SE end of Penguin Island we observed they bore NE½N and SW½S of each other[1] and somewhere about Twelve or Fourteen Miles apart – At a quarter after Twelve a breeze springing up from the Westward forged us ahead and at Four Cape Melville bore NNE Penguin Island N¾E – and Martin's head NNW½W – From this position the land stretched to the SW as far as the Eye could discern but a little distance to the Southward of Martin's head it abruptly broke off to the WNW forming to appearance in a deep sound[2] – At 7 We altered our Course to WSW for although the land was precluded from our sight by haze, the smoothness of the Water bespoke its vicinity – At ½ past 9 We again saw it bearing West and at Midnight had Moderate breezes and hazy Weather with smooth Water – A

Friday 28th.   heavy bluff point[3] NNW 7 or 8 Miles At 2 The Bluff bore N[b]W½W the land from it extending to WNW. In the course of the forenoon we saw several Whales principally in Shoals –

January <u>1820</u>   At Noon we had light and variable airs – An Ice Island NE[b]E½E – The extremes of the Main from SW to NW making of great height and every atom covered with Snow[4] – Our Latitude was 62°.49′.43″S Long*itude* 60°.00′.45″W – At 1 a Moderate breeze sprung up SW which by Four had encreased to a Fresh one – We then tacked and at 6.40 again put her round, the North Eastern extreme of the land N[b]E – A bluff bold head with a black rock shewing off it North and

---

[1] This is the exact magnetic bearing between the headlands, which are 11 miles apart.

[2] This sound is now known as Admiralty Bay.

[3] Ross Point (62°21′S, 59°07′W), the south-west extremity of Nelson Island.

[4] Livingston Island, 39 miles long. Originally called Frieseland (in various spellings), was first called Livingston's Island by Robert Fildes in 1821: Hattersley-Smith, 1991, II, p. 356.

another steep headland NW[b]W which appeared the North Western extremity of all – Between these Two Capes a deep bay ran up to the NW[b]W[1] but the Evening being far advanced rendered it imprudent to attempt its entrance – The land about it composed of rude crags and barren ridges covered with Snow to the Water's Edge may easily be imagined to present but a dreary Scene – All the day we had Penguins, Snow birds, Pintadoes, and Albatrosses around the Brig besides several Whales – At Midnight a heavy fog with small rain and smooth Water –

Saturday 29th. The following Morn*ing* was ushered in by a thick fog which however soon after Four clearing away we tacked to regain the Coast – In this we were for a short period disappointed by a relapse of the Weather which made it necessary to shorten sail, that we might not close it too hastily –

January 1820 a temporary relief about Eleven oClock favoured us with a glimpse of very high Mountains bearing North of us and at about Noon it had so far cleared up as to distinguish the extremes of the Main[2] from NW[b]W½W to NNW and Two Icebergs NE. Soon after this with Fresh breezes, thick fog and small rain the coast again for a time became enrobed remaining so until 50 minutes after 3 when land was perceived on the Weather bow, the extremes of which at Four bore from North to W[b]N the nearest part NNW about 4 Miles[3] – The breezes freshening we reduced our Sail to

[1] It is not easy to make a positive identification of these headlands. Bransfield's chart shows what is now known as McFarlane Strait and its eastern entrance point has an island off it. Assuming the 'deep bay' is the entrance to McFarlane Strait, and the noon position puts the *Williams* off this entrance and south of it, the 'North Eastern extreme' then becomes Robert Point (62°27'S, 59°23'W), the 'bluff bold head with a black rock shewing off it' Fort Point (62°33'S, 59°35'W) and the 'steep headland' Renier Point (62°36'S, 59°49'W). Although it is difficult to see how the latter could be described as appearing to be 'the North Western extremity of all', it could possibly be thought of as the north eastern extremity of all, if Livingston Island was regarded as the end of the mainland.

[2] Livingston Island, the south side of which is a continuous ice face backed by high mountains which rise to Mount Friesland 1770 m (5807 ft) in the middle and about 3 miles within the coastline (see also p. 128, n. 4 above).

[3] The land WbN was probably Barnard Point (62°46'S, 60°20'W) the southern extremity of Livingston Island while that to the north was probably in the vicinity of Brunow Bay (62°43'S, 60°08'W).

Plate 19. Typical weather like that experienced by Bransfield in Bransfield Strait (1970). Photograph Capt. R. J. Campbell.

Plate 20. Iceberg in Bransfield Strait (1970). Photograph Capt. R. J. Campbell.

double reefed Topsails under which we Wore and hove too but on Sounding found no bottom with 180 *fathoms* of line – The Barometer falling very rapidly apprized us of portending wind[1] which we amply guarded against by Close reefing the Topsails, Furling the Courses and setting the fore Trysail. Before 8 was proved the correctness of our Glass, the wind having encreased to Strong Gales – At 8.50 We Wore to the Southward and at Ten experienced heavy Squalls with a short and topping Sea – which at Midnight was accompanied with small rain –

January <u>1820</u>

Sunday 30th.

At ½ past 3 on the ensuing Morning while standing to the Southward we made a Group of small Islands extending from SE to E[b]S. for the purpose of weathering them we shook out the 2nd reef of the Fore Topsail – Set the Courses and boom Mainsail close reefed, and while thus employed perceived Two Islands on the Weather bow – Without the possibility of being able to effect our design at 20 minutes after Four we Wore, the whole range stretching from E[b]N to SW. The Winds at this time were Strong and a hazy Horizon which occasionally shut and opened to view an unknown Coast abounding with rocky Islets – At 8 The extremes of what we deemed the Main[2] bore from SW to W[b]N and at 9 from North to SW Twenty minutes after we tacked to the Southward and at ½ past 11 set the Land WSW 3 or 4 Leagues – At Noon our Latitude by a Meridian Altitude was 63°.3′.30″S Long*itude* by Chronometer 60°.25′.30″W At ½ past 12 the Haze thickening we Made more sail standing to the Southward and as it would appear by the bearing of the land at Noon away from it – At 3 our notice was arrested by Three very large Icebergs and 20 minutes after we were unexpectedly astonished by the discovery of land S[b]W –

January <u>1820</u>

We continued however to stand on, when at 4 the haze partially clearing away we found ourselves half encompassed with Islands spreading themselves from NE to East –

[1] Text amended to read: 'of the approach of wind'.

[2] From the noon position the vessel must have been running down the east coast of Deception Island which lies between 62°54′S and 63°00′S in 60°30′W. Plate 21.

between two of these we could perceive a range of Breakers in contact with each and immediately after this was discernable a high and rude range running in a NE and SW direction the centre of it bearing SE 6 or 7 Miles – a steep and roundish Island about 5 Miles distant SSW and a small circular Island SSW½W – the whole of these formed a Prospect not easily described and our apprehensions were not a little encreased by becoming re-immersed in fog and in a situation we knew not Where – Altho' a great part appeared to join still we were not able with certainty to determine it,[1] so unaccomodating was the Atmosphere but by setting the Land WSW at Noon proved we were engulphed but whether by Islands or the Main [still] remained to be determined – On sounding we struck bottom with 80 *fathoms* of line Coarse black sand & rocky – Our theme of conversation was the Idea of having by the direction the land took found what might possibly lead to the discovering of the long-contested existance of a Southern Continent[2] –

Soon after this we Wore and stood to the Northward fearfull of a change of wind –

January <u>1820</u>	We can positively assert that we saw land in 64°S still trending to the Eastward – In this Bay or Gulph we saw a very favorable share[3] of Whales and what is seldom found but where shelter may be obtained a great quantity of Seaweed apparently but freshly parted from the rocks – At 10 Having cleared the several Icebergs driving about us we Hove too and at Midn*igh*t had Moderate breezes with hazy Weather –
Trinity Land	The part forming like the Main M^r. Bransfield named "Trinity Land"[4] in compliment to the Trinity board and the small circular Island in Lat*itude* 63°.29′S Long*itude* 60°.34′W

[1] Text amended to read: 'we were ignorant of – Altho a great part of the land so seen appeared to be connected yet we were not able with certainty to determine the land'.

[2] Text amended to read: 'Our theme of conversation encouraged by the direction which the land took was the Idea of having by the direction the land took discovered what might possibly lead to the determination of the long-contested question as to existance of a Southern Continent'.

[3] Text amended to read: 'tolerable quantity'.

[4] This would appear to be the continental mainland and part of the Antarctic Peninsula. The part seen by Bransfield is now known as Palmer Coast. Trinity Peninsula is the name given to the

Plate 21. Deception Island from the east (1970). Photograph Capt. R. J. Campbell.

Tower Island
Monday 31st

"Tower Island" on account of its proximity[1] – We continued to lay to until 3 oClock on the proceeding[2] morning and then bore up ENE to ascertain most positively the true direction of the Coast With Mode*ra*te breezes and tolerably clear Weather we made all Sail when at Noon the Man at the Mast head reporting "fields of Ice ahead" we altered our Course to ESE our Latitude was 62°.50′S Long*itude* 57°.25′W Soon after one we descried a small low Island SE[b]E and in ten minutes after the Main land – Satisfied of its

northern extremity of the Antarctic Peninsula while the large island further west is known as Trinity Island (63°45′S, 60°45′W).

[1] This presumably refers to the fact that the Tower of London is adjacent to Trinity House on Tower Hill. The present Trinity House building was completed in 1798 although the Corporation of Trinity House of Deptford Strond, whose first charter dates from 1514 in the time King Henry VIII, was established in Water Lane in 1660 and remained there with various gaps until the present building was occupied: Mead, 1946, pp. 152–4.

Tower Island is shown in position 63°29′S, 60°00′W on Bransfield's chart, Plate 31. On modern charts it is 63°33′S, 59°48′W (northern end), 305 m (1000 ft) high and 5 miles by 3 miles in size. See p. 172.

[2] Text amended to read: 'following'.

'Trinity Land and Islands'

'Hope Island'

'O'Brien's Islands'

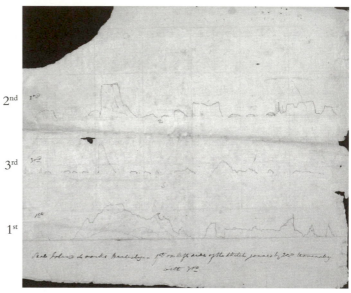

2nd

3rd

Sea Islands & rocks
westerly.   1st
'1st on left side of the
sketch joined by 2nd
terminating with 3rd'

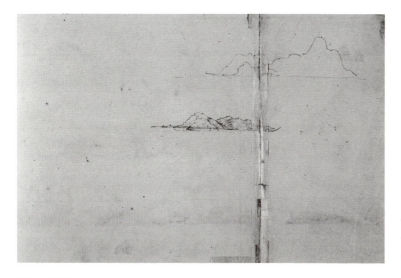

Untitled and
unfinished view
on two lines.

Plate 22. Poynter's Journal views.

direction we Shortened sail and Wore, the Island SE½S 6 Miles and the extremes of the supposed Main from East to South – This Island in Latitude 63°.5′S Longitude 56°.44′W[1] was named "Hope Island" from the hope

Hope Island

January 1820

we entertained that the range might continue to stretch Easterly untill joined by the Thule – That portion between the bearings of East and NEbN appeared level and tolerably clear while that in the SSW rose in Mountains of considerable height their summit entirely capt in Snow. As we drew inshore we had been passing several Icebergs some of them of great size and at 3 we counted no less than Thirty one – a few justly deserving the name of Islands – At 6 With our head off we shortened sail to Topsails and soon after lost sight of the land enveloped in a bank of Mist – At Midnight with clear Weather we had light breezes from the Westward – On the ensuing Morning – at 4 oClock we Bore up ENE for the purpose of making the land – At 6 The Wind shifted to the Northward – At 7 It became very thick which at 8 was accompanied with small rain – On trying for Sounding we were not able to strike bottom with 190 *fathoms* of line – At 10 Infested by an exceeding thick fog we Tacked to the Westward and at Noon had Fresh breezes with the same[2] Atmosphere – In the Afternoon we remarked a confused cross sea and at 4 not being able to distinguish half the Brigs length around we Tacked, fearful of again falling in with Ice, a predicament not very pleasant to encounter in so [Sun] blind a situation –

February 1820
Tuesday – 1st.

February 1820

Wednesday 2nd.

At 5 The wind had encreased to Strong breezes accompanied with small rain and at 10 minutes after Six the fog had partially cleared away – At 8 We shortened sail At 10 Tacked to the Westward with Strong winds and rainy Weather – At 2 the next morning we Tacked At 4 Had Strong breezes with rain At ½ past 6 Wore to the Westward and made sail – At 10 minutes after 9 By the carelessness of the Helmsman a Sea broke on board us which unshipped the Skylight, washed

---

[1] Present position 63°02′S, 56°50′W. Hope Island is 32 m (105 ft) high.

[2] Text amended to read: 'no better'.

overboard various[1] sundries but luckily effected no serious damage – At Noon we had Fresh gales with hazy Weather and a very heavy Sea – Being on a lee shore with the additional misfortune of perceiving the Barometer falling very rapidly we were under the necessity of keeping the Brig under a press of Canvas for the purpose of dragging her off – At 5 Finding her overpressed we reefed the Fore Topsail and Boom Mainsail, the Weather squally with a very thick fog – Soon after Six we saw a Hoop floating past which gave rise to some speculation but on enquiry finding [that] Two had been hove overboard in George's Bay [we] concluded it must have proceeded from thence none having been cast away elsewhere –

Shortly before 7 we perceived the Sea violently breaking over three very large rocks SW[b]W of us between 2 and

February 1820

3 miles distant[2] – In this unpleasant situation we Tacked and cracked on all Sail, the Brig was with safety able to bear; the gales fresh with very heavy Squalls – Our position rendering it absolutely necessary, the Officers and Men were ordered on the alert at a moments warning and every precaution being taken in case of accident, the whole Watch were kept on the look out – At ½ past 10 the breeze was rapidly dying away, the Barometer as low as 28°–¼ and still inclined to fall – To add to the whole we were driving fast in shore, the land running as we supposed in a N Easterly direction – At Midnight with foggy Weather and a very heavy Swell from the Northward it fell Calm, which circumstance directed our

Thursday 3rd.

hopes to a favorable change – About 15 minutes after Midnight a breeze springing up from the SW caused a degree of pleasure not easily to be described and with light hearts every one but the Watch retired to their beds – This was immediately taken advantage of but at One it having encreased to Strong Gales with heavy Squalls and showers of

---

[1] Text amended to read: 'a parcel'.

[2] From the subsequent course to O'Briens Islands and the track shown on the Norie chart (Plate 8), these rocks would appear to lie off the eastern end of King George Island. The probability is that it was Simpson Rock (61°58′S, 57°23′W), 9 m (30 ft) high, seven miles east of King George Island, although the reference to 'driving fast in shore, the land running as we supposed in a NEly direction' might be taken to indicate that they thought the *Williams* was in the vicinity of Cape Melville.

Plate 23. O'Briens Islands from the south (1994). Photograph Dr J. L. Smellie.

Sleet we were obliged to close reef the Topsails and boom Mainsail, being greatly overpressed – Soon after Midnight we had the

February <u>1820</u>   satisfaction of remarking the rise of the Glass which we greatly depended on from our having before proved it a correct instrument – and at Four it encreased to 28°½₀ We had still Strong Gales with Sleet although Moderate at intervals – Just before 8 We descried Two high Islands NE^bE and ENE and at Noon the centre of them bore E^bS 4 or 5 Leagues –

O'Briens
Islands   These were named "O'Briens Islands" in compliment to Captain O'Brien of HMS Slaney[1] and lie in Latitude 61°.30′S Longitude 56°.16′W – Steering to the Northward at ½ past One we perceived more land East to appearance making in

[1] Captain Donat Henchy O'Brien. Born in March 1785, described himself as a descendant of one of the ancient monarchs of Ireland. He entered the Navy on 16 December 1796 as ordinary on board HMS *Overyssel*, 64, Captains John Young and John Bazely. He remained in her until 1800 seeing action at the Helder where as master's mate in command of a flat-bottomed boat he assisted in the landing of the army. In January 1800 he joined HMS *Atlante*, 16, Captain Anselm John Griffths, acting as lieutenant before returning to the *Overyssel*. After serving in a number of different vessels he was, in HMS *Hussar*, 38, Captain Philip Wilkinson, when she was wrecked on the southernmost portion of the Saintes on 8 February 1804, and he became a prisoner of the French

Islands and at ½ past 3 made the Main,[1] to clear which we bore up NNE. At 4 The extremes bore from NE^bE to SE^bE At ½ past 5 We hauled up North, a small Island with several rocks trending Northerly from it ENE 5 or 6 Miles The extremes of the Main from East to S^bE½E – The portion between these bearings seemed to run about NNE and SSW of a Moderate height and the major part clothed in Snow – At 8 We had fresh Breezes from the Westward with cloudy Weather the extremes of the Main from E^bS to SE^bE, the small Island SE½E – At Midnight we Tacked with Moderate breezes and a Westerly Swell –

February <u>1820</u>
Friday 4th.

At a quarter after three on the ensuing Morning we again made the Land SE and at Four the extremes bore from East to SE^bE – Kept away ENE running along it – At 6 The haze rendered it undiscernable and a little before 9 the fog coming on exceedingly thick we hauled our wind on the Larboard tack – Passing a Log of wood afforded us another theme for argumentative speculation which however remained a quere[2] none could solve – At ½ past 9 It partially clearing up induced us to bear up ESE and at Noon we had Fresh breezes with hazy Weather – Several Whales and Seals playing around us – About a quarter after three we altered our Course to SSE and 25 minutes after made the Land along which we hauled up SSW – At 4 The centre of an exceeding

---

at Brest. After three attempts at escape, on all of which he was re-captured, he got away from the fortress at Bitche on 14 September 1808 and reached Trieste in November where he got on a boat from HMS *Amphion*, 32, Captain William Hoste, and after further adventures rejoined the fleet at Malta where Admiral Collingwood promoted him lieutenant on 29 March 1809. He continued serving in the Mediterranean, with distinction, principally under Captain Hoste, until 1813 when he was promoted commander 'entirely by his own exertions, unassisted by interest' (night-order issued by Captain Hoste, HMS *Bacchante*, Malta, April 20th, 1813, quoted in O'Brien, 1839, p. 486) and returned to England. He next obtained employment in command of HMS *Slaney*, 20, and was promoted post captain 5 March 1820, on 21 October, 1821, he was relieved and returned to England in HMS *Owen Glendower*, 36. He was promoted rear admiral on the Reserved half pay list, 8 March 1852, and died 13 May, 1857: O'Byrne, 1849, pp. 827–8; *Navy Lists*; *DNB*.

The islands are charted in position 61°28'S, 55°57'W. They are now named individually. Aspland Island is the largest, 3 miles long and 734 m (2408 ft) high, and the most northerly, with Eadie Island, 450 m (1476 ft) high, close to it and O'Brien Island with three peaks the highest of which is 420 m (1378 ft) high, a little further south-west.

[1] This is the western end of Elephant Island.

[2] Text amended to read: 'however raising a question which …'.

Plate 24. Cape Bowles from the south (1975). UK HO HMS *Endurance.*

high Mountain little inferior in its Altitude to the Peak of Teneriffe[1] SW 6 or 7 Miles – At 10 minutes before 6 We hove too, the Southern extreme bearing West 4 or 5 Miles. The Whale boat being hoisted out M[r]. Bransfield proceeded in her to plant another Union Jack with a similar inscription to that erected in Georges Bay on whatever part he could effect a landing – Having succeeded he planted it at the foot of a tremendous Snow precipice in a small cove affording a confined landing place on shingle bearing SW[b]W of us –

February <u>1820</u>

The Weather threatening to thicken he did not deem it prudent to remain longer than necessity required and had only time to remark it abounding like every other part of the Coast we had seen in Seals and Penguins – We could distinguish from the Brig various Streams descending in Cascades from the high land, but the margin of the shore appearing

---

[1] The 'Peak of Teneriffe' is Pico de Teide 3715 m (12,188 ft); this was Mount Irving, the highest point on Clarences Island, 1924 m (6312 ft).

Saturday 5th.

lined with rocks, must render water difficult to be obtained At 7 Perceiving the boat pulling off, we stood in to pick her up, which having done we hauled our Wind on the Larboard tack – At 8 The beach bore SWᵇW½W 6 Miles – the extremes from NW to SW At Midnight we had Fresh breezes with drizzling rain – At 4 oClock on the following Morning, the Atmosphere resumed its annoyance[1] which however soon after Five cleared away – Availing ourselves of the opportunity we tacked, Made sail and stood in to make the Coast left in the preceding Evening At ½ past 7 We made it bearing SW of us – At 8 Had Fresh breezes with fine hard Weather which by ½ past 10 had decreased to Light baffling airs – At Noon the extremes bore from WNW to WSW – the whole range appeared to incline in a NNW and SSE direction Not perceiving Land to the Southward of the Mountain under which the Jack was planted we bore up ESE

February <u>1820</u>

Cape Bowles

Having ascertained the Latitude and Longitude of this Southern extreme to be – 61°.19′S and 54°.10′W,[2] it was named "Cape Bowles" in compliment to the Commodore of the South American Station[3] – Our Lat*itude* at Noon was

---

[1] Text amended to read: 'annoying thickness'.

[2] Present position 61°19′S, 54°05′W.

[3] Commodore William Bowles, subsequently Admiral of the Fleet Sir William Bowles KCB. He was born in 1780 and entered the Navy 9 September 1796 as first-class volunteer on board HMS *Theseus*, 74, Captains Augustus Montgomery and John Aylmer, in the Channel and off Cadiz. After service in various ships he was appointed acting lieutenant in HMS *Cambrian*, 40, Captains Barclay and John Poo Beresford, 22 July 1803. He was confirmed 30 August while serving on the Halifax and North America Stations. He was promoted commander on 22 January 1806 and appointed to HMS *Zebra*, bomb, on 25 March 1807 for service with Lord Gambier off Copenhagen. He was promoted post captain on 13 October the same year and to command of HMS *Medusa*, 32, frigate, in 1808 and HMS *Warspite*, 74, 1809 and *Medusa* again in 1810. In 1811 he commanded HMS *Aquilon*, 32, in which frigate he conveyed Lord Cathcart as ambassador to St Petersburg and served for some time in the Baltic. In 1813 he proceeded to South America where he was employed until April 1814 when he returned home. In May 1816 he was again on the South America Station where he was Commodore, Commander in Chief until 1820.

On his return to England he married the Hon. Frances Temple, sister to Lord Palmerston. He then commanded the royal yacht *William and Mary* and was subsequently Comptroller General of the Coast Guard until promoted rear admiral 23 November 1841. He hoisted his flag in 29 May 1843 in HMS *Tyne*, 26, later transferring it to HMS *Caledonia*, 120, in which he remained until 1844. From 1844 to 1846 he was a member of the Board of Admiralty. He was elected MP for Launceston. He was promoted Admiral of the Fleet shortly before he died in 1869: O'Byrne, 1849, pp. 108–9; *Navy Lists*.

61°.16′.37″S Longitude 53°.35′.15″W – The abrupt break of the land to the Southward appearing to terminate its boundary, unless by taking a circuitous rout to the Westward it should resume a bend Easterly, determined us upon making an East course by steering which until arrived[1] in the Fiftieth degree West, and then due South, the question whether it was likely to communicate with Thule might very reasonably be decided – With Fresh breezes and fine Weather we soon lost sight of the Coast – At 9 We shortened sail and hove too with our head to the Southward – The Variation of the Needle by an Azimuth was found to be 20°.46′ Easterly and an Amplitude gave 19°.52′ Easterly –

Sunday 6th.

At 2 oClock in the following Morning with Moderate breezes and fine Weather we Bore up SE and Made sail but shortly before Four a thick mist coming on, obliged us as consistent with prudence to haul our wind on the Larboard tack – At Noon we had Light airs inclinable to Calm and a thick fog – At 1 The mist in some measure dispersing we Made sail but at ½ past 2 it became as bad as ever – We however continued standing to the SE until Four oClock

February 1820

and then hauled to the NW – The atmosphere continuing intensely thick without the slightest appearance of a change at 7 oClock we bore away NW^bN giving up the Idea of proceeding Southerly which could not be effected in such Weather without undergoing a continued series of harassings, which our People were but ill prepared to stand, for having been some time in a temperate climate they had contrived to get rid of their warm clothing for a lighter supply and when engaged on this Service [they] had not wherewithall to repurchase so necessary a suit[2] – At 8 We had moderate breezes with a thick mist and slight frost – On the

Monday 7th.

following Morning – the fog continuing so very thick as to

[1] Text amended to read: 'and to steer in that direction until arriving …'.

[2] Text amended to read: 'protection'. Bearing in mind that the crew of the *Williams* were accustomed to sailing round Cape Horn, it would seem probable that this remark refers to the party from HMS *Andromache*.

render our standing on imprudent at One oClock We hove too and at 4 it again clearing away Bore up WNW At 8 With fresh breezes and fine Weather we Altered our Course to WSW with the object of regaining the land – At Noon our Lat*itude* by a Meridian Altitude was 60°.39′.35″S Long*itude* by Chronometer 53°.15′.15″W – With Moderate breezes and clear Weather we hauled dead in for the land At 3.40 We descried it and at 4 Set the headland

February <u>1820</u>

to the Northward of Cape Bowles S^bE½E about 5 Leagues – At ½ past 4 We altered our Course to SW^bW but soon after 7 the breeze dying away delayed our approach to the part of the Coast we were endeavoring to attain At 8 With light airs enclinable to Calm Weather we particularly noticed a very confused Sea similar to that occasioned by a restless tide and making a noise like two meeting in opposite directions – In this situation a prodigious high Mountain garbed in Snow, projecting to Seaward and forming a remarkable promontory bore S^bE½E between 4 and 5 Leagues – The land to the Westward trended S W*esterly* and a high ridge whose summit was entirely clear of Snow SE^bE extended in the direction of East and West – At Mid*night* We had Light airs from the ESE

Tuesday 8th.

with Fine Weather and a Westerly Swell – As the Morning dawned we perceived land SSE and at 4 the extremes bore from South to ESE At this time a small Island[1] was perceptible to the Southward open with the great range and in a line with a reef of rocks S½W between 4 and 5 Leagues distant – The Main to the Southward of this Island trended in a SSW direction At 7 With light airs from the Southward we hauled

February <u>1820</u>

our wind and at Noon the Island bore SSE 6 or 7 Leagues – Our Lat*itude* by a Meridian Altitude was 60°.41′.58″S and at 2 the Longitude by a Lunar Obs*ervation* 53°.39′.45″W – At 4 The weather was Calm and fine – the land spreading itself from E^bS½S to S½W and running in an ENE and WSW direction; that shore between the bearings of E^bS½S and

---

[1] Probably Seal Island (see p. 145 below).

NE^bE[1] formed like an Island while from SE to S½W appeared like a continuation of the Main. At 7.30 A light air sprung up from the SW and at 8 The extremes of the land bore from E^bS½S to S^bW At Midnight We had light airs and fine Weather. The whole of the afternoon being beautifully clear displayed the line of Coast which lies in the parallel of

Wednesday 9th. 61°S – With light breezes and a cloudy atmosphere at 3 oClock on the ensuing morning we Tacked in shore and at Daylight the main body bore SE^bE At 7 the haze partially thickening a confined portion of it was only perceptible in the SE which at 10 became entirely enveloped – a long rugged Island with several rocks stretching from it SE between 5 and 6 Miles distant Soon after noon this gloomy Weather was accompanied with rain which with fresh breezes occasioned a heavy Swell from the Westward – About this time we shortened sail for the night and at Midnight had thick hazy Weather with a very confused Sea

February 1820
Thursday – 10th. At 2 on the following morning we Wore to regain a situation ready for taking any advantage the Weather might allow us – At 5 The breeze having greatly increased obliged us to close reef the Fore Topsail and at ½ past 9 we Tacked and furled the Square Mainsail At Noon we had Strong Gales with thick gloomy Weather and a heavy confused Sea – by 8 it had become more moderate – at 9 We Wore ship and at Midnight had Strong gales with heavy Squalls of Rain and

Friday 11th. Sleet – At 6 It became moderate which we took advantage of by shaking out the reefs of the Topsails and making Sail At ½ past 10 a thick fog came on which at Noon somewhat cleared away At 3 It again thickened and shortly after we Tacked to the Northward to procure an offing – At Midnight a continuation of thick rainy Weather with fresh breezes –

Saturday 12th. With the Idea of securing a situation for nearing the Coast

---

[1] The position would appear to be about 20 miles north of Elephant Island. The extreme limits are from the left hand edge of Clarences Island, at Lloyds Promontory (61°07′S, 54°00′W), to the right hand edge of Elephant Island in about 61°03′S, 55°21′W. The shore between the bearings of EbS½S and SEbE (not NEbE as stated which would appear to be an error) is Clarences Island, while that between SE and S½W is Elephant Island, shown on Bransfield's chart (Plate 31) as part of the mainland.

should the Weather in the Morning prove favorable we Tacked, jogging in shore until 3 oClock in the afternoon we again tacked and stood off, the winds blowing strong and accompanied with rain and sleet – We managed however in the forenoon by a glimpse of the Sun to procure sights for the Chronometers which at Noon gave 56°.27′W – Lat*itude* Obs*erved* 60°.52′S At Midn*ight* we had Fresh breezes with dark, heavy cloudy W*eathe*r and very heavy Westerly Swell –

February <u>1820</u>
Sunday – 13th.

At one on the ensuing morning with Fresh breezes we Bore up to make the Coast which at 50 minutes after 5 we descried making in small islands and bearing S^bW½W of us – For the purpose of nearing them we hauled our wind on the Larboard tack and Set Foresail At ½ past 7 the haze entirely clearing away shewed us the Main in the back ground – On heaving too we struck soundings with 79 *fatho*ms of line on a coarse rocky bottom At 8 The Wind had died away to light airs approaching to a Calm – the extremes of the Coast from S½W to E½N, the nearest part SSE between 3 and 4 miles – Between the Main and Largest Isle appeared a passage and from the latter a range of breakers trend about 4 Miles in the direction of SW^bW the outer one of which bore WSW of us – These rocks, to appearance, a huddled mixture of uncouth crags and inaccessable precipices seem to have been the remaining scraps not worked up, but thrown away by Nature as useless[1] and unprofitable except for the production of the Seal which by the report of Mr. Smith who landed here abound in myriads – While standing off and on during the period Mr. Smith was away, several Shags similar to those in Georges Bay paid us a visit and were so far from being shy

February <u>1820</u>

as to allow themselves to be struck with pieces of wood &c from the brig – Their plumage is a white breast with a black head and wings, bill long, narrow and sharp, the upper jaw with an abrupt curve overhanging the under one – Among a flock of Penguins we witnessed[2] three or four entirely white, the only ones of that colour we saw on the Coast – At Noon

[1] Text amended to read: 'of Natures Materials not worked up, but cast aside as useless …'.
[2] Text amended to read: 'saw'.

Seal Island

we determined the Latitude of the largest Island to be 61°.2′S Longitude 55°.32′W which afterwards received the name of "Seal Island"[1] – The Eastern end of this Island on with the point which forms the entrance of the passage bore SSE and the extremes of the Coast from E¾N to S½E. At 2 An exceeding high Mountain discovered itself S½W and in half an hour after The boat returned with 80 very fine fur skins and a piece of rock as a specimen resembling kennel coals[2] – On a fine but very limited sandy beach Mr. Smith effected a landing and this he reported to be so completely covered with Seals as to render it dangerous to go among them – he described them as regularly stowed in bulk[3] and sallying among them made such havoc that he left upwards of three hundred carcases not being able to stow them in the boat – They eyed him with

February 1820

vacant astonishment while destroying their comrades until it became their turn – and then received the blow with great seeming indifference yet they were so tenacious of life as to require the labour of Two men to keep them in a state of insensibility until it came to their turn to be skinned: indeed one that was brought on board, cut from the throat to the breech, besides round each flipper, shuffled along the deck when handed up the side – A Sea Elephant was also seen, Penguins innumerable and quantities of Marine birds who were so voracious as to partake of the carcases as the people were skinning and required to be knocked down with clubs to prevent interruption – After dinner Mr. Smith again proceeded on shore to obtain the Carcases he had left, but the tide having risen between 16 and 20 feet had washed nearly the whole of them away and those indeed that remained were so torn by the birds as to render the skins unfit for use – The expedient of procuring more being resorted to, great

---

[1] Present position 61°00′S, 55°22′W. The largest island is 92 m (302 ft) high.

[2] 'Kennel coals': probably 'cannel coal' formerly known as 'candle coal', which is a type of hydrogen-rich sapropelic coal used in the nineteenth century to produce gas for lighting or to burn in domestic fires. It is dull black sometimes with a waxy lustre and burns easily with a bright flame.

[3] Today (1997) Seal Island has a fairly small (but increasing) population of antarctic fur seals (*Arctocephalus gazella*) and both chinstrap (*Pygoscelis antarctica*) and macaroni penguins (*Eudyptes chrysolophus*) which breed in good numbers.

slaughter took place which ended only when a sufficiency was obtained for Specimens which we were particularly ordered to procure by Captain Shirreff previous to sailing –

February <u>1820</u>

Monday – 14th.

On perceiving the boat making her way off we stood towards her for the purpose of picking her up which having accomplished we Made sail to the Northward for the night – At Midn*ight* we had Squally Weather with rain – At 2 oClock on the following Morn*ing* with Squalls of rain and sleet and a heavy Swell from the NW we Tacked to the Eastward and at 4 had Calm and cloudy W*eathe*r. At 8 a Breeze having sprung up from the Westward we Bore up for the land and Made sail – at ½ past 10 we Altered our Course to SE and at Noon Saw the land extending from SE to SW, the nearest part of it South 9 or 10 Miles – The lower part was discernable only[1] the fog concealing its summit – Sights for the Chron*omete*rs taken in the forenoon gave our Long*itu*de 55°.31′W Lat*itu*de Observa*tio*n 60°.55′S On working up the board was deduced a very wide difference from the Observ*atio*n which fully confirmed what we had suspected – a set driving us to the Eastward – At One we altered our Course to ENE and soon after Four perceived a very high and rugged Mountain thro' the haze South to close which we hauled up SSE shortly after this we descried the Main ENE. At ½ past 4 The Man at the Mast head reporting Breakers to leeward we tacked, the Mountain bearing

February <u>1820</u>

Valentines head

WSW and the Eastern shore NE½E When about, we perceived the supposed breakers was a very strong ripple occasioned by a sluicing tide running in a Northerly direction between these two headlands, and indeed the rapidity of it may with propriety entitle it to the name of "a Race". This Eastern headland which we ascertained to be in the Lat*itu*de of 61°.3′S Longitude 54°.48′W was named "Valentines head"[2] in remembrance of the day – At 3 We bore up NE^bE

---

[1] Text amended to read: 'The lower part only was discernable …'.

[2] Cape Valentine (Valentines Head) is shown on Bransfield's chart (Plate 31) and Poynter's chart (Plate 30) as the eastern extremity of Elephant Island, present position 61°06′S, 54°40′W. From the comments on 15th February it appears Poynter is referring to Valentines Head as the eastern extremity of Cornwallis's Island. This must be a mistake as the position he gives for Valentines Head in Longitude 54°48′W is west of that given for Cornwallis's Island in Longitude 54°36′W.

Plate 25. Elephant Island east coast with Valentines Head at right (1996).
Photograph Dr J. L. Smellie.

Plate 26. Valentines Head looking west (1994). Photograph Dr J. L. Smellie.

147

Tuesday – 15th.

to prove whether as we suppose it was an Island, but before our object could be effected it came on a thick fog which obliged us to haul our wind The centre of the supposed Island SE about 4 Miles dist*ant*. At Midn*ig*ht we had Moderate Breezes with thick hazy Weather and a heavy swell from the Westward At one oClock on the ensuing Morn*ing* – we stood in and At 8 Made the land SSE 3 or 4 Miles – The haze rendering it imprudent to make a nearer approach we Wore until 9 when the Weather having a little brightened up we again stood in – Soon after 11 We perceived Cape Valentine SSE 5 or 6 miles and other land East which we altered our course to close While drawing in we ascertained beyond dispute the certainty of Cape Valentines forming one extreme of an Island the centre of which at ½ past 11 bore SSE

February <u>1820</u>

**Cornwallis'
Island**

**Wednesday 16th.
Sunday 20th.**

This Island which was high and nearly clear of Snow we found to lie in Lat*itu*de 61°S Long*itu*de 54°.36′W[1] It was named "Cornwallis's Island" in compliment to the Right Hon*oura*ble Admiral Lord Cornwallis[2] – At Noon we hauled upon a wind, the extremes of the Island from SSW to WSW Twenty minutes after One we descried land forming like islands West of us and one NW^bW – On perceiving them we tacked the Weather Squally and very hazy – At Midn*ig*ht We had light airs inclinable to Calm with a Westerly Swell and thick fog – From the 16th to the 20th. we were buried in a continual fog which for most part of the time was so exceedingly thick, that any object at the brigs length would not

---

[1] Present position 61°04′S, 54°29′W, 7 miles ENE of Valentines Head. The island is two miles long by one mile wide and rises from the sea to sharp crests 470 m (1542 ft) high.

[2] Admiral Sir William Cornwallis, fourth son of Charles Cornwallis and First Earl, 1744–1819. He entered the Navy in HMS *Newark*, 80, in 1755 and fought in HMS *Dunkirk*, 60, at the battle of Quiberon Bay. He was promoted lieutenant in July 1762, and commander in HMS *Wasp*, 8, Sloop in October, where he remained until 1765 when he was promoted to post captain in HMS *Prince Edward*, 44. In 1788 he became Commander in Chief East Indies, and was promoted rear admiral in February and vice admiral in July 1793. In 1796 he was made Commander in Chief West Indies. He was promoted admiral 14 February 1799 and in 1801 succeeded Lord St Vincent in command of the Channel Fleet where he remained until he was relieved by Lord St Vincent again in 1806. His flag ship during this period was HMS *Ville de Paris*, 110, Captain T. R. Ricketts, in which Bransfield served as an ordinary and later able seaman. He was MP for Eye 1768–74, 1782–84 & 1790–1807 and for Portsmouth 1784–90. He died 5 July 1819: *DNB*.

have been discernable – In the forenoon of the latter we obtained sights for the Chronometers which gave our Longitude 52°.5′W Latitude Observed 60°.31′S – The Sun setting tolerably clear gave the Variation by an Azimuth[1] 23°.52′ Easterly –

Monday 21st. The following day afforded partial fogs and clearances but during the intervals both in the fore and after noon we procured sights which in the former gave our Longitude 52°.23′.45″W and in the latter 52°.44′.15″W the Latitude Observed 61°.30′S. In the afternoon we passed thro' a strong ripple occasioned by sets meeting from North & South –

February 1820
Tuesday – 22nd.
At Four oClock on the following Morning, with the Intention of prosecuting a research to the Southward we Bore up – Fancy had already pictured to us, as having penetrated into the Antarctic Regions which may appear somewhat plausible when it is related that not a particle of Ice had been seen by us on the Eastern coast or that part we had left – This however it was not destined we should effect although allowed to hover on the verge of that Circle and indeed considering the advanced state of the Season our disappointment was not so great as it otherwise would have been – With a fine breeze from the NE after 43 Miles had been run down Icebergs became discernable and before the Evening had closed in we met with several pieces of loose Ice – As it would have been the very height of imprudence to have continued all night proceeding amid floating Ice we laid our head to the Eastward – until 3 oClock on the following

Wednesday 23rd. Morning and then made sail to effect our design – Passing truant Icebergs about 8 oClock several fancied they discovered the loom of land on the lee beam to prove which we Kept away SW for about the period of Twenty Minutes when the deception disappearing disclosed an Horizon chequered by straggling Bergs –

February 1820 Having resumed our Course we perceived about 11 a range of field Ice to leeward the sea at times breaking heavily over

---

[1] Since this observation was taken at sunset it was probably an amplitude.

it – To give it a wide berth we hauled our wind to the West-ward the extremes of the field bearing W^{b}S to South – At Noon giving up every Idea of proceeding farther to the Southward or to the Westward which we had proposed doing if possible we Tacked ship with Fresh breezes and cloudy Weather in Lat*itude* 64°.56′S Long*itude* 56°W[1] Thirty eight Bergs and fields of Ice being then around us – In a vessel not prepared for such an attempt – at Sea the sev-enth day after being engaged,[2] – picking her way thro' Ice in the latter end of the Month of February in 64°S amid 8 hours of darkness must plead some excuse to the liberal minded for relinquishing a project which had it failed from accident would have prevented the possibility of our fate being ascertained no other consort accompanying us – an assistance very necessary in every undertaking of the Kind – for should one meet a check, the result of what has already been done is not altogether lost – All the afternoon with Strong breezes accompanied with occasional showers of Snow we passed through quantities of loose Ice and at 6 the Weather somewhat Moderated with a thick wet fog.

February <u>1820</u>
Thursday – 24th.

Soon after 8 We tacked to the Eastward an Iceberg South – 1 Mile – At 1 oClock on the proceeding Morning we Tacked to the Northward and continued all day plying in that direc-tion attended by continual falls of Snow and Sleet – at inter-vals passing thro' loose Ice At 8 Veiled in a thick fog we shortened sail – At 11 We hove too with our head to the Eastward and at Midnight had light breezes with dark cloudy W*eathe*r and a hard frost, much Ice having formed itself on our decks and rigging – At 4 oClock with Mode*ra*te breezes

Friday – 25th.

---

[1] This position was presumably by account. The longitude, if correct, would indicate that if the *Williams* followed a reasonably direct route, she would have passed close east of the Danger Islands (63°26′S, 54°38′W) on the way south and between them and Joinville Island on the way north. It would appear that the position is based on steering south (magnetic) and allowing a speed of about six and a half knots with five to six hours hove to during the hours of darkness (without a specific record of the courses steered and speeds logged this can only be a guess), however the Norie chart (Plate 8) and Admiralty chart 1238 both show a course generally south (true) which seems more likely to be correct as that would have kept the *Williams* clear of the Danger Islands, which would otherwise almost certainly have been sighted and commented on.

[2] I.e. having been engaged on 12 December and put to sea on 19 December, 1819.

and a very hard frost we Bore up North and Made Sail –
With constant light breezes and thick fogs interrupted at
intervals by heavy Showers of Snow and Sleet we continued

Sunday – 27th.
Monday – 28th.

until the 27th creeping to the Northward – At Daylight on
the 28th the Summit of the towering snow –clad land in the
vicinity of Cape Bowles became discernable by the clearance of the fog – To near the coast we altered our Course to
NNW and at 8 Cape Bowles bore W½S between 3 and 4
Leagues distant – About Ten the Weather becoming tolerably clear we perceived the land between Cape Bowles and
the Northern extremity to run in a N[b]W and S[b]E direction
At Noon our Long*itude* deduced from sights taken in the
forenoon to be 54°.35′.15″W – Latitude Obser*ved*
61°.13′S[1]

February – 1820

At ½ past One the Northern extreme bore W½S Cornwallis' Island just opening with it[2] – Ranging along the Eastern
side we perceived on the haze clearing away the whole to be
an Island about 14 Miles long and 9 broad, running North
and South, completely iron bound,[3] not affording the least
appearance of landing place – Having ascertained the
Northern headland to lie in Lat*itude* 61°.6′S and Long*itude*

Lloyds
Promontory

54°.16′W it was named "Lloyds Promontory"[4] and the
whole that of "Clarences Island" in compliment to His

---

[1] This position is about 20 miles west of the position as defined from the land fixes (allowing for
the 10′ longitude difference – see p. 173) i.e. west of Clarences Island. From the text it is clear the
Williams proceeded up the east coast of Clarences Island the southern extremity of which had been
placed in longitude 54°10′W (present longitude 54°05′W) on 5 February. It would therefore seem
probable that the position has been incorrectly transcribed; the latitude agrees with the land fixes.
    The position is shown on the track chart, but has not been included in the track which follows
the land fixes.

[2] See Plate 27.

[3] 'Iron bound': see p. 1, n. 1.

[4] Present position 61°07′S, 54°00′W. No reason is given for this name. William Smith in his
second visit to the South Shetland Islands in October 1819 gave the name Lloyd's Land to the
island now know as Greenwich Island, as indicated on Foster's Chart, Plate 3, and in the diagram
in the *Edinburgh Philosophical Journal*, Plate 5, account of the discovery by Miers. The extracts from
Smith's journal quoted by Captain Shirreff in his letter to the Admiralty (p. 47) and by Weddell,
1825, pp. 130–31, both contain the statement 'I thought it prudent as having a Merchant cargo on
board', and 'and perhaps deviating from the insurance to haul off to the Westward', as the reason
for not conducting a more extensive examination on 18 October. It may therefore be that the
name was given for Lloyds of London and when it was not used by Bransfield for Greenwich

Plate 27. Lloyds Promontory from the east with Cornwallis's Island just open (1975). UK HO HMS *Endurance*.

Clarences
Island

Royal Highness the Admiral of the Fleet[1] – At 5 a thick fog coming on with Snow and sleet we Shortened sail and hauled our wind to the NW. At Midnight We had fresh

Island (which is not distinguished on his chart) it was transferred to this cape. The other names used on Foster's chart and that in the *Edinburgh Philosophical Journal* are North Foreland (see p. 110, n. 3 above and pp. 46 and 51), Smith's Cape, Williams's Point, Nelson's Island, Shireff's Cove, and Hoseason's Aim. Smith and Williams presumably refer to the master and his ship, Nelson was presumably the admiral and victor of Trafalgar, Shireff is stated to refer to Captain Shirreff of HMS *Andromache*, Hoseason was probably on board the *Williams* and certainly made subsequent voyages to the area, so it possible that there was a local connection to one of the crew of the *Williams*.

[1] His Royal Highness Prince William Henry, third son of King George III, born at Buckingham Palace 1765. He was created Duke of Clarence and St Andrews and Earl of Munster in 1789 and succeeded to the throne as William IV in 1830 on the death of his elder brother George IV. He died in 1837. He went to sea at fourteen and in due course commanded his own ship. He became an Admiral of the Fleet in 1811. In May 1827 Canning revived the post of Lord High Admiral and William was invited to accept it, which he did. It would appear that this was intended as a sinecure to keep William from embarrassing the government. He, however, believed in leading his fleet in person which produced rapid disagreement with the Council of Admirals and in particular with Vice Admiral Sir George Cockburn and John Croker the Secretary. On 12 June 1828 a Tory government under the Duke of Wellington assumed power and when further disagreements came to a head, George IV and the Prime Minister directed and the Lord High Admiral resigned.

Tuesday – 29th.	breezes with cloudy Weather and heavy rain – Shortly after Midnight we Wore round and at 2 had Strong gales with rain – At 4 We close reefed the Topsails the Weather having encreased to Hard Gales, with a very high Sea At 5 We furled the Foresail and Fore Topsail and set the fore storm staysail – Hard Gales with violent gusts and heavy rain – At 8 We carried away the Weather main Topsail sheet which we rove afresh and furled the same – The brig being uneasy At 4 We again set it close reefed At Midnight We Wore with Fresh breezes, clear Weather and a very heavy Sea from the SW.

February 1820
March
Wednesday – 1st.

The breeze kept continually dying away until 4 oClock on the following Morning when it became perfect calm with a thick fog – We took this opportunity of bending new Topsails which as soon as brought to were set – At 11 A breeze springing up from the Eastward we trimmed Sails and stood to the Southward – During the afternoon we had dark gloomy Weather but at Midnight it had become beautifully clear, which we took advantage of by keeping away SSE for the land –

Thursday – 2nd.

At 5 we Set the Courses and at 8 descried the Land SE At ½ past 9 We altered our Course to SW the Centre of a high bluff Island SE, the line of Coast running in an ENE and WSW direction 9.45 Lloyds Promontory bore E^bS¾S Cornwallis' Island SE and Valentines head S^bE½E. Soon after Ten the whole became enrobed in a shower of Snow and 30 minutes after we hauled to the NW under easy sail – At Noon we had fresh breezes with heavy Snow – All the afternoon we had thick Weather with partial falls of Snow and at ¼ after Six our head breaking off to SSW we Wore round.

Friday 3rd.

At 2 on the following Morning it was Calm but a breeze springing up about Four we stood in under

March 1820

all Sail to close the land which before 8 we discerned extending from SE to South – At 9 We lost sight of it in fog which at 10 obliged us to stand to the Northward – The fog clearing away about 2 was succeeded by rain which continued without intermission until Midnight – At 4 oClock on the ensuing morning it was Calm – At 8 We tacked with a

Saturday – 4th.

Plate 28. Clarences Island from west with Cape Bowles at right hand end (1994).
Photograph Dr J. L. Smellie.

Plate 29. Valentines Head, Corwallis's Island and Clarences Island from southwest with Cape
Bowles at right hand end (1994). Photograph Dr J. L. Smellie.

light breeze from the Southward and soon after Ten discerned the high land in the neighbourhood of Cape Bowles S^{b}E½E and a range of Coast running to the Westward – At Noon we were in Longitude 54°.22′.30″W[1] – Latitude Observed 60°.38′S Cape Bowles bearing SSE Lloyds Promontory SSE½E Cornwallis' Island S½W Cape Valentine S^{b}W the Western extreme of Seal Island SW½S – At 6 Cape Bowles bore S^{b}E½E. At 9 We Tacked to the SW Clarences Island S^{b}E½E between 16 and 17 Leagues distant –

Sunday 5th. At 2 oClock on the following Morning we stood to the Northward and at ½ past 7 Tacked, plying along the Coast – Until 10 PM we continued plying to the SW and then again

Monday – 6th. stood to the Northward – At 4 (AM) We again tacked to the SW and at Noon were in Longitude 56°.1′.45″W Latitude Observed 60°.57′S. A Lunar taken in the forenoon and worked up gave 55°.54′W At 8 With Strong Breezes and dark Weather we Altered our Course to WSW

March 1820
Tuesday – 7th. and at 11 hauled on a wind SW. During the proceeding Twelve hours we continued plying to the Westward for the purpose of attaining Cape Shirreff and at Noon had Fresh breezes with a long rolling ground swell – our Longitude was 58°.47′W Latitude Observed 61°.15′S – Soon after we bore up S^{b}E to make the land which about four we succeeded in by discerning an Island SE and allmost immediately after the Main land – At 6 The extremes bore from E^{b}N to SSE displaying a complete string of rocks or islets lying along it At Sunset we found the variation of the Needle by an Amplitude to be 23°.21′ Easterly At 8 We struck soundings with 120 fathoms of line on a fine dark sand and at Midnight Wore

Wednesday 8th. to the Southward. Soon after Four oClock we descried the land E^{b}N and at ½ past 5 Wore round and obtained Soundings in 115 fathoms – fine dark sand – At 8 It proved calm – a small remarkable rock NE^{b}E the Northern extreme of the Main land ENE between 9 and 10 Leagues – Southern Ditto.[2] S½W 8 or 9 Leagues. The coast between these

[1] Allowing for the 10′ correction to the longitude (see p. 173) the bearings of the land agree remarkably well with the observed position.

[2] 'Southern Ditto', i.e. the southern extreme of the mainland S½W 8 or 9 leagues.

extremes which lie NE^bN and SW^bS of each other is profusely scattered with rocks and Islets many of which are between 4 and 5 miles offshore – Soon after a breeze sprung up from the Westward

March – <u>1820</u>

and at 10 we Wore to the SE. At Noon the extremes bore from NE^bE to S^bW, the Northern portion partly buried in fog and the Eastern Island which we supposed the same as seen on the morning of the 22nd. of January[1] to the Westward of Cape Melville NE^bE 6 or 7 Leagues – Our Lat*itude* by a Meridian Altitude was 61°.54′S Long*itude* deduced from sights taken in the forenoon 58°.59′.15″W Shortly before One we Tacked to the NW and determined the Island to lie in Lat*itude* 61°.50′S Longitude 58°.20′W – This at the

Ridleys Island

request of M^r. Smith was named "Ridleys Island" in compliment to Sir Matthew White Ridley MP[2] – for the place the Brig belonged to – It is situated about 3 Miles from the Main and 2 Miles in length – very high and craggy, and at this time partially covered with Snow – At 4 With Moderate breezes and fine W*eathe*r we again tacked and at 6 the extremes bore from ENE to South – We now stood off for the night and at Sunset found the variation by an Amplitude to be 23°.40′

Thursday – 9th.

E*aste*rly. At ½ past 3 We tacked and at 6 Made all sail to regain a situation inshore – At 9 We discerned Land SE and at Noon with Light breezes and fine clear Weather we eagerly sought so favorable an opportunity of closing it for the purpose of procuring

March <u>1820</u>

a correct view – the extremes bore from East to SSE that

---

[1] The bearing of this island and the noon position make it the island now known as Ridley Island (61°51′S, 58°01′W), which had been first sighted on 21 January. That first sighted on the morning of 22 January was Penguin Island in George's (now King George) Bay, so it may be that the date has been given incorrectly. The island is two miles long and two miles offshore, rising to a peak 254 m (833 ft) high and prominent from all directions, so that it fits the description reasonably well.

[2] Matthew White Ridley of Blagdon, Northumberland, 3rd Bart., MP for Newcastle upon Tyne, as his father had been before him and son and grandson were to be after him (the latter becoming Home Secretary and 1st Viscount Ridley). He was born 18 April, 1788 and died 14 July 1836. He married Laura daughter of George Hawkins on 13 August, 1803. They had four sons, two of whom became Major Generals, one went into the church while the other succeeded to the baronetcy and became MP for North Northumberland: Burke, *Peerage*.

portion lying to the Westward veiled in haze – Our Longitude was – 59°.3'W – Latitude 61°.48'S – Shortly before Four drawing in with Breakers we tacked to the Northward and struck soundings with 24 fathoms of line on a bottom of sand and rock – a high prominent headland[1] entirely clad in Snow East between 2 and 3 Miles distant – a flat table Island SW and a towering ragged rock with a profusion of lesser ones around it NE – The coast trending in the direction of NE^{b}N and SW^{b}S is lined with numberless rocks – breakers and miserable Islands against which the Sea breaks with enfuriated violence – and these with a back ground of cliffs of Snow may impart some Idea as to the aspect of the whole – At 6 The Table Island bore SE 5 or 6 Leagues distant – All

Friday – 10th. the following morning we were plying to the Westward but the wind being dead in our teeth together with a strong current to struggle against rendered our progress but extremely slow – At ½ past 9 It became thick with a Squall of rain which made it necessary to shorten sail – A partial clearance shewed us the land from SSE to ENE but it being of short duration we soon lost it again.

March 1820 At 1 We tacked to the NW and almost immediately after discerned the 3 rocks which lay to the Westward of Ridleys Island NE^{b}E about 9 miles distant – The Weather proving very Squally with heavy Rain we reduced our Sail to close reefed Topsails and at Midnight had Heavy Gales with fre-

Saturday 11th. quent Squalls – From the 11th. in Latitude 5̶9̶°̶.̶3̶0̶'̶S̶ 61°.12'S Longitude 56°.50'W we were reluctantly driven to the Eastward (by the continuance of adverse winds and thick

Tuesday – 14th. Weather) until the 14th. when we found we had decreased our Latitude to 59°.30'S Longitude 54°W – All the afternoon

Wednesday – 15th. and following day the wind betrayed symptoms of veering

Thursday – 16th. to the Northward, and on the proceeding day its settling at

---

[1] This is probably Stigant Point (62°01'S, 58°42'W), 64 m (210 ft) high and described as conspicuous in the *Admiralty Sailing Directions*. Davey Point (6 miles NW of Stigant Point) and Round Point (9 miles NW) are also described as conspicuous but do not seem so likely as the 20 fathom depth contour extends beyond the danger line off Stigant Point but not off the other two points). The 'towering ragged rock' is probably Jagged Island (61°54'S, 58°27'W), 66 m (216 ft) high, two miles off Round Point, and the 'table island' may be Atherton Islands (62°05'S, 58°57'W), 44 and 40 m (145 and 132 ft) high, and 8 miles SW of Stigant Point.

Friday – 17th.

North and the Weather clearing up urged us to make all possible sail to the Westward being particularly desirous of landing at Cape Shirreff previous to our bidding farewell to this newly discovered tract – At Noon our Lat*itude* was 61°.6′S Long*itude* 59°.32′W At 4 We bore away for the land but at 6 the Weather becoming Squally we close reefed the Topsails, Furled the Main Sail – and T*op*G*allant* Sails and hauled our wind to the Westward – On the ensuing morning the wind continued to encrease until ½ past 8 when having hard Gales with violent Squalls – and a very cross confused Sea rising we furled the fore Topsail – At Noon however we

March 1820

Sunday – 18th.

we procured sights which placed us in Long*itude* 62°.15′.45″W Lat*itude* 61°.39′S during the afternoon it gradually became more Moderate and at Mid*night* we set the Fore Topsail close reefed – At 6 We Wore and at 8 Bore up and Made sail for Cape Shirreff – The last heavy Weather together with the continued wet fogs we had experienced on the Coast having caused numberless chafes about the rigging all hands were now employed in setting all to rights by parcelling[1] &c – At 4 oClock in the afternoon we descried the land SE*b*E upon which the fore Tops*ail* was hove aback and soundings obtained in 85 *fathoms* on a bottom of fine dark sand and ooze – The fore Topsail being close reefed and those of the Main mended we stood to the Northward eager for the dawn of day anticipating the result of the morrow

Sunday – 19th.

Smiths Islands

At 4 oClock with Fresh breezes we Wore and Made all sail in shore and at Noon discovered land SE*b*S which afterwards proved the Islands made by the Brig in February 1819 – These were named "Smiths Islands" in compliment to the first discoverer – Excellent sights placed us in Long*itude* 60°.35′W Lat*itude* 62°.11′S – With a Moderate breeze and beautifully clear Weather our eyes were eagerly roving for a landing place where M*r*. Bransfield wished to plant another Union before the undertaking was

---

[1] 'Parcelling': narrow strips of old canvas daubed with tar were wound round a rope like bandages, prior to its being served, i.e. having spun-yarn bound round it and tightened with a serving-board or mallet. This was done to prevent wear and chafing: Falconer, 1769, s.v. *parcelling*; Smyth, 1867, pp. 517 and 608.

March – <u>1820</u>

was relinquished for the Season – the sweeping current seeming to have conspired against our attaining Cape Shirreff where it was first intended to have been planted – At 2 The Southernmost of Smiths Islands bore South about 6 or 7 miles distant – Western end of Desolation Island SSW and a small Table Island ENE – This Island which we determined to lie in Latitude 62°.18′S Longitude 59°.56′W was named "Falcons Island" in compliment to Captain Falcon of HMS Tyne[1] – When between 4 and 5 miles off we bore away NE along the Coast and at 3 were obliged to alter our Course to NE^{b}N for the purpose of avoiding breakers lying off the North Western shore of the island between 3 and 4 miles distant – We had now traversed the whole line from the Start point to Cape Bowles which seemed to partake of an equal share of sterility – and between Desolation Island and Cape Melville, the whole range appeared defended by an unconnected chain of rocks, breakers and small Islands – Soon after Sunset we had the last view of New South Britain whose shores afford nothing more than an excellent and plentiful fishery which it is to be hoped may confer abundant benefit to our Country – From the Start point in Longitude 61°.27′W we traced the Coast to Cape Bowles in 54°.10′W

March <u>1820</u>

making the distance of 7°.17′ in the direction of East and West and from the Latitude 61°S until we became engulphed

---

[1] Captain Gordon Thomas Falcon. He entered the Navy as an able seaman in 1794 on board HMS *Sheerness*, 44, Captain William George Fairfax, flagship of Rear Admiral Henry Harvey in the Channel, and shortly became a midshipman. He remained with Captain Fairfax in HMS *Repulse*, 64, and *Venerable*, 74, the latter flying the flag of Admiral Duncan. He was present at the battle of Camperdown, 11 October 1797. He spent some time as an acting lieutenant before being confirmed on 15 May 1800 in HMS *Wright*, 14, Captain Thomas Campbell. He continued at sea until 8 March 1811 when he was promoted commander into HMS *Melpomene*, troop-ship. He was promoted post captain 29 October 1813 and next year while in command of HMS *Cyane*, 32, with her consort HMS *Levant*, 20, after a furious action, he was captured by the American ship *Constitution*, 54, and became a prisoner of war. He was soon released and in 1817 was appointed to HMS *Tyne*, 26, on the South America Station. He continued to serve at sea until 1836. In 1845 he became captain of the *Royal Sovereign*, yacht, and Superintendent of the Dockyard at Pembroke. He was promoted Rear Admiral of the Red on 1 August 1848 and died in 1854: O'Byrne, 1849, p. 346; *Navy Lists*.

Falcons Island is now known as Table Island and lies in position 62°21′S, 59°49′W.

in 64°S the land still running in that direction. That it extends to the Westward of the Start is proved by Mr. Smith having seen it in 63°W and little doubt can remain of its running still further by his having been beset with Ice in 67°W in the La*titude* of 62°.12′S In all probability it may prove of considerable extent which on an examination to the Westward where the climate is milder may be found to be productive of vegetation, for what we explored I conceive to be Islands lying off the extreme of a tract of greater magnitude – That New South Britain may add another Fishery to the Crown of Great Britain remains only to be proved by the arrival of a few ships on her shores whose expedition in filling will at once decide how profitable a harvest may be reaped – and this will be found to consist of Whale oil, Sea Elephant oil and Seal skins – That the range we traversed is Islands I have not the least doubt of and indeed in some parts we saw passages but the advanced state of the Season rendered it imprudent to attempt their examination – There is great reason to premise that between them good shelter may be obtained but the

March <u>1820</u>

disadvantages of deep Water and sluicing tides must naturally be expected to be found where the land towers to a great elevation, situated in a high Latitude – Between the Latitudes of 62° and 64° the Whale harvest appeared by far the most abundant some thousands having been seen by us on that portion of Water – Whether these were of the right sort I shall not presume to give my opinion but they appeared between Forty and Sixty feet in length of a rusty brown colour, with long shelving and flat heads and have a short stumpy fin on the back about One third the length of the Fish from the tail[1] – When we first came on the coast they

---

[1] It is not possible to say precisely which sort of whales are being described here, but the head-shape and stumpy fin exclude right whales. If the length is accurate all but sperm whales and the medium-large baleen whales can be excluded. Blue whales are longer than 60 feet. The head shape is inconsistent with sperm whales, leaving fin, sei and humpback. Of these only the latter is brownish. However 'rusty brown' suggests that the whales may have been covered in diatoms, which might make even a grey body appear brown. Since humpback whales have long and noteworthy flippers, which are not mentioned, the probability is that these were a mixture of fin and, to a lesser extent, sei whales. See also Robert Fildes's remarks at p. 106, n. 2 above.

were plentiful in all parts but at this period appeared to have deserted the Northern shore – They may in all probability as the Winter solstice approaches emigrate to the Southward for the purpose of procuring shelter among the Ice and this may appear more plausible when I relate that the shoals we saw latterly were all making progress in that direction[1] – The East and Western shores furnish the retreat of the Seal, myriads of whom swarm on every rock wherever it is possible to effect a landing. Where the surf breaks with great violence, these they

March 1820

seem to prefer – and every spot of sand in such a situation is literally covered with them – the more sheltered situations however appear the haunt of the Sea Elephant such as Georges Bay &c and I have no doubt but that between the Islands they will be found in immense herds – They delight in miry places where they lay more than half covered amid the fæces &c of Penguins in large Societys – The only Fish we saw were Grampuss' Porpoises,[2] a small fish about the size of a half grown sprat and the limpet in Georges Bay – No land Animal and only two birds The White Pigeon, and a small one about the make of a Wren,[3] displaying a similar plumage with a longer tail, flew strong and quick and appeared not the least fatigued altho' at a considerable distance from the shore – Many of the former we procured but notwithstanding every precaution was taken for their preservation, they were destroyed by the rats who proved during the voyage an inveterate Enemy and unavoidable nuisance – The Sea birds were the same as in others parts consisting of Penguins of 5 different Species Albatrosses – Gulls – Petrells,

[1] Whales are known to migrate and are thought to leave this area for warmer waters around March/April returning to higher latitudes in September/October. However recent evidence on their movement has tended only to show how little is really known about their migrations.

[2] Grampus is the name that has been used for Risso's dolphin (*Grampus grisea*) which is a very widely distributed species but unknown in the polar waters round the Antarctic Peninsula. Grampus has also been used to describe the killer whale (*Orcinus orca*) which is a common and conspicuous species in these waters and this seems therefore the most likely identification.

[3] No land birds are found today as far south as 62°– 64°S. From the description this might be a pipit, either the correndera pipit (*Anthus correndera*), widely distributed in South America and the Falkland Islands, or the endemic South Georgia pipit (*Anthus antarcticus*).

Snow-birds – Shags – Pintadoes or the Cape Pigeon &c &c &c –

March <u>1820</u>   On the Northern coast we constantly experienced a sweeping current setting us to the Eastward[1] which together with a Westerly trade wind[2] must point out how absolutely necessary it will be to make land well to the Westward from whence with a flowing sheet an easy and sure progress will

[1] Robert Fildes (UK HO, Misc Papers, vol. 57, Ad 5i) includes a long section on the tides on this coast which, with modifications, was repeated by John Purdy, 1837, pp. 132–3, (and in subsequent editions) and by the British Admiralty in the *South America Pilot*, Part I, 1874, pp. 365–6. It is still included in the *Antarctic Pilot*, 1974, pp. 157–8. In this, among other things, he states:

The tides on the north coast of New Shetland are very irregular, it being sometimes high water for 24 hours together; at other times it flows tide and half tide, and remains about 3 or 4 hours high water and then ebbs again; although there is in general one flood and one ebb every 24 hours ....

When the brig Williams was on the survey, I have been told that they found the current always running strong to the eastward, but as they appear to have only taken a line of coast, it being without doubt dangerous for a single vessel to approach too near; they could not be expected to have had as good an opportunity of experiencing how the tides run in the proximity of land, which those who have been continually passing and repassing in shore, could not fail to observe.

In a SW gale I have seen the tide, at a distance of a league from the coast, run directly to windward, at a rate of 2 or 3 knots, and vice versa, to the eastward again. When the brig Williams [on William Smith's voyage sealing, after completing his charter to the Royal Navy] and ship Indian were both blown out of Blythe Bay [on the south side of Deception Island] at the same time by a gale of wind from the eastward. the Indian, onboard of which I was, drove to the westward of Rugged Island, and the Williams, although lying to drove up to the eastward directly to windward, two thirds of the way to Table Island; which evidently shewed that the two vessels had received the impulse of two contrary streams of the tide.

From all the observations I have been able to make, I think the flood and ebb, in moderate weather, runs backwards and forwards as far in the offing as 2 leagues from the outer points of the land, taking the sweep of the bays. Nevertheless sometimes it runs much longer both ways, and likewise stronger than it does at others; and its distance from the coast also varies. Outside these limits I have found the current run, at least a knot in the same direction that the wind blows.

[2] Robert Fildes also wrote on the winds (UK HO, Misc Papers, vol 57, Ad 5i) and these remarks were also reproduced in Purdy, 1837, pp. 131–2, (and in subsequent editions) and by the British Admiralty in the *South America Pilot*, Part I, 1874, p. 366. They last appeared in the *Antarctic Pilot*, 1930, p. 71.:

Nearly all the misfortunes that have happened in South Shetland, have been in gales of wind from Eastward, which prevail here a great deal, and blow with tremendous fury; generally accompanied with heavy falls of snow. No less than seven vessels have been lost, and all with easterly gales except the Clothier, which struck on a sunken rock.

In the years 1820, 1821 & 1822 four fifths of the gales were from eastward: we had all

be secured in the opposite direction – To beat up against this will be tedious and uncertain besides the forfeiture of a considerable portion of time which cannot fail of being attended with much loss, the season being but limited – The most preferable for the fishery must be the Months of November, December and January for after that period if we are allowed to judge, the whole is buried in an almost continual fog – although we experienced much wet, it was unaccompanied with severity and but only three times did Ice shew itself on board – Remaining until the Sun had begun his Declination to the Northward we took our leave of the Coast building in the hopes of being again sent on the following Year when by being on the ground by the latter end of October the whole might be satisfactorily completed before the commencement of the foggy Season –

March <u>1820</u>	We continued plying to the Westward until 25th.
Saturday – 25th.	On the 29th. our sights placed us to the Westward of 80° on
Wednesday – 29th.	which we altered our Course to NNW
<u>April</u>	On the 7th. April we were in Longitude 79°.14′.20″W Lat-
Friday – 7th.	*itude* 35°.13′S the Island of Juan Fernandez bearing
Saturday – 8th.	N 12°.8′E 90 Miles – With the dawn of day on the following

morning it was perceived NNW of us and as it had been the intention of M^r. Bransfield to touch there we steered for its eastern extreme – The uncouth and extremely irregular aspect it presents on making it bespeaks little in its favour, but on a nearer approach these crags and apparently inaccessible precipices are seen clothed with lofty woods interspersed

---

looked for harbours sheltered from the westward, under the impression that we should have most to fear from that quarter.

In fine weather, the winds from SW and NE are about equal, not keeping long in either quarter. Indeed with very few exceptions the winds are here always along the land, which renders this coast far less dangerous when under sail, than it otherwise would be.

The south-westers here much like north-westers at home, are attended by a fine clear sky, and generally sweep away all the fog and sleet of the light north-westers.

During two seasons I recollect only one gale from NW which was very heavy. I was then in Blythe Bay, and it was perfectly smooth although the sea outside was in a manner overwhelming.

with patches of luxuriant vegetation on which herds of Bullocks, Horses and Goats are seen feeding – About 4 oClock in the afternoon we were abreast of the East end and ranging along the North Eastern shore eagerly sought for Cumberland Bay – The night however closed in before we were rightly able to discern it and just as it grew dark lights were seen in the supposed bight – No Vessel lying there, and judging they might be shewn by some poor fellows in distress, or as a Signal of direction Mr. Smith proceeded in the Whale boat towards them, but on landing saw nothing more than the lights gliding among

April <u>1820</u>

Sunday – 9th.

the bushes, and although our people hailed both in English and Spanish, they were not able to entice them to a discovery – The boat having returned we stood off and on during the night using our best endeavours to preserve a situation for obtaining an Anchorage in the Mor*ni*ng – On the break of day we stood in and at 7.30 Came too with the Chain cable in 17 *fath*oms on a bottom of sand and Coral at about 2 Cables' lengths from the shore – The West point of the bay – NNW½W – East point E^bS. Garrison W½S and the bottom of the bay SSW. Having veered 60 *fath*oms of Chain we steadied her with the Kedge[1] – As soon as she was satisfactorily secured we sent our people on shore for a run who on returning brought on board quantities of Peaches, Apples, Vegetables &c while the remaining few left on board had amply performed their parts by Taking with hook and line a large store of excellent and delicious fish – During an excursion I made in the afternoon I stumbled on Two wild bullocks who were so shy that I could not obtain a shot at either altho' I had provided myself with a Musket and its necessary appurtenances – Thinking it more than probable that one or more might be obtained after

April <u>1820</u>

dark with Five hands I took my Station at the head of an

[1] 'Kedge': a small anchor used to keep a ship steady and clear from her bower anchor while she rides in harbour, particularly at the turn of the tide: Smyth, 1867, p. 417.

Avenue, skirting a Rivulet which rippled at its foot conceiving this from the many tracks likely to be one of their Watering places – but altho' we frequently heard them around us, the darkness of the surrounding woods skreened them from our sight, the break of day terminating our unsuccessful speculation – Nature may be said to have lavished her Beauties on this delightful Island blending the whole so as to present both an aweful and Magnificent Landscape – The Northern part composed of irregular inaccessible precipices are nevertheless on their very summits covered with trees, while the Valleys in the neighbourhood of Cumberland Bay are composed entirely of Aromatics among which the Myrtle proves the most conspicuous – Vegetation is so prolific that seeming as if neglected amid the wilds in view fruit trees suddenly burst forth from their bosoms affording from their overloaded boughs a profuse offspring not inferior in size or flavour to what are reared by the nourishment of Cultivation – The Vegetables we found here and which proved very acceptable were Cresses, Turnip tops, Radishes, Mint &c

April <u>1820</u>

all very good of their kind altho' the radishes were somewhat stringy – The fish we took consisting of Cod, Cavallies, Silver fish, Breams, Maids, Congers &c were so extremely plentiful that during the very short time we laid here independent of what we used in the Cabin and before the Mast, retaining one days fresh stock besides, two whole casks were salted down to prevent their spoiling – These were all taken with the hook and line, the rocky state of the bottom not being adapted for hauling the Seine – The Village of S[t]. John the Baptiste is rather prettily situated defended by the fort of S[t]. Joseph but is now entirely in ruins, the Chilanos having brought away the Spanish prisoners and Garrison at the commencement of the Revolution and the whole being built of Wood have been taken down by the several vessels who touch here for firewood – The Anchorage although open from NNW to E[b]S is entirely sheltered from all but the Northerly winds and these never blowing with any force but during the winter solstice makes it in the Summer Months a very desirable bay – To let go an Anchor about a Cable and a half's length from the shore on the Western side, and mooring her head and stern with

April <u>1820</u>

a hawser and kedge will be found much better than remaining at single Anchor for the Southerly winds which set in strong being confined by the height of the land come with tremendous gusts down the vallies which acting like so many funnels serve to encrease their violence – these causing a Vessel to sheer about, fouls her Anchor, and in the end shouldering it takes the whole to Sea – With an artificial horizon we settled its Latitude to be 33°.38′.56″S Long*itude* 78°.57′W – All the forenoon and part of the Afternoon we were employed in rafting off wood and procuring Water which being completed by 5 oClock we Weighed the Chain; but the heavy winds down the vallies causing us to swing wildly about we clapt a slip buoy on the Kedge and let it go, standing out of the bay – When clear we hove too and sent the boats in to weigh it but the buoy rope being too short had sunk the log and the boats were under the necessity of returning without having effected their purpose.

Friday – 14th.

At Daylight on the 14th. we Made the land to the Southward of Valparayso but having found the fore Topmast sprung we were obliged to heave too to

April <u>1820</u>

secure it – Point Coroumilla[1] N½E. Soon after 8 we Bore up NNW and shewed our Colours to the Signal Station – Just after Noon we rounded the Point of Angels when we perceived HMS Hyperion lying in the Bay – On M[r]. Bransfield's waiting on Captain Searle all our Logs, Charts and every document relating to the Voyage were ordered as customary[2] to be immediately delivered in and at the same time

---

[1] Punta Curaumilla (33°06′S, 71°45′W) lies at the western entrance point to Bahía Valparaíso, and is recommended in the *Admiralty Sailing Directions* today as the landfall for Valparaíso.

[2] This practice was of long standing. 'The Instructions given by the Right Honourable the Lords in Council to M. Edward Fenton for his voyage to the East Indies and Cathay dated 9 April 1582', recorded in Hakluyt, 1598–1600, III, p. 756, contain a similar provision at Item 18.

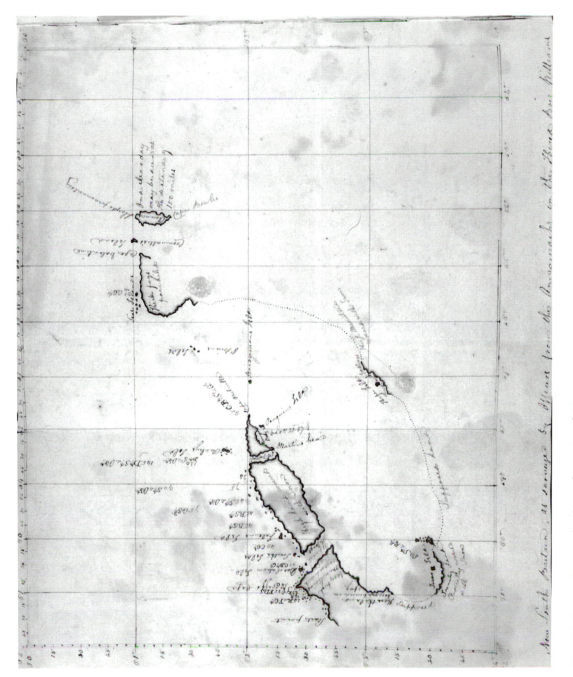

Plate 30. Poynter's Journal. Chart of New South Britain.

167

strictly forbidding any particular point of the result to be spoken of –

Sunday – 16th.   At 2 (PM) We anchored in 20 *fathoms* and on Sunday the 16th. struck the Pendant –

C. W. Poynter

CHAPTER 7

BRANSFIELD'S SURVEY

A large number of bearings and directions is recorded in the text of Poynter's journal, but nowhere is it stated whether these have been corrected for magnetic variation or not. Under normal circumstances they would have been recorded uncorrected in the log and the variation applied later when working out the account and plotting the survey. There are two places where the actual bearings can be measured from modern charts. On leaving George's Bay the bearing of Cape Melville in line with the SE end of Penguin Island is stated to be NE½N which is 039° magnetic, magnetic variation is given in the Journal as 24° E, giving 063° true, while on a modern chart it is 062°; on 28 February Lloyds Promontory is stated to bear W½S (264° magnetic, variation 20° E, i.e. 284° true) with Cornwallis's Island just open, and again on a modern chart this is 284°. The plan of George's Bay is drawn on magnetic north and the bearings quoted all appear to fit if accepted as magnetic. In a number of places the trend of the coast is given and this too appears to be magnetic. On the other hand on 17 January the latitudes of Cape Shirreff and Desolation Island are given, being nearly the same and it is stated that Desolation Island lies ten miles due east from the Cape. The untitled plan of Barclay Bay (Plate 11), on which these features are shown, is drawn on true north and this is stated on it. The only other mention of a direction qualified by 'due' is on 5 February in the plan of proceeding to the 'Fiftieth degree West and then due South'. Here it would seem appropriate that the vessel intended to proceed true south (but see p. 150, n. 1).

It has therefore been accepted that the bearings given in the Poynter's journal are all magnetic (unless qualified by 'due'), and positions shown on the track chart (Plate 9) have been plotted making this assumption. In general these plot well on the features indicated in the notes, which have been identified by descriptions, where possible, from the *Antarctic Pilot*, 1974, and consideration of the distance it would have been practicable for the *Williams* to have sailed in the time available. In very few cases is the course stated and frequently we are told they hauled their wind, wore or tacked, without being told whence the wind blew so that no attempt has been made to produce an accurate track; this would be impracticable on the information available today, indeed it is probable they would have been doubtful exactly where they had been at the time. Positions of which we can be reasonably certain are indicated together with their time and date, and these are joined by a dotted track.

Observed positions quoted are apparently based on meridian altitudes of the sun for latitude, while longitude is based on the chronometer. Two lunar sights are recorded.

Although chronometers are mentioned on a number of occasions in the plural, there is no mention of a chronometer having been transferred from HMS *Andromache*. The chart of George's Bay which is reproduced by Robert Fildes[1] gives the same position as the journal for Martin's Head and states that the Longitude is by Captain Smith's chronometer. It would seem reasonably certain therefore that there was only the one onboard.

The Remark Book of HMS *Andromache*,[2] while in Valparaíso states:

> Latitude of the ship in the Roads 33°02′ South Longitude by the mean of several lunar observations taken at opposite sides[3] of the Bay 71°37′ West. The distances to ascertain the Longitude were measured under the western Battery and the altitude of the sun and moon found by calculation as will appear by my former Remark Book, Variation of the Compass 14° East.

The former Remark Book[4] shows that lunars were taken on 29 May and 11 June, 1818, the first a set of two observations with the sun east of the moon and the second a set of four observations with the sun west of the moon. The computed longitudes were 71°19′30″W and 71°55′15″W respectively with a mean of 71°37′27″W.[5] This position agrees almost exactly with the modern position. Since it was used by HMS *Andromache* on subsequent visits to Valparaíso, and obtained before the brig was chartered, it seems safe to assume it was used by

---

[1] UK HO, Misc Papers, vol. 57, Ad5i: Harbours etc in South Shetlands by Robt. Flides, presented to Captain Beaufort by Mr Purdy, 11 Nov 1829. Also in PRO ADM 55/143.

[2] UK HO, Misc Papers, vol. 54, Ad1.

[3] This would appear to mean that the observations were taken with the sun and moon on opposite sides of each other, and not that the observations were taken in different positions.

[4] UK HO, Misc Papers, vol. 55, Ad2. The working of the sights is given in full.

[5] The hand writing of this Remark Book is the same as that in the Remark Book of HMS *Goldfinch*, 10, Captain Edmund Waller, 29 December 1813 to 30 June 1814 (UK HO, Misc Papers. vol. 106, De3) which is signed by Bransfield who was master of that ship at that time. It is thus safe to conclude that it is in Bransfield's own hand. Above the calculations he states: 'I took the under distances …', and under the 'Directions for Sailing in and out of Valparaiso' he writes: 'I have sounded all parts of the Bay and found nothing like danger within 2 cables length of the shore. The Bottom is good in the Roadstead …'. Thus it would appear that Bransfield himself took the observations on which the position of Valparaíso was based.

Bransfield to obtain the initial error of the chronometer, and that in consequence this was known correctly. There is no mention of how the chronometer was rated, if indeed it was. In view of the speed with which the expedition was set up it seems unlikely that Bransfield was able to take observations before departure, however William Smith may have done this as a matter of course before the expedition was organized. The only possibility of rating the chronometer during the voyage occurred in George's Bay, at the end of January, 1820, but no mention is made of it in the journal and since the astronomical observations and surveying done by Bransfield are duly recorded it seems most unlikely that it was done.

The journal states that the majority of the positions quoted are noon position and this has been assumed to be the case throughout, unless it is specifically stated that they are not.

There are a large number of positions quoted only a few of which are given with land bearings taken at the same time. The latter together with some seventeen named land features (which are listed in the following table) can be checked – always assuming the features have been correctly identified, and a comparison made. Due allowance for the fact that the same point of the feature may not be used in both cases should be made. Apart from the longitudes in George's Bay and Cumberland Bay, which were observed ashore using an artificial horizon, it is not stated how the land features were fixed, except to say they were positioned from sea.[1] This probably means a magnetic bearing and an estimated distance. Today this sounds highly inaccurate but mariners then were used to judging their distance offshore and it was possible using a table of distances to the horizon for various heights of eye to obtain comparatively accurate results out to about 10 to 15 miles.[2] It was also possible to use the distance the ship ran in a given time as a base and obtain the range from the change of bearing.

---

[1] The chart of the bay south of Cape Shirreff (Plate 11) has two notes '⧾ Latitude determined at Sea' and '☉ Longitude by Time Keeper at Sea' shown on it (last two lines of the text at lower right) and the two symbols then appear on Start Point, Shirreffs Cape and Desolation Island.

[2] Phipps, 1774, p. 100, states:

Seamen, though they judge very accurately of thier distance from places upon coasts well known to them, are very often mistaken when they fall in with land they have never seen before; of which we had, at first, some instances in this voyage, the height of the mountains, before we knew the scale of this coast, making us always think ourselves nearer the land than we really were.

Phipps, in HMS *Racehorse* and *Carcass*, was commenting on his arrival off Spitsbergen, in 1773. However he only had the problem 'at first' and was only two months in the area, so that it is reasonable to suppose that if Bransfield had a similar initial difficulty it was rapidly overcome.

Date 1820	Name	Journal Posn.		Modern Chart		Dif. Long
		Lat S	Long W	Lat S	Long W	
17 Jan	Start Point	62°42′	61°27′	62°35′	61°13′	−14
17 Jan	Cape Shirreff	62°26′	60°54′	62°27′	60°47′	−7
17 Jan	Desolation I.	62°27′	60°35′	62°27′	60°23′	−12
23 Jan	Turret Point	62°04′	58°06′	62°05′	57°57′	−9
25 Jan	Cape Melville	62°01′	57°44′	62°01′	57°34′	−10
25 Jan	Martin's Head	62°12′	58°20′	62°12′	58°15′	−5
30 Jan	Tower Island	63°29′	60°34′	63°33′	59°48′	−46
	Ohlin Island			63°32′	60°05′	−29
31 Jan	Hope Island	63°05′	56°44′	63°02′	56°50′	+6
	Bransfield Chart	63°05′	57°08′			−18
3 Feb	O'Briens Is.	61°30′	56°16′	61°28′	55°57′	−19
	Bransfield Chart	61°30′	56°27′			−30
5 Feb	Cape Bowles	61°19′	54°10′	61°19′	54°05′	−5
13 Feb	Seal Island	61°02′	55°32′	61°00′	55°22′	−10
14 Feb	Valentines Hd	61°03′	54°48′	61°06′	54°40′	−8
15 Feb	Cornwallis's I.	61°00′	54°36′	61°04′	54°29′	−7
28 Feb	Lloyds Promy.	61°06′	54°16′	61°07′	54°00′	−16
8 Mar	Ridleys I.	61°50′	58°20′	61°51′	58°01′	−19
19 Mar	Falcons I.	62°18′	59°56′	62°21′	59°49′	−7
13 Apl	Cumberland B.	33°39′	78°57′	33°37′	78°50′	−7

The small round Island referred to as Tower Island in the journal is probably not that which now bears that name. The latter is shown on Bransfield's chart (Plate 31) and is 5 miles long and 3 miles wide. Bransfield's chart also shows a small island in the position given in the journal, which has no name; it is now known as Ohlin Island and it appears to be this island which is called Tower Island on the chart in the journal.

The position given for Hope Island in the journal appears to be in error. Working from the noon position quoted, 62°50′S 57°25′W, a course ESE for one hour and ten minutes, allowing a speed of about 5½ knots, thence SE½S 6 miles plots in about the position shown on Bransfield's chart, furthermore Poynter's chart (Plate 30) shows Hope Island in about the same position.

O'Briens Islands are much nearer the position given in the journal than that shown on Bransfield's chart. On the 1839 Admiralty chart[1] they are placed in 55°52′W.

[1] British Admiralty Chart 1238, *The South Shetland and South Orkney Islands with the tracks of the*

If we accept that, due to their uncertainty, these three should be left out, the average error is −10′ of longitude with a spread between −5′ and −19′, which, due to the convergence of the meridians towards the pole, represents about six nautical miles on the earth's surface in this latitude . The mean error in latitude is +¼′ with a spread between −7′ and +4′[1] i.e. 11 nautical miles. It is not surprising that the final latitudes are more accurate than the longitudes in view of the relative ease with which latitude could be determined by a meridian observation of an heavenly body.

The position of the land on the track chart, Plate 9, is the same as that on the modern chart, the noon positions have therefore all been plotted with 10′ deducted from their longitudes to bring them into line with the land fixes and the land itself.

On two occasions at sea lunar observations were taken. For neither of these is it clear if the longitude has been calculated for the time of the sight or adjusted to noon, nor are land bearings available to check their accuracy. In view of their isolated nature they are unlikely to have been used to check the chronometer, and there is no indication in the journal that they were so used or indeed used to position land features. They have not therefore been used in the track.

Apart from unknown chronometer errors, observational errors also produced inaccuracies in the longitude. For example in a sight taken three hours either side of noon in 60°S with a declination of the sun at 10°S an error of 2′ in the observed altitude will produce an error of 5′ in longitude and an error in the assumed latitude of 2′ can produce 3′ in longitude. Using a sextant on the deck of a brig in conditions of relatively poor visibility, a realistic expectation of accuracy for a practised observer might well not be better than 5′, which might be reduced to 2′ by taking a series of observations and using the mean.

A further interesting point about the longitudes is that although they are all based on chronometer determinations, there is no indication of a progressive error as one might expect from a chronometer whose rate was not known accurately. It could be that once a point had been fixed subsequent positions were adjusted so that it was kept in the same place, but if this had been done it would seem probable that it would have been mentioned. It is also possible that corrections were applied on return to Valparaíso when a comparison with the known

---

several Discoverers 1819–1843. Published according to Act of Parliament at the Hydrographic Office of the Admiralty Septr 7th 1839 – Additions to 1844. UK HO.

[1] Including all observations but accepting that Tower Island is indeed Ohlin Island, that a mistake has been made with the position of Hope Island and using the charted position, and ignoring the charted position of O'Briens Islands does not alter the mean latitude error or spread and only increases the mean longitude error to −12′ with a spread of −5′ to −29′.

longitude would have provided an accumulated error which could have been applied retrospectively, but again there is no indication that this has been done and indeed since the journal was apparently impounded on arrival[1] it would seem to have been impracticable. The conclusion must therefore be that the rate was known to such a degree of accuracy that any error has been obscured by the random error of the observations.[2]

Taking into account the difficulties involved in making the observations and fixing the land from positions at sea, the overall accuracy and spreads are astonishing and one can only admire the remarkably high standard achieved.

Bransfield's original charts were passed to the Hydrographic Office. These, together with the published versions are:

1. Manuscript chart[3] (untitled) signed by Edward Bransfield showing the South Shetland Islands and Trinity Land. This chart is described in Hinks, 1939 and in Gould, 1941 with a tracing of the original showing the manuscript notes except the note on Elephant Island, 'Here the Land was in a SW Direction could get no opp^y of going along it always being veil'd with Fog Season being Late', which is given in Gould's notes. There is no border round the chart, but a graticule covers an area from latitude 60° to 64°S and longitude 52° to 63°W, 76 by 61 cms (30 by 24 inches).

2. Manuscript chart[4] (untitled) showing South Shetland Islands with boxes drawn on it for the views, for the engraver to work from. The topography follows 1 exactly except that Smith's Cape and the Fields of Ice north of it are taken from Foster's chart (Plate 3). Manuscript notes are similar to those on 1 except that the note inside the coastline of Elephant Island is not given. Some abbreviations are expanded and natures of the bottom are given in abbreviated form. Area covered: latitude 59°25' to 64°35'S, longitude 52°00' to 67°22'W, 61 by 44 cms (24 by 17½ inches).

[1] According to Poynter's entry in his journal for 14 April, Captain Searle, of HMS *Hyperion*, the senior officer in Valparaíso when the *Williams* arrived, directed that all documents should be 'immediately delivered'. However Bransfield's letter covering the delivery of these documents is dated 4 May (Appendix 3) allowing time for the production of fair records so that an adjustment of positions cannot be entirely ruled out.

[2] Leaving out the same three suspect observations as before the mean Longitude errors per month are: January (6 observations) −9'·5, February (5 observations) −9'·2, March (2 observations) −13', and April (1 observation) −7'.

[3] UK HO, s 92, Shelf Ae1, currently (1997) not available for examination. A copy of this document was presented to the Scott Polar Research Institute by Vice Admiral Edgell, Hydrographer of the Navy, in August 1941 (SPRI MS 355/2) from which this information has been taken.

[4] UK HO, f42 Shelf Ae.

3. Published chart[1], from 2 above, titled *A Chart of New or South Shetland, seen in 1819 by Willm Smith, Master of the Brig Williams, Surveyed by E. Bransfield, Master R.N. in 1820, NB. This Land was known to the Old Navigators and said to be first discovered by Theodore Gerrards in 1599*, Published according to Act of Parliament by Capt. Hurd R.N. Hydrographer to the Admiralty 30th November 1822. 61 by 43½ cms (24 by 17 inches). (Plate 31.) There are eleven views on this chart. Those of *O'Brien's Islands ESE 4 or 5 leagues* and *Hope Island SE½E 5 or 6 miles* appear to have been taken from the views in Poynter's journal, Plate 22. *View of Seal Islands and Reef* has the same outline as that in the journal, which appears to be unfinished so that there may have been another intermediate state. The *First appearance of land discovered by Capt. Smith … might*, with some imagination, be based on view C to K on Midshipman Foster's chart, Plate 3. Apart from these no originals for the views on this chart are known to exist.

4. Published chart[2] titled *A Chart of New Shetland, with the tracks of Mr Bransfield, HMS Andromache, 1820*, London, Published as the Act directs January 1st 1822, by J. W. Norie & C° at the Navigation Warehouse and Naval academy, N° 157 Leadenhall Street. 33 by 26½ cms (13 by 10½ inches). (Plate 8). This chart states that it was 'further explored by Mr Powell, Commander of the Sloop *Dove* in 1821 & 1822 and by Captain Weddell 1823. Hughes's Bay is added from Mr Hoseason's Survey in the Ship *Sprightly*, 1824.' (Another chart titled *Chart of South Shetland, including Coronation Island, &c from the exploration of the Sloop Dove in the years 1821 and 1822 by George Powell, Commander of the same*, was published by R. H. Laurie and dated 1 November, 1822[3].)

5. Manuscript chart[4] titled *Georges Bay* signed by Edward Bransfield with three views on it showing Martin's Head, Penguin Island and Cape Melville. 64 by 38½ cms (25 by 15 inches). It is not aligned with either true or magnetic north vertical although a compass shows magnetic bearings. It is similar to that in Poynter as well as to that on the chart which accompanied Smith's Memorial, which are both on a smaller scale, and do not have the views on them[5].

6. Manuscript chart[6] titled *Plan of Georges Bay South Shetland by E Bransfield,*

[1] UK HO, C74 Shelf Gy.

[2] UK HO, L9945 Shelf Tw.

[3] UK HO, A 508 Shelf Ae1.

[4] UK HO, s 90 Shelf Ae1, currently (1997) not available for examination. A copy of this document was presented to the Scott Polar Research Institute by Vice Admiral Edgell, Hydrographer of the Navy, in August 1941 (SPRI MS 355/1), from which this information has been taken.

[5] The same plan, without the views, is also reproduced by Robert Fildes, PRO ADM 55/143 and UK HO, Misc Documents, vol. 57, Ad 5i.

[6] UK HO, s 90/2, Shelf Ae1, currently (1977) not available for examination. This chart is reproduced in Blewitt, 1957.

Master RN. 1820. This is a manuscript prepared from 5 above for the engraver to work from; no chart appears to have been published, but see below.

Bransfield knew that his survey was exploratory and that the peninsula depicted on his chart was probably a group of islands, as Poynter remarked in his journal under 19 March (p. 160) when summing up their work 'for what we explored I conceive to be Islands lying off the extreme of a tract of greater magnitude' and again 'That the range we traversed is Islands I have not the least doubt of and indeed in some parts we saw passages but the advanced state of the Season rendered it imprudent to attempt their examination'. It is not surprising therefore that his chart was soon superseded. Indeed it was known to be out of date even before it was published in November 1822. When the Admiralty produced *A General Chart of South America from a drawing by Lieut. A. B. Becher, R.N. combined with the best English and Spanish Surveys in the Hydrographical Office* dated 4th November 1824, it showed South Shetland, including Powell's Group[1] (now known as South Orkney Islands) in the same form as they were shown on Powell's chart of his work in the *Dove* in 1821–22 (see 4 above).

British Admiralty Chart 1238, *The South Shetland and South Orkney Islands with the tracks of the several Discoverers* was first published in 1839 (without the number) and shows only that portion of Bransfield's track from 20 February to 2 March, 1820 when the *Williams* made the long passage from the vicinity of Clarences Island south to 64°56'S and back again to the same area[2]. This track agrees with that shown on the Norie chart (4 above) which appears to be the only contemporary track now available.

When the Admiralty published Chart 3205, *South Shetlands and Adjoining Islands and Lands* in 1901 George's Bay had become St George Bay and the chart carried a plan 'St George Bay Anchorage, Surveyed by E. Bransfield, Master R.N. 1820'.

---

[1] Copy in UK HO. It also showed the Isles of Aurora; pp. 188–9, and 189, n. 2.
[2] Copy in UK HO with additions to 1844. It also shows the tracks of Bellingshausen 1821, Powel 1821, Weddel 1821, Foster 1829, Biscoe 1832, D'Urville 1838 and Ross 1843.

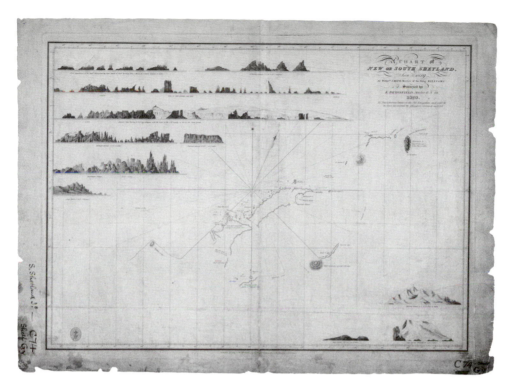

Plate 31. A Chart of New or South Shetland (1822). UK HO, C 74 Gy.

This chart is reproduced on the following eight pages to the same size as the original, 61 x 43½ cms, as follows:

178	179	180	181
182	183	184	185

First appearance of the land discovered by Capt. Smith in 1819. bearing from S.W.b.S. to S.E.b.E. distant 12 mi...

S.b.E.¾E.

E.N.E.   Sheriff's Cape bearing E.N.E. by compass with the la...

Ridley's Island S.S.E. 3. miles

Desolation Island   S.S.E. ... miles

178

S.E. b E. distant 12 miles

O'Brien's

View of Seal Islands and Reef

by compass with the land to the S.W. nearly as far as the Start point

Falcon's Island E.N.E. 7 or 8 miles

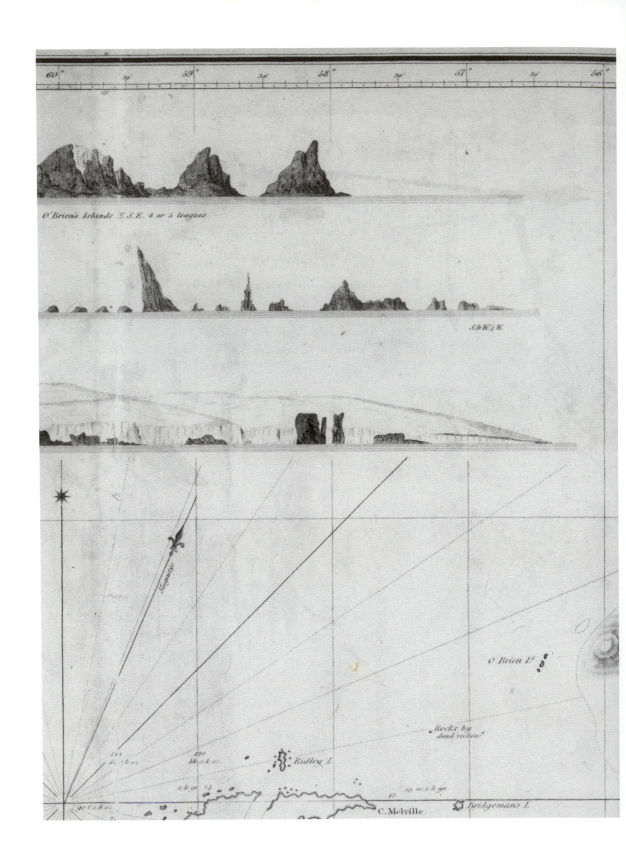

O'Brien's Islands S.S.E. 4 or 5 leagues

S.bW.½W.

Magnetic

O'Brien I.ˢ

Rocks by
dead reckonᵍ

Ridley I.

C.Melville

Bridgeman's I.

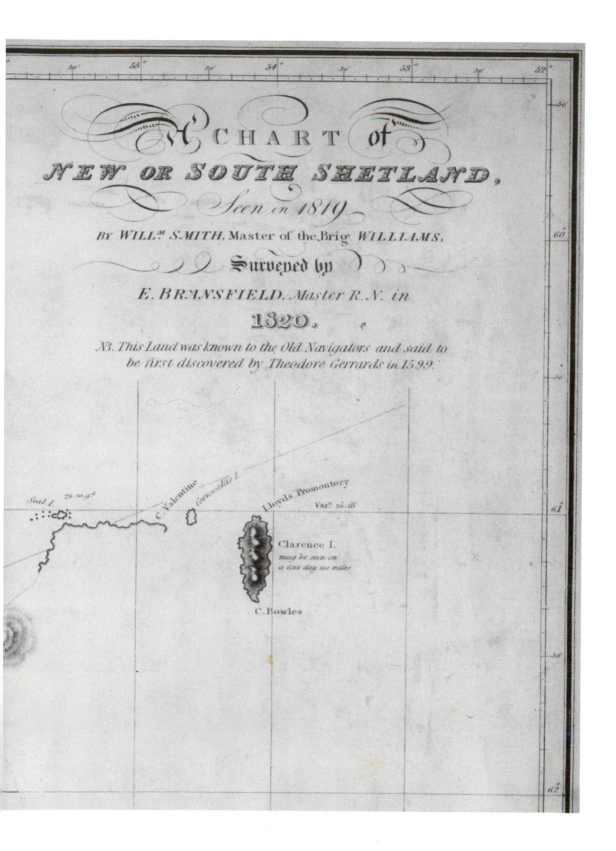

A CHART of
NEW OR SOUTH SHETLAND,
Seen in 1819

BY *WILL.M SMITH*, Master of the Brig *WILLIAMS*,

Surveyed by

E. BRANSFIELD, Master R.N. in
1820.

*NB. This Land was known to the Old Navigators and said to
be first discovered by Theodore Gerrards in 1599.*

Seal I.   79.00.9.t

C. Valentine   Cornwallis I.

Lloyds Promontory

Var.ⁿ 20.18'

Clarence I.
*may be seen on
a fine day 100 miles*

C. Bowles

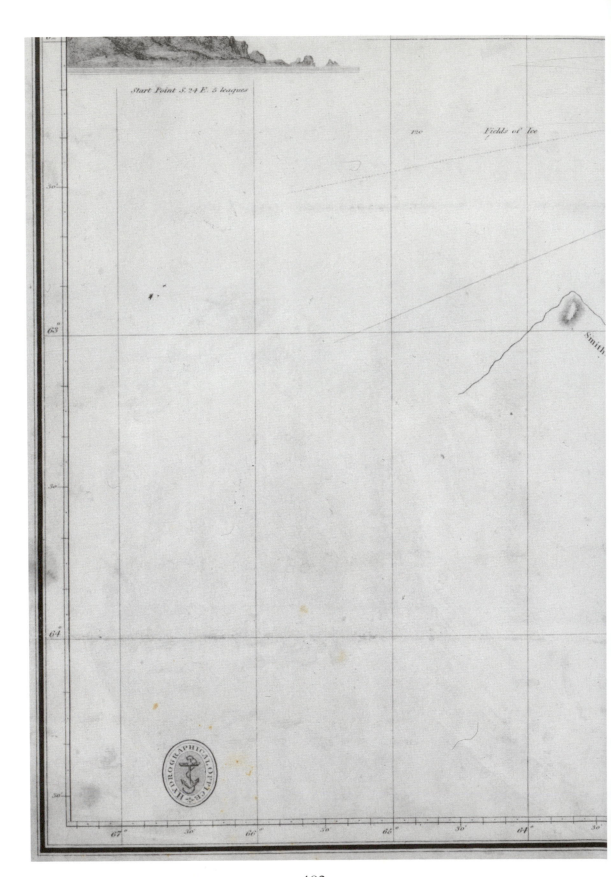

Start Point S.24 E. 5 leagues

120

Fields of Ice

Smith

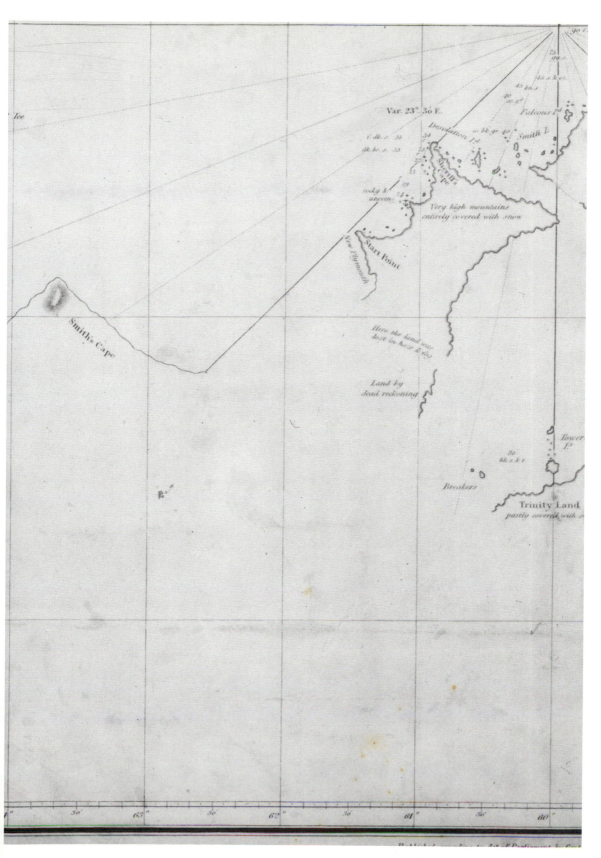

Var. 23° 30 E.

Ice

Desolation I.d

Falcons I.d

Smith I.

Smith's Cape

Very high mountains
entirely covered with snow

New Plymouth

Start Point

rocky &
uneven

Smith's Cape

Here the land was
lost in lat. & 60,5

Land by
dead reckoning

Tower
P.t

Breakers

Trinity Land
partly covered with s

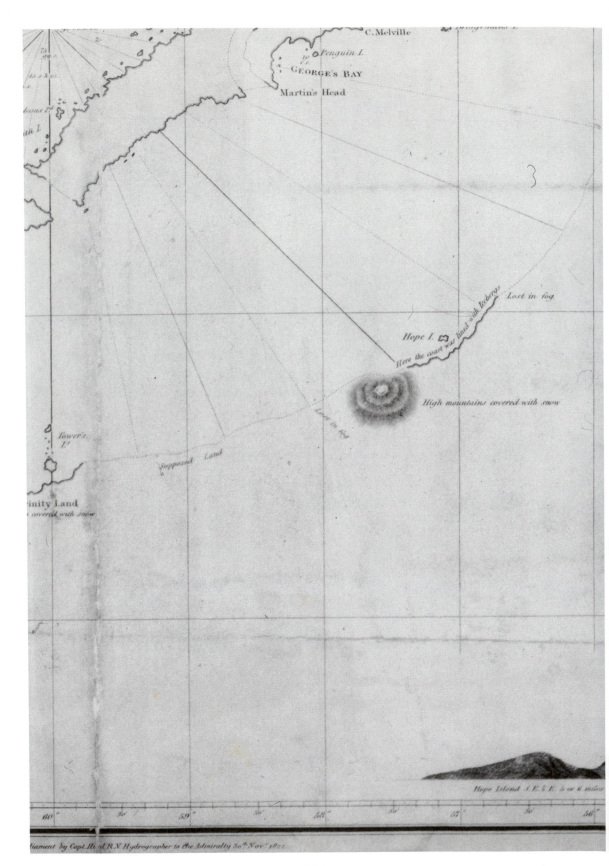

C. Melville

Penguin I.

GEORGE'S BAY

Martin's Head

Lost in fog

Hope I.

Here the coast was lined with Icebergs

High mountains covered with snow

Lost in fog

Tower's I.

Supposed Land

Trinity Land

covered with snow

Hope Island S.E. ½ E. 5 or 6 miles

60°   30'   59°   30'   58°   30'   57°   30'   56°

...liament by Capt. H. of R.N. Hydrographer to the Admiralty 30th Nov.r 1822.

184

Clarence Island, a S. 20° E. dist. 27 miles

Cape Bowles S.W. b W ½ W 3 or 4 miles

supposed Land

J. Walker Sculpt.

185

CHAPTER 8

OTHER EXPEDITIONS
IN THE 1819–1820 SEASON

It is generally accepted that three other vessels visited the South Shetland Islands and took seal skins during the period when Edward Bransfield was surveying them. The brig *Hersilia*, Captain James P. Sheffield, sailed from Stonington, Connecticut, on 22 July 1819, returning to Buenos Aires on 27 February and Stonington on 21 May 1820 with a cargo of 8868 skins. Dr W. S. Bruce stated, in 1918, that he had been informed by Mr H. G. A. Mackie, British Consul General in Buenos Aires, that the Argentine polacre *San Juan Nepomuceno*, Captain Carlos Timblon, left Buenos Aires on 25 August 1819 and returned on 22 February 1820 with a cargo of 14,600 skins for trans-shipment to Don Adam Guy[1] (in London). It has been assumed that, in view of the depleted state of fur seals on known beaches, she had been to the South Shetland Islands, but nothing further is known about her voyage. The third was the brig *Espírito Santo*, probably commanded by Captain Rodrigo[2] with Mr Joseph Herring, late mate of the brig *Williams*, on board.

The log of the *Hersilia*, covering the period 11 January 1820, when the vessel sailed from Staten Island until 20 May off Stonington, came to light in 1956 and, together with a number of other records was used by Kenneth Bertrand in his reconstruction of her voyage,[3] which was planned for exploring, sealing and trading. Captain Edmund Fanning states that he was 'in possession of the corrected survey of the Spanish corvette, Atrevida's position of the Aurora Islands, also of the manuscript of Captain Dirck Gherritz's discovery of land to the south of Cape Horn',[4] and the master and supercargo (William A. Fanning, Captain Fanning's son) were:

[1] Interdepartmental Committee, 1920, p. 38, note.

[2] Headland, 1989, p 113; Bertram, 1971, pp. 55–6.

[3] Bertrand, 1971, pp. 41–59. Since the log was not available to Stevens, 1954, his account of the voyage has not been used. He does, however, reproduce the crew list, pp. 34–5, and some other useful information.

[4] Fanning, 1834, p. 428.

directed in their instructions, to touch first at the Falkland Islands, there to fill up their water and refresh the crew, thence to proceed in search of the Aurora Islands, and should seals be there found, to procure their cargo, if not, to return westward to Staten Land, and after wooding and watering, to stand to the southward, keeping as nearly in the latitude of Cape Horn as the winds would admit, until they arrived in the latitude of 63° south, then to bear up and steer east, when it was confidently expected they would meet with land.[1]

[1] Fanning, 1834, p. 429. Stackpole, 1955, p. 11, states 'This, [that *Hersilia* was despatched purposely to discover any new land to the south of Cape Horn] of course, is hardly creditable in view of other evidence …' and he quotes a letter from James Byers, Fanning's erstwhile partner, to General Daniel Parker dated 25 August 1820 (National Archives of the United States, Records of the Dept. of State, Miscellaneous Letters, August–October 1820) which states that Captain Sheffield heard a report of the new islands, went to look for them, and found them in December, 1819.

Bertrand, however, considers that it is unlikely to have been an afterthought on the part of Fanning in that he wrote to the *New England Palladium and Commercial Advertiser*, Boston, 5 December 1820:

The fact is I do not consider this land [South Shetland Islands] as a new discovery. It was first seen by a Dutch Captain in the latter part of the 15th Century, and Frazier saw it in 1712 and called it South Iceland. This came to my knowledge in 1799, and I now have before me a manuscript chart of this *New South Iceland* as we call it to an extent 11 and 12 degrees of longitude and of between 5 and 6 degrees of latitude. (Given in full in Stevens, 1954, pp. 57–9.)

While Fanning will undoubtedly have known about the remarks in Dalrymple's work on Gherritz voyage it is quite certain that the manuscript chart he refers to was not by Dirck Gherritz, who did not visit the area (pp. 17–18 and p. 17, n. 2). It is, however, quite possible he was referring to a chart produced by Captain Sheffield.

Amédée François Frézier sailed as an officer in *St Joseph*, 36, 350 tons, 135 men, commanded by Sieur Duchêne Battas with the *Mary*, 120 tons (Sieur du Jardais Daniel) as store ship from St Malo on a trading voyage to the west coast of South America, in 1712. They passed through the Strait of Le Maire and rounded Cape Horn on the way out going south to 59°58′S without sighting land to the southward (May 1712). Frézier returned to France in the *Mary Anne* of Marseilles (Monsieur Pisson) rounding the Horn in March 1714. Frézier's account, published in French in Paris in 1716 and translated into English and printed by Jonah Bowyer, 1717, records (at pp. 283–4 of the English version) that they sighted an iceberg in 58°40′S at least 200 feet high and above 3 cables long, which was at first taken for an unknown island 'but the Weather clearing up a little, it perfectly appear'd to be Ice, whose blewish Colour in some Parts look'd like Smoak.' They then:

spy'd at E. and by N. about a League and a Quarter from us, another Float of Ice, much higher than the former, which look'd like a Coast four or five Leagues long; the End whereof we could not well see, by reason of the Fog…. Tho' those Parts have been frequented for 14 Years past, at all Times of the Year, very few Ships have met with Ice, so that it was not apprehended. Only the *Assumption,* commanded by *Poree,* in 1708, saw a vast Float, like a Coast.

He then adds (p. 284):

If it be true, as many pretend, that the Ice in the Sea is only form'd of the fresh Water, which runs down from the Land, it must be concluded that there is Land towards the South Pole; but it is not true that there are any more to the Northward than 63 Degrees of Latitude for the Extent of above 200 Leagues, from 55 of Longitude to 80; for that Space has been run over by several Ships, which the S.W. and S.S.W. Winds have obliged to stand far to the Southward to double the End of the Lands. Thus those Southern Lands, or *Terra Australis* generally laid down in the old Charts, are meer Chimeras, which have been justly left out of the new Charts.

It is worth adding that Frézier set Cape Horn in 55°50′ or 56°S and only 40 leagues from the Strait

According to Captain Fanning[1] the brig called at the Falkland Islands, relocated the Aurora Islands and reported that they had no landing places 'even for amphibious animals, on them'[2] and turned west for Staten Land as instructed. Having taken on board wood and water they turned south following their instructions and in 63° south turned east and

> at 10 A.M. to their great joy, a high and round mountain island was discovered, covered with snow, although in the month of February, and the last summer month in this region. From its singular form they named it Mount Pisgah Island.[3]

Other accounts indicate that the second mate, Nathaniel B. Palmer, was left at

---

of Le Maire while his charts had it in 57½° or 58°S and 100 leagues from the Strait (p. 285). The current position is 55°59'S about 100 miles or 33 leagues from the Strait, which gives an indication of the accuracy of his navigation.

Burney, 1803–17, IV (1816), pp. 490–505, also gives an account of Frézier's travels but makes no mention of sighting the ice (or land) south of Cape Horn, he does however give some information on Porée's voyage (IV, pp. 455–6):

> In July 1708, a ship named l'Assomption, commanded by M. Porée of St Malo, fell in with a land which he believed a new discovery being by his reckoning 100 leagues to the East of Isles Nouvelles, or John Davis's South Land [Falkland Islands], and he ran along its North coast, Frézier, however believed that what Porée saw was no other than the Isles Nouvelles; and in his chart accordingly, he marked the Northern coast of those Isles as the land of the Assomption. Porée saw also a great bank at a distance, and was doubtful whether it was ice or land: the place of the ship is not specified.

Frézier, 1717, pp. 288–9, gives his reasons for his belief, quoted by Burney above, concluding: the most convincing is, that we and our Comrades must have run over that new Land, according to the Longitude in which it was laid down in the Manuscript Chart; and it is morally impossible that a Ship should have had no Sight of it, being about 50 Leagues in Length E.S.E. and W.N.W.

Neither the French account of Frézier's voyage published in Paris 1716, the English translation of it, 1717, nor those published in French in Amsterdam, 1717 and Paris 1732, nor that in Dutch in Amsterdam 1718, make any mention of South Iceland or the discovery of land south of Cape Horn.

The letter quoted by Bertrand was written after the return to Stonington of the Hersilia (21 May, 1820). It would therefore appear probable that Stackpole is correct in his assessment. It is also interesting to compare the instructions Fanning states were given to Captain Sheffield (Fanning 1834, 429) with the Directions printed by Blunt in The American Coast Pilot, 1827, p. 523, for a vessel sailing from the coast of Patagonia to New South Iceland – see pp. 196–7.

[1] Fanning, 1834, pp. 429–30.

[2] The Aurora Islands were first reported in 1762 by the Aurora. They were supposedly sighted again in 1790 and surveyed by Captain Bustamante y Guerra in the corvette Atrevida in 1794. They do not exist and it is generally considered that the Shag Rocks were identified. See Stommel, 1984, pp. 84–97.

[3] The island is now known as Smith Island but the peak is named Mount Pisgah. The name is thought to have been given because of the resemblance to the double-topped Mount Pisgah in the town of Durham, Connecticut (Alberts, 1981, p. 665) however there may also be an element of its biblical connotation as the Mount from which Moses looked on the promised land (Deuteronomy 34:1–4). See Plate 4.

the Falkland Islands and heard of the newly discovered islands, but not their position from the captain of *Espírito Santo* which called while he was on shore.[1] From the log, land was discovered at 0400 on 18 January, and on 23 January they came to anchor in 8 fathoms, sandy bottom, in company with a brig from Buenos Aires,[2] in Hersilia Cove on the north-east side of Rugged Island. Reconstruction of their track indicates that these five days were spent in the vicinity and north of a line joining Smith and Snow Islands. Sixteen days later, on 7 February, *Hersilia* sailed having embarked all the skins salt was available to cure. Departure was made sailing WNW and NW and north for Staten Island, which was not sighted. The vessel passed east of the Falkland Islands and after calling at Buenos Aires reached Stonington on 21 May, 1820.

The *Imperial Magazine* for August 1820 carries the account of Mr Herring (see below), who had apparently sailed with William Smith in the *Williams* on her first voyage, and fitted out a vessel on speculation in Montevideo which arrived in the area on 25 December 1819. He makes no mention of meeting the *Hersilia*, but it took thirty-three days to embark their cargo so that if his vessel was that met by *Hersilia* he would have almost completed by the time she arrived. He also states that the cargo was sold in Buenos Aires. Since the skins embarked in *San Juan Nepomuceno* were consigned to Adam Guy in London, the probability is that Herring was embarked in *Espírito Santo*.

Imperial Magazine August 1820:[3]

IMPORTANT DISCOVERY

About two years since, a seafaring man named Herring, who had long been employed in the Falmouth Packets, came in a ship to Liverpool; from which port he sailed to Buenos Ayres. Arriving thither, he engaged himself as mate of a ship, then about to sail into the southern ocean round Cape Horn. While prosecuting this voyage, they visited a high southern latitude, where at a distance they discovered land, and found themselves surrounded by multitudes of seals. They, however, accomplished their voyage, and returned to Buenos Ayres without visiting the land they had perceived. Mr Herring, who had marked its situation, prevailed upon some British merchants in Buenos Ayres, to fit out a vessel on speculation, being satisfied that the prospect of taking seals would fully justify the experiment.

On the 25th of December, 1819, the vessel reached this land, which he found to consist of a group of barren islands, the largest of which he conceives to be about ten

---

[1] Bertrand, 1971, p. 46.

[2] According to Captain Thomas Davidson, who was not on board *Hersilia*, this was the brig that Nathaniel Palmer had met in the Falkland Islands, i.e. *Espírito Santo*: Bertrand, 1971, pp. 55–6.

[3] *Imperial Magazine or Compendium of Religious, Moral, and Philosophical Knowledge*, 2, 1820, cols 674–6.

miles long. The whole surface was covered with snow; but in no part could he discover either tree or shrub, and vegetation was exceedingly scanty. The snow alone furnished them with water. They, however, succeeded in finding a tolerably good harbour, and safe anchorage in a sandy bottom; and their landing was easily effected on a sandy beach.

On getting on shore, Mr. Herring being fully persuaded that his was the first human foot that had ever made an impression in the sands, or that trod upon the rocks, hoisted the British flag; and he and his companions drank his Majesty's health in a glass of grog.

The seals, which were the great object of the voyage, they found in countless multitudes, varying in dimensions from the size of a sheep to that of a small ox. Of these, in 33 days, they killed vast numbers, the skins of which they sold at Buenos Ayres at a very low rate. Some sea elephants were occasionally on the shore, which he conceives would be productive of oil, but they were rather shy. The seals, on the contrary, were so tame, that even while they were killing some, the survivors made no effort to get away, but would even come and smell round them while they were skinning those they had previously knocked down. Among the rocks they also found many gulls resembling those of England, and a species of very large bird, such as they had never seen before. These birds were so tame, that they sometimes dragged them from their nests; but to these they instantly returned, even while the men were standing by their sides.

On returning to Buenos Ayres, they found every thing in a state of confusion, through the calamities of war; and although an offer was made to Mr. Herring to go on another voyage, he declined it, and seizing the first opportunity, sailed for Liverpool, which he reached a few days since.

Some merchants, to whom he has imparted the latitude and longitude of these islands, are decidedly of opinion, that they have never been noticed by any of our circumnavigators, and that they have no existence in any map or chart yet published.

The fur on the seal-skin is remarkably fine in texture; and some hatters to whom it has been shewn, tell him, that they think it exceedingly valuable. We have been favoured with a small piece of this beautiful article, which may be inspected at the Caxton Printing-Office.

July 3, 1820.

APPENDIX 1

Accounts by Purdy, 1822, Weddell, 1825, Noric, 1825 and Blunt 1827.

Purdy, 1822, pp. 38–9

Weddell, 1825, pp. 129–31

Norie 1825, pp. 10–11

For the first notices of this discovery [South Shetland], the world is indebted to Mr. William Smith, commander of the brig Williams, of Blythe, by whom the land was first seen in the month of February, 1819. The Williams was, at this time, on a voyage from Buenos Ayres to Valparaiso, and stretching far to the south. On the 19th, land or ice was seen in latitude 62°40′, and near the longitude 60°W., then bearing S.E. by S. about two leagues. Hard gales, with flying showers of snow, and fields of ice, a combination of adverse circumstances, prevented, at this time, an exploration of the coast; and, on the brig's return to the River Plata, in the month of May, similar circumstances prevented any

The discovery of this archipelago, as already mentioned, was made by Mr. William Smith, commander of the brig William, on a passage from Monte Video to Valparaiso in 1819, as stated in the following extract from that vessel's log-book.
'After taking our departure from Monte Video, nothing material occurred until I got into

It had long been an object of controversy whether the existence of a southern continent was real or imaginary, and the voyages of Captain *Cook* seemed to have silenced all expectation on the subject, when Mr. Wm. *Smith*, of the brig *Williams*, in *February* 1819, on a voyage from *Buenos Ayres* to *Valparaiso*, steering out of the usual track round *Cape Horn*, and going far to the southward, being in latitude 62°34′S. and in the longitude of 60° West, saw what he imagined to be land, bearing S.E. by S. distant about two leagues, but adverse circumstances would not at that time allow him to explore it; on a subsequent voyage,

Purdy, 1822, cont.

further discovery: but, on a subsequent voyage from Monte-Video to Valparaiso, in October of the same year, the Williams again made the land. Captain Smith, in his journal, says, 'I, to my great satisfaction, discovered land on the 15th October, at six *p.m.* in latitude 62°30', and longitude 60°W., by chronometer, bearing distance about three leagues; hazy weather; bore up and sailed towards it; at four miles distant sounded in 40 fathoms, fine black sand; an island bearing E. by S. At S.E. by E. bearing, sounded in 60 fathoms, same bottom; hauled off during the night to the northward; at daylight stood in for the land again, at three leagues distance. From the body of the islands sounded again, 95 fathoms, fine sand and oaze; at eight, weather clear and pleasant, saw the main land bearing S.S.E., distant from the islands about three leagues. Having ran as far as the cape, we found the land trend off to the N.E. Coasting to the eastward, and sounding, found it

Weddell, 1825, cont.

the latitude of Cape Horn, with a fair wind to go to the westward, and steering S.S.E. with an intention to make the island again, and continuing this course for a few days, I, to my great satisfaction, discovered land. On the 15th October, at 6 P.M., in latitude 62°30'S., and longitude 60°W., by chronometers, bearing S.E. by E. about three leagues, hazy weather, bore up and sailed towards it. At four miles' distance sounded in 40 fathoms, fine black sand. Island bearing E. by S. to S.E. by E., sounded in 60 fathoms, same bottom. Hauled off during the night to the northward. At daylight stood in for the land again, at three leagues' distance from the body of islands. Sounded again 95 fathoms, fine sand. 'October 18th. Weather clear and pleasant, saw the main land bearing S.S.E., distance from the island about three leagues; having ran as far as the Cape, we found the land trend off to the N.E., coasting to the eastward; I sounded, found it similar

Norie, 1825, cont.

from the *River Plate* to *Valparaiso,* in *October* of the same year, Mr. *Smith,* with the intent of ascertaining a confirmation of his suspicions, again sought a similar latitude, and made good his discovery; for on the 15th of *October,* being in latitude 62°30' and longitude 60°, he perceived land at the distance of 3 leagues, the weather being hazy, when he bore up towards it, and found, at 4 miles distance soundings of 40 fathoms, fine black sand, an island bearing E. by S. at the time; when this island bore S.E. by E. soundings of 60 fathoms were obtained; he therefore stood off during the night, but at day-light made again for the land; when within 3 leagues distance, he sounded again in 95 fathoms, sand and ouze; the weather was clear, and the mainland appeared S.S.E. distant from the island 3 leagues, and stretching off to the N. Eastward. Mr. *Smith* now coasted along to the eastward, finding soundings of fine sand all the way; a remarkable point of land now bore E.½S.

Purdy, 1822, cont.

similar to the former, fine sand. The point called North Foreland bearing E.½S., hauled in for it, got the island to bear N.W. distance half a league. Soundings regular from 20 to 35 fathoms, good bottom sand and gravel. Finding the weather favourable, we down boat, and succeeded in landing; found it barren and covered with snow. Seals in abundance.
'The boat having returned, which, when secured, made sail off shore for the ensuing night; in the morning altered the course so as to keep the land to the southward in view; at eleven *a.m.* the North Foreland bore S.E. by E five leagues. The land then took a south-easterly direction, varying to the eastward; weather thick and squally, with snow. I thought proper, having property on board, and perhaps deviating from the assurance, to haul off to the westward on my intended voyage. Strong variable winds. Made Cape Williams; could perceive some high land to

Weddell, 1825, cont.

to the former, fine sand. The point called North Foreland E. by S.; hauled in for it; got the island to bear W.N.W. distance half a league; sounded regular from 20 to 35 fathoms, good bottom, sand and gravel. Finding the weather favourable, we lowered down the boat, and succeeded in landing; found it barren and covered with snow; seals in abundance. The boat having returned, and being secured, we made sail off shore the ensuing night. In the morning, altered the course so as to reach the land to the southward in view. At 11 A.M. the North Foreland bore S.E. by E. five leagues; the land then took a south-easterly direction, varying to the eastward; weather thick and squally, with snow.
'I thought proper, having property on board, and perhaps deviating from the insurance, to haul off to the westward on my intended voyage. Stormy, variable winds; made Cape Millan; could perceive some high land to the westward of the Cape, stretching in a south-west

Norie, 1825, cont.

which he called the *North Foreland*, from its similarity in appearance to the *English* coast so named; he then hauled in for the land, getting the island to bear N.W. distant one mile and a half, having regular soundings from 35 to 20 fathoms, good ground of sand and gravel, when, finding the weather favourable, he landed. The shores were barren and covered with snow; seals and penguins were in great abundance. The next morning, keeping the land in view, he made sail, and at eleven A.M. brought the *North Foreland* to bear S.E. by E. distant 5 leagues: the shore then took a south-easterly direction, inclining to the east, when the discovery being secured beyond dispute, Mr. *Smith* hauled off, and proceeded on his commercial pursuits, to the westward; but before he quitted the vicinity of his first discovery, he observed high land stretching to the westward of *Cape Williams*, in a S. Westerly direction; and having sailed to the westward about 150 miles, he saw another headland,

Purdy, 1822, cont.

the westward of the Cape, and stretching in a S.W. direction. The weather becoming thick and squally, we made sail to the westward, having sailed 150 miles to W.S.W. The weather moderating, saw another head-land bearing by observation E.N.E., distance ten leagues; very high. Observed in latitude 62°53′S., and longitude, by chronometer 63°40′W. of Greenwich; named this Smith's Cape. Found the land to extend from the cape in a southerly direction. Shaped my course for Valparaiso, where I arrived on the 24th November, after a passage of sixty days from Monte Video.'

Weddell, 1825, cont.

direction; the weather becoming thick and squally, made sail to the westward. Having sailed 150 miles on W.S.W., the weather moderating, saw another head-land bearing E.N.E., distance 10 leagues; very high; observed latitude 62°52′ south, longitude, by chronometers, 63°40′ west; named this South Cape; found the land to extend from the Cape in a southerly direction. Shaped my course for Valparaiso, where I arrived on the 24th November after a passage of 60 days from Monte Video.' (Signed) 'Wm. Smith.'★ ★ Accounts of this discovery were originally made known to the British public in the Literary Gazette.

Norie, 1825, cont.

bearing E.N.E. distant 10 leagues; this he named *Smith's Cape*, the land appeared then to run off to the southward; the extend of land thus partially seen being near 3 degrees.

Blunt, 1827, pp. 520–23

Purdy's version of William Smith's text, also contains his copy of Dr Young's account of Bransfield's voyage, and a number of other remarks from subsequent voyages of American and British sealers. All these were copied directly by Edmund Blunt and first appeared in the eleventh edition of *The American Coast Pilot,* 1827, which also included the following:

Directions for sailing from the Coast of Patagonia, *or* Falkland Islands, *to* New South Icelands:

After obtaining sight of Statten Land, bring Cape St. John's to bear west, five or six leagues distant; then, on account of the N.E. set off Cape Horn, endeavour to make a course good south, until you arrive in the latitude 62°50′S. then steer east keeping between the latitude of 62°50′ and 63°5′S. until you make the land, which will be *Mount Pisgo Island;* when you have got sight of this island, bring the centre of it to bear S.W. five leagues distant. If, when in this situation, the weather should set in thick or foggy, keep this situation by lying by, or on short tacks, until the weather lights up, then steer N.E.½E. until you make Castle Rock, situated off the south chop of Strait Despair; leave Castle Rock broad on your starboard bow, and keep steering north and eastward past the mouth of the strait, when you will make Ragged Island, which keep off your starboard bow and beam until you open the pass between the N.W. end of Ragged Island and the Main Island; then steer into the pass E.S.E. keeping Ragged Island shore nearest onboard, and anchor in the harbour around the second point of Ragged Island, in 6 or 8 fathoms. Double this second point well on board, to avoid the reefs that lie off in the pass abreast of the harbour of *Port Sheffield*, in Ragged Island.

There are some reefs in the offing off the mouth of Ragged Island pass, and in it, but with care, and a good look out, they are easily avoided, as the breakers or ripples will show where they are.

N.B. Mount Pisgo is a very high round island, with a bold shore all around it, and may be seen in clear weather at least thirty leagues.

Ragged Island is now know as Rugged Island. Port Sheffield, presumably called after Captain James P. Sheffield, captain of the brig *Hersilia* (see Chapter 8), would appear to be Hersilia Cove, which is off the north-east end of Rugged Island, in the entrance to the harbour between Rugged Island and Livingston Island, known to the American sealers as President's Harbor. The latter is shown as New Plymouth on Bransfield's chart by which name it is known today. It is tempting to suspect that these directions were obtained by Edmund Blunt either directly or indirectly from Captain Sheffield himself since not only is his name used for the harbour, but they reflect the track taken by the *Hersilia*.

This whole section was deleted from the next edition in 1833, presumably to reduce the size of the volume since a large amount of new information had been added on South America from the surveys carried out by British naval officers, and it had been recognized that vessels were no longer using the South Shetland Islands for sealing.

APPENDIX 2

Covering Letter from Captain Shirreff enclosing:
Logbook of the Brig *Williams,*
Orders for Edward Bransfield,
Charter Agreement.

'Duplicate'

His Majesty's Ship Andromache
~~Panama February 16ᵗʰ 1820~~
Valparaiso 19 Dec 1819[1]

Sir,

Herewith I have the honour to enclose you an extract from the log book of William Smith Master of the Brig Williams, [pp. 46–8] as well as a sketch and a rough chart of a coast discovered by him in latitude 62°.53′S and longitude 63°.40′W[2] from whence he ran along the shore nearly 200 miles to the Westward (on his passage from Monte Video to this port), and as it does not appear from the most minute examination to have been laid down in any chart either new or old, though it is not impossible that it may be connected with that land which Cook calls Southern Thule and Sandwich land, I have thought it a matter of considerable importance to the interests of Great Britain, as well to obtain an accurate survey of its coasts, and harbours, as to ascertain whether its soil and climate are capable of sustaining a population (which from the reports of Mʳ Smith, of the mildness of the weather I am led to believe) since from its vicinity to the Pacific Ocean it appears to me well calculated as a Naval depot, and if the account given by the Crew of the Brig be correct, it swarms with such an abundance of Sperm Whales, Otters and Seals, as must make it an object of the greatest importance to the interests of our Whale fisheries. –

I have therefore in consideration of the above mentioned circumstances considered it my duty to hire the aforementioned Brig under the terms mentioned in the enclosure Nᵒ· 2 [below] being a Vessel well calculated for surveying and have sent her under the direction of Mʳ Bransfield Master of this Ship, who from my own observation, I know to be well qualified for the undertaking, for the purpose of putting in execution the enclosed instructions which you will find marked Nᵒ· 3 [pp. 70–72]. –

---

[1] The date is corrected in pencil in a different hand. There is a note in the margin which reads 'duplicate copy of sketch and charts of land mislaid'. This is in the same hand as the letter indicating that these documents were not forwarded by Captain Shirreff.

[2] This chart and sketch must have been based on the same original as Miers's chart published in *The Edinburgh Philosophical Journal* (Plates 5 and 6) and Midshipman Foster's chart (Plate 3), see also p. 43, n. 2.

I request you will be pleased to lay this information before the Lords Commissioners of the Admiralty, who I trust will conceive the object for which I have sent this Vessel of sufficient importance to warrant such an act, and that they will accordingly approve of my having so done. –

I have the honor to be

Sir

Your obed.^{t.} humble Servant

W H Shirreff

To/ J. W. Croker Esquire
&c – &c – &c.
Admiralty
London

Across the corner is written in Croker's hand:

> May 2
> Own rec.[1]
> Capt Hurd[2]

Charter Agreement between Captain Shirreff and Captain Smith[3]

It is covenanted, concluded and agreed upon this Sixteenth day of December, in the year of our Lord one thousand eight hundred and nineteen and in the fifty ninth year of the reign of our Sovereign Lord George the 3.rd. by the grace of God, of the United Kingdom of Great Britain & Ireland, defender of the faith &c. &c. by and between William Smith of the good Brig called Williams of Blythe, whereof the said William Smith is now Master, of the burthen of two hundred and sixteen tons, register tonnage, now riding in the Port of Valparayso, of the one part; and W^{m.} H^{y.} Shirreff Esquire, Captain of H.B.M. Ship Andromache and Senior Officer on the Western Coast of South America, for and on the behalf of His Majesty, on the other part, in the manner following; that is to say the said Wm. Smith for and on the behalf of himself, and all and every of the part owners of the said Brig, hath granted, and to hire and freight, letten and by these presents, doth grant and to hire and freight, let the said Brig to the said W^{m.} H^{y.} Shirreff Esquire, to receive on board at Valparayso all such Officers and Men, as shall be ordered by him to be put on board her, and to proceed therewith to such part or parts, and on such service as he shall be directed to perform by the Senior Officer on board, or in the event of his death the next in rank to him. –

And the said W^{m.} H^{y.} Shirreff Esquire, for and on the behalf of His Majesty, has hired the said Brig for the said service accordingly. – Viz.^{t.} The said Wm. Smith doth covenant,

---

[1] This appears to be a note of the action taken. The meaning is not immediately clear, but subsequent letters in PRO files have a similar note which, in some cases is written out in full 'Own receipt'. The remark is ticked and what appears to be '2c&rec.^d' written beside it in a different hand. Possibly this indicates the action taken by John Croker's private secretary, Mr L. C. Biggs.

[2] Captain Thomas Hurd, Hydrographer to the Admiralty 1808–23.

[3] PRO ADM 1/2548.

promise and agree, that the said Brig be strong, firm, tight, staunch and substantial, both above water and beneath, and shall be equipped, fitted, furnished and provided with Masts, Sails, Sail Yards, Anchors, Ropes, Cords, Tackle, Apparel; also with three proper boats and gratings to her hatchways necessary for such a voyage; and also with furniture, and all other materials and things necessary and proper for such a voyage and service, and not to have less than three large Cables of 120 fathoms each, or so many together as will make up 360 fathoms, and one Stream Cable all in good condition, and to have all proper sails, and not less than two Mainsails, two Maintopsails, two Foretopsails and two Foresails, with a complete set of small sails, and also to be manned with twenty five Men and Officers, fit and capable to manage and sail her, and shall have at least four Carriage Guns mounted, not less than four pounders, twenty five Muskets, twenty five Cutlasses, and three pair of Pistols, and be provided with powder and Shot, not less than twenty rounds of each for each Gun, and all things necessary and answerable thereunto, with a proper place, or Magazine, for the security of the powder; and also with good and wholesome victuals, sufficient for the said Men during the said service and employment; and the said W^m. Smith for and on the behalf of himself, and all and every of the part Owners, doth hereby covenant, conclude, and agree to receive such amount of pay per month for the hire of the said Brig, as the Commissioners of His Majesty's Navy shall think adequate to the service performed, provided, nevertheless, and it is agreed between the said parties, that upon the loss of time, breach of orders, or neglect of duty by the said Master, being made appear, the said Commissioners shall have free liberty, and be permitted to mulct, or make such abatement out of the freight and pay of the said Vessel, as shall be by them judged fit and reasonable – And it is further covenanted and agreed by W^m. Smith for and on behalf of himself and all and every of the part Owners, that if the said Brig shall happen to be burnt, sunk, or lost in any other way during the aforesaid Service as it shall appear to a Court Martial, that the same did not proceed through any fault, neglect, or otherwise, in the Master or Ships Company, he shall receive such allowance, as the said Commissioners shall think adequate to the said loss. –

To the true performance and keeping all and every the covenants, conditions, and agreements abovementioned on the part and behalf of the said W^m. Smith to be kept, done and performed, he, the said W^m. Smith bindeth himself, his heirs, executors, and Administrators and the said Brig, with her tackle, Apparel, Ammunition, freight and furniture, unto the said W^m. H^y Shirreff Esquire for and on behalf of His Majesty, in the penalty, or sum of five hundred pounds of lawful money of Great Britain, to be recovered and paid by these presents. – In witness whereof the said W^m. Smith hath set his hand and seal to one part hereof, and the other part hereof, the said William Henry Shirreff Esquire for and on His Majesty's behalf, has signed his name and caused his seal to be affixed, the day and year first abovementioned – It is hereby also agreed between both parties, that the said Brig Williams shall enter into pay from the day she proceeds to sea. –

Signed, Sealed and delivered   W. H. Shirreff,

                W Smith

in the presence of   W^m. Turner, Witness

                D. H. D. Brill [?] Witness

APPENDIX 3

Additional Naval Reports

Report of the discovery by Commodore Hardy

Commodore Hardy, in HMS *Tyne*, 26, at Buenos Aires, received a private report of William Smith's discovery from Valparaíso and wrote to John Crocker, Secretary to the Admiralty on 6 January, 1820. The report must have been dispatched from Valparaíso about the time the *Williams* sailed on her voyage with Edward Bransfield, since the regular time for the post between there and Buenos Aires was twenty days although the express covered the distance of 1365 miles in twelve days.[1] His letter[2] was carried in HMS *Creole*, bringing Commodore Bowles home. She sailed from Buenos Aires on 12 January and reached Portsmouth on 29 April, 1820. The letter is marked 'R*eceived* 30 April' and minuted 'Own rect'[3] and 'Captain Hurd' (the Hydrographer of the Navy) by Croker on 1 May. The date stamp for its receipt is 17 May 1820 – the same date as that on Captain Shirreff's report (Appendix 2).

Nº 6.
H.M. Ship Tyne Buenos
Ayres, 6th January 1820

Sir,

Be pleased to acquaint my Lords Commissioners of the Admiralty, that by private accounts from Valparaizo, I learn that an Island has been discovered, in Latitude 62°40'S. and, running from 60° to 63°40'W. by Mr Smith Master of the Merchant Vessel, Williams, on her voyage from Monte Video to Valparaizo – he landed, – and observed a great many Seals, and speaks of it as likely to be of advantage to the Southern Whale Fishing – I am told Captain Shirreff has sent to Survey it – as soon as I can gather more correct information on the Subject, I will forward it to their Lordships – I have examined the Charts and Maps of the World, and cannot find any land placed in that Latitude and Longitude, or even the Track of any Ships having passed near it. –

I have the honor to be
Sir,
Your most obedient
humble servant
(Signed) T. M. Hardy Commodore.

John Wilson Croker Esq – Admiralty London

[1] Norie, 1825, p. 21.
[2] PRO ADM 1/25.
[3] See p. 199, n. 1. This also has a line through it and what might be a similar hieroglyphic to that on Captain Shirreff's letter.

Bransfield's report to Captain Searle on return from his voyage.[1]

Valparaiso 4th May 1820

Commodore

Sir

In compliance with your Order of the 15th April – Herewith you will receive the Log Book of the Hired Armed Brig Williams of Blyth, under my Command on a Voyage of Discovery to the Southward, together with the Charts and Views of the Land discovered and surveyed by me, between the 19th December 1819 and the 16th April 1820 the receipt of which I beg you will be pleased to acknowledge.

I have further to state that the late time of the Year, which I was ordered on this service, put it entirely out of my Power to complete the Work; but should what I have done meet the Approbation of the Commodore, I beg leave to offer my services to finish it the next Season, being of opinion there is a great deal more to be done and as to its utility to Great Britain my Log will best explain –

I have the Honor to be

Sir

With due respect, your

Most Ob^t H^ble Servant

(Signed) E Bransfield Master

HMS Andromache

To

T. Searle C.B. Captain of His Majestys Ship Hyperion and Senior Officer on the Western side of South America.

The Public Record Office copy of this document is marked 'Copy' and is signed by Commodore T. M. Hardy, indicating that he had seen it. The Admiralty date stamp is 'November 16 1821'.

[1] PRO ADM 1/2548

APPENDIX 4

Selection of Additional Newspaper and Journal reports in Chronological Order.

The Courier, 2 May 1820:

BUENOS AYRES, JAN. 7.

The Spanish seventy-four, *San Telmo*, which sailed from Cadiz, was supposed to have foundered, having been left making much water, and rudder lost, by a ship arrived at Callao, from Cadiz with a cargo worth 7,500,000 dollars. The ship got into Callao during an absence of seven days of Lord Cochrane's squadron, which went to a small port at the south to repair damages sustained in an unsuccessful attack. The frigate *Prueba* had escaped from Callao, and gone to Guyaquil.

A new island has been discovered off Cape Horn, in lat. 61 deg. long. 55 deg. by the ship *William*, on a voyage from Monte Video for Valparaiso. The same ship having been despatched again by Capt. Sherriff, of the *Andromache* frigate, to survey the coast, had explored it for 200 miles. – The Captain went ashore, found it covered with snow, and uninhabited. Abundance of seals and whales were found in its neighbourhood.[1]

Gentleman's Magazine May 1820, p. 462:

A new island has been discovered off Cape Horn, in latitude 61 deg. longitude 55 deg. by the ship William, on a voyage from Monte Video for Valparaiso. The same ship having been dispatched by Captain Sheriff, of the Andromache frigate to survey the coast, explored it for 200 miles. The Captain went ashore, and found it covered with snow, and uninhabited: abundance of seals and whales were found in its neighbourhood. He has named the island New Shetland.

The Courier, 20 July 1820:

By a passenger landed at Falmouth, from Rio de Janiero, it is said that in the very early part of the year, one of His Majesty's ships cruizing on the Brazil Coast, fell in with in lat. 62. long. 62. some unknown land, found the same for some miles uninhabited; but the coast full of seals. This information given at Buenos Ayres, gave rise to speculation with

---

[1] This is presumably based on an independent report and not on Commodore Hardy's letter (p. 201) since the position of the new land differs from that in the latter which likewise makes no mention of the new land being covered in snow or uninhabited – it does not mention the loss of the *San Telmo* either.

some vessels, and which had brought back about 15,000 seals, after a very short time, which they sold at five dollars each at Buenos Ayres.[1] – It is the general opinion at Buenos Ayres, from the different reports, that the land forms part of a continent. Several other vessels were fitting out for the same coast on the seal fishery. – *Cornwall Gazette.*

Literary Gazette and Journal of Belles Lettres, 5 August 1820, pp. 505–6:

ARTS AND SCIENCES

IMPORTANT DISCOVERY

An opinion of the existence of an Antarctic Continent has prevailed ever since the discovery of America rendered us more intimately acquainted with the figure of the earth; nor, when all the circumstances that led to it are considered, can it be called an unreasonable opinion. The vast quantity of floating ice in the higher southern latitudes, justly indicated its origin to be in fresh water rivers and lakes, at no great distance. And again, the immense space of ocean, in the southern hemisphere, in the absence of such a continent, led to an inference that that beautiful arrangement and disposition of land and water, so conspicuous in the northern, was overlooked, and the equilibrium neglected in the southern hemisphere.

These considerations led many voyagers to search for this Terra Incognita, and particularly influenced the last voyage of Captain Cook. But is it not surprising that it should have escaped the observation of the circum-navigators of all nations, and have baffled the laborious perseverance of Cook himself? and that the numerous vessels (whalers and others) that have navigated the sea contiguous to such land for nearly two centuries, should have remained in ignorance of its existence? Yet such is the fact; and it is equally surprising, that the honour of its discovery should have been reserved for the master of a small trading vessel, nearly fifty years after the question seemed to be set at rest by the unsuccessful result of Captain Cook's navigation.[2]

---

[1] This presumably refers to the voyage of *Espírito Santo* the skins from which Mr Herring said were sold in Buenos Aires at 'a very low rate.' p. 191.

[2] [Footnote in original] Captain Cook first explored the Southern Ocean between the meridian of the Cape of Good Hope and New Zealand; consequently far to the east of the land now discovered. In November, 1773, he left New Zealand, and employed several weeks between 180° and 90° West longitude, and 45° to about 72° South latitude; so that he never approached within 30 degrees (on the Antarctic circle) of the new continent. The only passages we think it necessary to quote from him, as illustrative of our present subject, are the following:-

"In lat 67°20′, long 137°12′," he says, "While we were taking up ice, we got two of the antarctic peterels so often mentioned, by which our conjectures were confirmed of their being of the peterel tribe. They are about the size of a large pigeon; the feathers of the head, back, and part of the upper side of the wings, are of a light brown; the belly, and under side of the wings, white; the tail feathers are also white, but tipped with brown: at the same time, we got another new peterel, smaller than the former, and all of a dark grey plumage. We remarked that these birds were fuller of feathers than any we had hitherto seen; such care has nature taken to clothe them suitably to the climate in which they live. At the same time we saw a few chocolate coloured albatrosses; these, as well as the peterels above-mentioned, we nowhere saw but among the ice; hence one may with reason conjecture that there is land to the South. If not, I must ask where these birds breed? A question which will perhaps never be

In the absence of a more detailed narrative of this important discovery, which we presume is retarded for obvious reasons, resulting from the impolicy of making premature disclosures, the following few particulars may not only gratify curiosity, but will, in a great measure, we trust, counteract the ill effects of the garbled and incorrect statements, which are beginning to find their way into the periodical press.

One of the evils attending mis-statements, in the origin of an important discovery, is, that of involving the question in a labyrinth of contradictions, from which in after times, it is difficult to unravel the truth. In the present instance too, as in former cases, a meritorious and enterprising, though obscure individual, is in danger of being deprived of the credit he so justly deserves, by probably adding to his native country a new source of wealth; the full worth of which would only be truly known by its possession by a rival in commercial enterprize.

A Mr. Smith, Master of the William, of Blythe, in Northumberland, and trading between Rio Plata and Chili, in endeavouring to facilitate his passage round Cape Horn, last year, ran to a higher latitude than is usual in such voyages, and in lat. 62°30′, and 60° west longitude, discovered land. As circumstances would not admit of a close examination, he deferred it until his return to Buenos Ayres, when he made such further observations as convinced him of the importance of his discovery. On making it known in Buenos Ayres, speculation was set on the alert, and the Americans at that place became very anxious to obtain every information necessary to their availing themselves of the discovery, which they saw was pregnant with vast benefit to a commercial people. Captain Smith was however too much of an Englishman to assist their speculations, by affording them that knowledge of his secret which it was so necessary for them to possess; and was determined that his native country only should enjoy the advantages of his discovery; and on his return voyage to Valparaiso, in February last, he devoted as much time to the development of it as was consistent with his primary object, a safe and successful voyage.

---

determined; for hitherto we have found these lands, if any, quite inaccessible. Besides these birds, we saw a very large seal, which kept playing about us some time. One of our people who had been in Greenland, called it a sea-horse; but everyone else took it for what I have said."

Again in lat. 65°42′, long 99°44′: "I now came to the resolution to proceed to the North, and to spend the ensuing winter within the Tropic, if I met with no employment before I came there. I was now well satisfied no continent was to be found in this ocean, but what must lie so far to the South as to be wholly inaccessible on account of ice; and that if one should be found in the Southern Atlantic Ocean, it would be necessary to have the whole summer before us to explore it. On the other hand, upon a supposition that there is no land there, we undoubtedly might have reached the Cape of Good Hope by April, and so have put an end to the expedition, so far as it related to the finding a continent; which indeed was the first object of the voyage. But for me at this time to have quitted the Southern Pacific Ocean, with a good ship expressly sent out on discoveries, a healthy crew, and not in want either of stores or of provisions, would have been betraying not only a want of perseverance, but of judgment, in supposing the South Pacific Ocean to have been so well explored, that nothing remained to be done in it. This, however, was not my opinion; for though I had proved that there was no continent but what must lie far to the South, there remained nevertheless room for very large islands in places wholly unexamined: and many of those which were formerly discovered, are but imperfectly explored, and their situations as imperfectly known. I was besides of opinion, that my remaining in this sea some time longer, would be productive of improvements in navigation and geography, as well as in other sciences.

He ran in a westward direction along the coasts, either of a continent or numerous islands, for two or three hundred miles, forming large bays, and abounding with spermaceti whale, seals, &c. He took numerous soundings and bearings, draughts, and charts of the coast; and in short, did everything that the most experienced navigator dispatched purposely for the object of making a survey, could do. He even landed, and in the usual manner took possession of the country for his sovereign, and named his acquisition, 'New South Shetland'. The climate was temperate, the coast mountainous, apparently uninhabited, but not destitute of vegetation, as firs and pines were observable in many places; in short, the country had upon the whole the appearance of the coast of Norway. After having satisfied himself with every particular that time and circumstances permitted him to examine, be bore away to the North and pursued his voyage.

On his arrival at Valparaiso he communicated his discovery to Captain Sherriff of H.M.S. Andromache, who happened to be there. Captain S. immediately felt the importance of the communication, and lost not a moment in making every arrangement for following it up; he immediately dispatched the William, with officers from the Andromache: and in this stage the last letter from Chili left the expedition, with the most sanguine expectation of success, and ultimate advantages resulting from it: and, if we are correctly informed, a fully detailed narrative has been forwarded to the government.

On taking a cursory view of the charts of the Southern Atlantic and Pacific Oceans, it will be seen, that though Captain Cook penetrated to a much higher latitude, and consequently drew his conclusion from observing nothing but vast mountains of ice, it will be seen also that his meridian was 45 degrees further to the west of New South Shetland, leaving a vast space unexplored on the parallel of 62° between that and Sandwich Land, in longitude about 28° west. He again made 67° or thereabouts, but in longitude 137° to 147° west. Perouse ascended no higher than 60°30′; Vancouver about 55°; other navigators passing the Straights of Magellan and Le Maire; most of them passing as close Cape Horn as possible, in order, as they thought, to shorten the passage to the Pacific, are circumstances that reasonably account for the protracted period to which so important a discovery has been delayed.

Morning Chronicle, 7 August 1820:

SOUTHERN or ANTARCTIC CONTINENT

This important discovery, which will be attended with incalculable advantages to our trade in the South seas, was made last year by a Mr Smith, Master of the William, of Blythe, in Northumberland. Our South Sea Traders, who, during hostilities between this country and Spain, have been subjected to the greatest difficulties and privations, will now be independent of Spain or any other power possessing South America. Mr Smith ran for two or three hundred miles along this continent which formed large bays, abounding with the spermaceti whale, seals, &c. The draughts and soundings taken by the discoverer, are in the possession of our Government. The following brief account has been given of the discovery:-

'A Mr. Smith, Master of the William, of Blythe, in Northumberland, …' [then as in the *Literary Gazette*, without the footnote].

206

The Globe, 7 August 1820:

The account is identical to that in the *Morning Chronicle*

The Times, 10 August 1820:

The Brig *Williams* had returned to Valparaiso from a survey of the land said to have been discovered to the south of Cape Horn, but Capt. Searle of the Hyperion, had prevented all intercourse with the shore which led to the opinion that some discovery of great importance had been made.

Morning Chronicle, 11 August 1820:

Sir,   Colchester, Aug. 9.

I beg leave to observe, upon the account given in your Paper of the 7th inst., of the late discovery made of an Antarctic Continent, that, while the failure of such a discovery by Cook, Perouse, and Vancouver, is noticed, no mention is made of Theodore Gerrard, who is recorded to have discovered land in the Great Southern Ocean so early as the year 1599, under nearly the same latitude and longitude as that given by Mr. Smith for his own observations.

Old Gerrard's discovery may be seen in Kitchen's Atlas, published in 1787, where the land is laid down as extending in a bay-formed shape for about two degrees from north-west to south-east. I am, Sir, your obedient servant,   E.W.

Literary Gazette and Journal of Belles Lettres, 12 August 1820, p. 524:

ANTARCTIC COUNTRY

It is stated in recent arrivals from Valparaiso, that the Brig Williams (an account of the despatch of which, by Captain Sheriff, to ascertain the nature of the country discovered to the southward of Cape Horn) had returned from the survey. On her arrival off the harbour, and making her report to Captain Searle, of the Hyperion, orders were given that no intercourse with the shore should be permitted. This has naturally led to the inference, that the discovery turns out to be important, and that this precaution is taken to prevent the interference or claim of any foreign nation, previous to the usual measures of taking possession in the name of His Britannic Majesty. The only draughtsman on the station, competent to perform the scientific part of the investigation, was Mr Bone, a son of the distinguished artist of that name; he accordingly went in the Williams, and made the drawings of the coast, &c.

Literary Gazette and Journal of Belles Lettres, 19 August 1820, p. 538:

THE ANTARCTIC COUNTRY

Government is, it seems, fitting out an expedition for the new country, and several of the Southern whalers have already sailed thither. The account which we gave of Captain Smith's voyage has led to various letters in the newspapers, and particularly in the Morning Chronicle, denying that this was a *discovery*, and asserting that the coast was known to the Dutch long ago. These strictures grow out of an utter misunderstanding of what we stated; for the whole gist of our remarks was laid on the failure of Captain Cook to make out a land *previously discovered,* though not accurately laid down in the charts of any navigator. Nor did we insinuate the slightest blame upon that justly renowned officer, of whose efforts, perseverance, and great achievements, none living entertain a higher opinion than we do. Captain Cook we consider to be one of the greatest ornaments of his profession, belonging to a country blazing with the glories of its sailors.

Blackwood's Edinburgh Magazine, August 1820, pp. 566–7:

Reprint of *Literary Gazette and Journal of Belles Lettres* articles of 5 August, pp. 505–6 and 12 August, p. 524 with rubric from *Morning Chronicle* of 7 August, 1820, and terminal acknowledgement to the *Literary Gazette*.

The Imperial Magazine; or Compendium of Religious, Moral, and Philosophical Knowledge, August 1820, cols 674–6:

Voyage of Mr Herring – text in Chapter 8, pp. 190–91.

No geographical position of the new land was given in this report.

Edinburgh Magazine and Literary Miscellany, August 1820, pp. 110–12:

ACCOUNT OF THE DISCOVERY OF NEW SOUTH SHETLAND; WITH
OBSERVATIONS ON ITS IMPORTANCE.

We have often of late regretted that we live in an age when no expected discoveries of strange lands can stir up enterprise, and reward our eternal desire for something new. When our minds have not been filled with the terror of revolutions, – the dread of subjugation, – or the joy of victory, (which have pretty well occupied these last thirty years,) we have longed for the return of those days of ignorance, every one of which brought to the ravished ears of our ancestors some golden tale of new worlds, more sweet than all the fables of the east. As we surveyed our Atlas, however, we were quite in despair, and concluded, that, except the interior of Africa, no part of the world, capable of bearing the foot of the wanderer or the keel of a ship, was so unexplored, that we could ever hope to hear of any new continents, or any more varieties of the human race. To our surprise reports have recently been circulated, that Terra Australasia has actually been seen by a British merchant ship. At first we treated this as an Irish or American report, both of which are generally famous for not being true; but our credulity has been conquered by the kindness of a friend, and the certainty of the discovery put beyond question. We hasten to lay before our readers an extract from the information which he has transmitted from Valparaiso. The whole, accompanied by a chart and view of the coast, will appear in the ensuing number of the Edinburgh Philosophical Journal, and we must refer such of our readers as desire further information to that publication.

Mr. William Smith, master of the brig Williams of Blythe in a voyage from Buenos Ayres to Valparaiso, fancying that Cape Horn might be weathered better by preserving a more than usual southerly course, being on the 19th of February 1819 in lat. 62°40′ south, and long. 62′ W. imagined he saw land, amidst fields of floating ice, at the distance of two leagues. At this time, encountering hard gales of wind, accompanied by flying showers of snow, he thought it prudent to haul off to the northward during the night. Next day, (February 20,) he again stood in for his supposed land, At noon his latitude by observation was 62°17′S., long. 60°12′W. by an excellent chronometer. The weather was moderate, and the atmosphere clear, when he again made *the land*. He was deterred from approaching nearer, by fearing blowing weather. He observed, however, to the westward more land, which he approached to the distance of ten miles. Both appeared to be islands, and bare, barren and rocky. Feeling himself in a responsible situation with regard to his ship and cargo, he contented himself with this distant survey, and on his arrival at Valparaiso, related to the English there every thing he had seen, who all ridiculed him for his credulity. He was not, however, to be thus easily laughed out of his own observation; and, on his return to the River Plate in June following, was determined, if possible, to verify what he had seen. He steered in the latitude of 62 ° 12′S. , but when he reached the longitude 67°W. he became so beset with loose pack ice, that he was alarmed for the safety of his ship and cargo, and obliged to give up the attempt.

On his arrival at Monte Video, he was again ridiculed for his credulity, and almost led to renounce his former conclusions. His account reached the ears of some American merchants, who endeavoured to obtain from him the true situation of the land, and offered to charter his ship on a voyage of discovery. He, however, to his credit, refused to disclose the longitude and latitude to any but a British born subject: though he honourably offered to conduct the vessel himself, and, if no land existed, to receive no freight; but that was not the object of the other party, and Jonathan[1] withdrew his contract. The honest Englishman, at length having obtained freight, a second time to Chili, set off on his voyage, and, on the 15th of October last, at 6 P.M., being then about the same latitude and longitude as before, he discovered the same land, bearing S.E. by E. three leagues, the weather being hazy. He bore up for it, approached within four miles, and proved it to be a large barren rock, inhabited only by innumerable penguins: he sounded in 40 and 60 fathoms, procuring a bottom of black sand. At day-light next morning he again stood in for the island; and at 8 A.M. the weather being very clear, he could plainly distinguish the main-land, bearing S. S. E. , the island being distant from it about three leagues. The main-land presented itself as a cape, to which the coast tended in a N.E. direction, having peculiar marks, of which he took rough sketches: he stood in, and ran along the land as far as the point, to which he gave the name of North Foreland, obtaining all the way regular sounding of sand and gravel, lessening gradually from 35 to 20 fathoms; the bottom was good and regular. The island bearing N.W., distant seven leagues, he observed the appearance of a good harbour, and sent a boat's crew and his first mate on shore, where they planted a board with the Union jack, and an appropriate inscription, with three cheers, taking possession in the name of the King of Great Britain. To the main-land was given the name of New South Shetland, on account of its lying in about the same latitude as the Shetland Islands. It was barren and

---

[1] 'Jonathan': a name often applied to Americans in general, but really appropriate to the Quakers in America, being a corruption of John Nathan: Smyth, 1867, pp. 413–14.

rocky, the highest points being covered with snow. At the place of landing the spot was barren, being stony, not of rounded pebbles, but of bluish-grey slaty pieces, varying in size from very large to very small. The harbour appeared to proceed inland as far as the eye could reach, and to afford a good anchorage. This place was called Shireff's Cove in honor of the Commanding Naval Officer in the Pacific. An abundance of birds were seen so tame, that they could be approached without disturbing them. The day drawing to a close, the boat pushed off, the master, with the most prudent views, hauling off the shore with his ship. The harbour appeared to abound with the real spermaceti whale. Seals and sea-otters abounded, as also an animal differing from the sea-otter. Next morning at day-break, he could perceive the land tend in a S.E. direction. Keeping his course to southward and westward, he saw several other islands, all about three leagues from the main-land, and all alike barren and rocky. He afterwards made a point of land which he called Cape William, and could distinctly perceive, with a telescope, trees which bore a resemblance to Norway pines: Indeed, he describes the whole appearance of the land, as being more like the Norwegian coast than any he ever saw.

The weather at daybreak next day becoming more settled, he descried another headland, which he named Smith's Cape: The weather being remarkably clear and fine, he proved it to lie in latitude 62°53'S. ; longitude 63°40'W. From Smith's Cape, the land appeared to extend in a south-westerly direction; but however eager his desire to extend his search, he concluded that he had fully attained his object, having proved the existence of the coast for the distance of 250 miles. He therefore shaped his course to the northward; and in the month of November reached the Port of Valparaiso. One may judge of the sensation produced in the breast of an Englishman on hearing the relation of Mr Smith; every one became struck with the advantages which a British settlement would offer, not only to our whale fisheries, but to our commercial interests in that quarter of the globe. Until the political arrangements of these countries (Spanish colonies) become in some degree settled, the consequences resulting from the animosities that may possibly arise between the many contending parties must necessarily be feared. Those who were here during the affair at Cancharayada well know the value of any thing like a British settlement, however miserable, to retire to. On the arrival of the Williams in November last there was a general and simultaneous feeling among the English merchants, who instantly set about taking up a vessel which should be chartered on a voyage of discovery at their own expense. Mr Smith, on his arrival, having transmitted his observations to the commanding officer in the Pacific, Captain Shireff of the Andromache, this excellent officer, ever alive as well to British interests as to the pursuit of objects of science and utility, instantly chartered the same brig Williams on Government account, in order to make an accurate and regular survey of the coasts and harbours. The Williams, refitted completely with every necessary for the voyage, put to sea in one week, (on the 19th December,) being placed under the charge of Mr Edward Bransfield, master of the Andromache, and several assistants, who were all ordered to observe, collect, and preserve every object of natural science during the prosecution of the more important objects of the expedition.

There is reason to believe this land has been twice before discovered, first by some

Spaniards or Portuguese prior to 1569, and afterwards by Theodore Gerrards, one of the first Dutchmen who passed into the South Sea. This, however, does not take from the merit of Captain Smith, nor make the re-found Continent less of a novelty to us, who never before heard any accurate account of its existence.

As yet it remains an interesting topic of conversation, whether New Shetland be an island of considerable size, or if it be part of a continent. It is by no means an improbable supposition, that it is connected with Southern Thule, the most southerly point of Sandwich Land seen by Captain Cook in 1775, and situated in 59°30′ lat. S., and 27°30′W. long., as there exists, according to the account given of Sandwich Land by Dr Forster, some resemblance between it and New South Shetland.

The climate of New Shetland would seem to be very temperate, considering its latitude; and, should the expedition now sent out bring assurances that the land is capable of supporting a population – an assumption which the appearance of trees and the abundance of birds seen on landing, render very probable – the place may become a colony of some importance.

Those who are aware of the extent to which the whale-fishery may be carried on in this hemisphere, must be immediately struck with the immense benefit which the acquisition of New Shetland might offer as a British settlement. There are at this time upwards of 200 American whale-ships lucratively employed in the Pacific, when Great Britain cannot boast of more than 30 or 40. This fact is enough to exhibit the advantage of this settlement; but we must also take into view the whole trade with Buenos Ayres, Chili, Peru, and the immensely extensive provinces of the interior, which is increasing with strides unknown, and establishing a demand for articles of British manufactures, that must eventually prove the channel for the consumption of British produce, and the employment of British capital. If we consider, too, that these countries must eventually become places of barter and entrepôt to our Indian and China trades, then must the importance of the situation, if it can admit of a settlement, be strikingly apparent. Comparing this spot with the Cape of Good Hope and New Holland, it will be seen that these three places form equi-distant depôts in the Southern Hemisphere, respectively situated so as to defend, if not command, a superiority of trade with more extensive markets than were ever offered to any commercial nation at any former period in the world; and this, too, at a time when the late eventful circumstances in the history of Europe have turned in no small degree British commerce out of those channels in which it has flowed uninterrupted for so many years.

No one can deny that the want of a British settlement contiguous to the coast of South America is seriously felt. Since the abandonment of the Falkland Islands, we have no possession, – not even a watering-place, – nearer than the Cape of Good Hope or New Holland; and no one can calculate upon the absolute necessity Great Britain may one day feel for such a possession. Under every point of view, as well national, commercial, and scientific, must the discovery of New South Shetland be valued; and without doubt the results of the present expedition will be anxiously looked for by every well-wisher to his country.

Valparaiso, Jan, 1820.

Gentleman's Magazine, September 1820, pp. 267–8:

NEW SOUTHERN CONTINENT

A great discovery has been made in Geography by Mr. Smith, master of the William, of *Blythe,* in Northumberland. Whilst trading between Rio Plata and Chili, in endeavouring to facilitate his passage round Cape Horn, last year, he ran to a higher latitude than is usual in such voyages, and in lat. 62.30 and 60. West long. discovered land. As circumstances would not admit of a close examination, he returned to Buenos Ayres; having again departed thence for Valparaiso in February last, he resolved to devote as much time to the purpose as was consistent with his primary object, a safe and successful voyage. – He ran in a Westward direction along the coasts, either of a continent or numerous islands, for two or three hundred miles, forming large bays, and abounding with the spermaceti whale, seals, &c. He took numerous soundings and bearings, draughts, and chart of the coast; and, in short, did every thing that the most experienced Navigator, dispatched purposely for the object of making a survey, could do. He even landed, and in the usual manner took possession of the country for his Sovereign, and named his acquisition New South Shetland. The climate was temperate, the coast mountainous, apparently uninhabited, but not destitute of vegetation, as firs and pines were observable in many places; in short, the country had upon the whole the appearance of the coast of Norway. After having satisfied himself with every particular that time and circumstances permitted him to examine, he bore away to the North and pursued his voyage. – On his arrival at Valparaiso he communicated his discovery to Capt. Sherriff, of his Majesty's ship Andromache, and a fully detailed narrative was forwarded to the Government. – The Conway sloop sailed lately for the South Seas; and it is not improbable but that she is intended to take a survey of the newly-discovered country.

The Imperial Magazine; or Compendium of Religious, Moral and Philosophical Knowledge, 2 September 1820, cols 755–8:

NEWLY DISCOVERED CONTINENT

In our last Number, col. 674,[1] we gave an account of an important discovery of land which had been made off Cape Horn. This information we obtained from a Mr. Herring, who had visited the coasts, and who was successfully employed in the taking of seals on its shores. It appears, however, from statements since published, that what he thought to be a group of barren islands, is a vast tract of land, which may be denominated a continent. Of this discovery, and the circumstances which led to it, we now subjoin the following particulars, as published in the Literary Gazette and some newspaper.

"A Mr. Smith, master of the William, of Blythe, in Northumberland, and trading ...." [then as in *Literary Gazette* of 5 August without the footnote].

It is well known to those who are acquainted with Captain James Cook's narrative of his circumnavigation, that he entertained a serious opinion, that a vast body of land was still undiscovered in the southern regions, and his last voyage was particularly, though unsuccessfully, directed to this important object.[2] Of its particular situation he could

[1] P. 190.
[2] This is presumably a reference to Captain Cook's second voyage.

know nothing but from geographical calculations, and those it appears led him into an error. His full persuasion that land somewhere existed, and his opinion respecting its situation, may be gathered from the following observations.

"In lat. 67°20′, long. 137° 12′," he says … [then as in *Literary Gazette* of 5 August, footnote, p. 204, until] … called it a sea-horse; but every one else took it for what I have said."

Of the great results to which the discovery recently made, may lead, we are unable to form any rational conjecture. The full extent of land is yet unexplored; and of the internal capabilities of the country, little or nothing is yet known. Adventurers no doubt will throng to this newly discovered world, and make their observation, on phenomena and productions with which both science and commerce may hereafter be enriched.

Edinburgh Philosophical Journal, October 1820, pp. 367–80:
Article by John Miers – text in Chapter 4, pp. 48–61.

Literary Gazette and Journal of Belles Lettres, 14 October 1820, p. 668:
Article on William Smith's voyages with extracts from his journal – text in Chapter 4, pp. 62–3.

The Globe, 2 November 1820:
Copy of article in *Literary Gazette and Journal of Belles Lettres* of 14 October.

Edinburgh Philosophical Journal, April 1821, pp. 345–8:
Article by Dr Young on Barnsfield's voyage. Text in Chapter 5, pp. 79–81.

Literary Gazette and Journal of Belles Lettres, 7 April 1821, p. 218:
Reprint of Dr Young's article in the *Edinburgh Philosophical Journal* of April 1821.

Literary Gazette and Journal of Belles Lettres, 3, 10, and 24 November 1821, pp. 691–2, 712–13, 746–7:
Extracts from Midshipman Poynter's journal and remarks by Midshipman Bone. Text in Chapter 5, pp. 82–90.

BIBLIOGRAPHY

Aker, R., 'Sir Francis Drake Discovered Cape Horn', *Mariner's Mirror*, 84, 1998, pp. 81–4.

Alberts, F. G., *Geographical Names of the Antarctic*, Washington DC, 1981.

Antarctic Pilot, HMSO, London, 1930, 1948, 1961 and 1974.

Armstrong, T., 'Bellingshausen and the Discovery of Antarctic', *Polar Record*, 15, 1971, pp. 887–91.

Balch, E. S., *Antarctica*, Philadelphia, 1902.

Barra, O.P. de la, 'El misterio del "San Telmo"', *Boletín Antártico Chileno,* 11, April 1992, pp. 2–5.

Beaglehole, J .C. ed., *The Journals of Captain James Cook on his Voyages of Discovery, II, The Voyage of the Resolution and Adventure 1772–1775*, London, The Hakluyt Society, extra series 35, 1961.

Belcher, Commander E., *A Treatise on Nautical Surveying*. London, 1835.

Belov, M. I., comment on article by T. Armstong, *Polar Record*, 15, 1971, pp. 890–91.

Berguño, J. B., 'Las Shetland del Sur: El ciclo lobero', *Boletín Antártico Chileno*, April 1993, pp. 5–13, and October 1993, pp. 2–9.

Bertrand, K. J., *Americans in Antarctica 1775–1948*, New York, 1971.

Blewitt, M., *Surveys of the Seas*, Macgibbon and Key, London and Bath, 1957.

Blunt, E., *The American Coast Pilot*, tenth, eleventh and twelfth editions, New York, 1822, 1827 and 1833.

Bourne, W., *A Regiment for the Sea*, edited E. G. R. Taylor, London, The Hakluyt Society, second series 121, 1963.

Bruce, W. S., 'The Story of the Antarctic', *Scottish Geographical Magazine*, 10, 1894, pp. 57–62.

——, 'The Weddell Sea: An Historical Retrospect', *Scottish Geographical Magazine*, 33, 1917, pp. 241–58.

Buache, P., 'Geographical and Physical Observations, including a Theory of the Antarctic Regions &c.', *Gentleman's Magazine*, 33, 1763, pp. 32–6.

Burney, J., *A Chronological History of the Voyages and Discoveries in the South Sea or Pacific Ocean,* 5 vols, London, 1803–17 (reprint Israel, 1967).

Callender, J., *Terra Australis Cognita or Voyages to the Terra Australis*, 3 vols, Edinburgh, 1766 (reprint Israel, 1967).

Calman, W. T., 'James Eights, A Pioneer Antarctic Naturalist' (Presidential Address), *Proceedings of the Linnean Society of London,* 1937, pp. 171–84.

Carruthers, W., 'John Miers', *Journal of Botany*, 1880, pp. 33–6.

Christie, E. W. H., 'The Supposed Discovery of South Georgia by Amerigo Vespucci', *Polar Record*, 5, July 1950, pp. 560–64.

——, *The Antarctic Problem*, London, 1951.

Colledge, J. J., *Ships of the Royal Navy,* 2 vols, 1969–70 (reprinted Bath, 1987–9).

Constantinescu, F. C. and Torrens, D. N., 'Análisis bioantropológico de un cráneo humano hallado en cabo Shirreff, isla Livingston, Antártica', *Boletín del Instituto Antártico Chileno*, serie cientifica, 45, 1995, pp. 89–99.

Cook, J., *A Voyage towards the South Pole, and Round the World &c.* 2 vols, London, 1777.

Dalrymple, A., *Memoir of a Chart of the Southern Ocean,* London, 1769.

——, *An Historical Collection of the Several Voyages and Discoveries in the South Pacific Ocean*, 2 vols, London, 1770–71, (reprint Israel, 1967).

——, *Essay on Nautical Surveying,* 2nd edn, London, 1786 (originally published 1771).

David, A. C. F., ed., *The Charts and Coastal Views of Captain Cook's Voyages*, vols I and II, London, The Hakluyt Society, extra series 43 and 44, 1988 and 1992.

Drake, Sir Francis, *The World Encompassed by Sir Francis Drake, 1628* (reprinted World Publishing Company, Cleveland, Ohio, 1966).

Eights, J., 'Description of a New Crustaceous Animal found on the Shores of the South Shetland Islands, with Remarks on their Natural History, *Transactions of the Albany Institute*, 2, 1833, pp. 53–69.

Falconer, W., *An Universal Dictionary of the Marine*, London, 1769.

Fanning, E., *Voyages Round the World; with Selected Sketches of Voyages to the South Seas*, London, 1834.

Forster, G., *A Voyage round the World in His Britannic Majesty's Sloop Resolution &c.*, 2 vols, London, 1777.

Frezier, A. M., *A Voyage to the South Sea, And along the Coasts of Chili and Peru, in the Years 1712, 1713 and 1714*, London, 1717.

Fricker, K., *The Antarctic Regions*, London, 1900.

Gould, R. T., 'The Charting of the South Shetlands, 1819–28', *The Mariner's Mirror*, 27, 1941, pp. 206–42.

——, 'The First Sighting of the Antarctic Continent', *Geographical Journal*, 65, 1925, pp. 220–25.

Grimble, I., *The Sea Wolf. The Life of Admiral Cochrane*, London, 1978.

Hakluyt, R., *The Principal Navigations, Voiages, Traffiques, and Discoveries of the English Nation, &c.*, 3 vols, London, 1598–1600.

Hasleden, T., *The Seaman's Daily Assistant &c.,* London, 1765.

Hattersley-Smith, G., *The History of Place-names in the British Antarctic Territory*, 2 vols, Cambridge, 1991.

Headland, R. K., *The Island of South Georgia*, Cambridge, 1984.

——, *Chronological List of Antarctic Expeditions and Related Historical Events*, Cambridge, 1989.

Herodotus, *The Histories*, transl. Aubrey de Sélincourt, London, 1954.

Hinks, A. R., 'On Some Misrepresentations of Antarctic History', *Geographical Journal*, 94, 1939, pp. 309–30.

Hobbs, W. H., *The Discoveries of Antarctica within the American Sector, as Revealed by Maps and Documents*, Philadelphia, 1939.

Inman, J., *A Treatise on Navigation and Nautical Astronomy*. Portsea, 1821.

Interdepartmental Committee, *Report on Research and Development in the Dependencies of the Falkland Islands*, HMSO, London, 1920.

Jones, A. E. G., 'Captain William Smith and the Discovery of New South Shetland', *Geographical Journal*, 141, 1975, pp. 445–61.

——, *Antarctica Observed,* Whitby, 1982.

——, 'Edward Bransfield, Master R.N.', *Mariner's Mirror*, 52, 1966, pp. 379–86.

Jones, A. E. G. and Chisholm, J., 'The Poynter Journal', *The Turnbull Record*, 30, 1997, pp. 9–24.

Kaye Lamb, W., ed., *The Voyage of George Vancouver 1791–1795*, 4 vols, London, The Hakluyt Society, second series 163–166, 1984.

King, Captain P. P. and FitzRoy, Captain R., *Narrative of the Surveying Voyages of His Majesty's Ships Adventure and Beagle,* London, 1839.

Lebedev, V. L., 'Geographical Observations in the Antarctic made by the Expeditions of Cook 1772–1775 and Bellingshausen-Lazerev 1819–1821', *Antarktika: Doklady Komissii (Antarctica Commission Reports) 1960*, Moscow, 1961 (transl. Jerusalem, 1966, pp. 1–19).

Lee, I., 'The Voyages of Captain William Smith and Others to the South Shetlands', *Geograhical Journal*, 42, 1913, pp. 365–70.

Lewis-Smith, R., 'Early Nineteenth Century Sealer's Refuges on Livingston Island, South Shetland Islands', *British Antarctic Survey Bulletin,* 74, 1987, pp. 49–72.

Longitude, Commissioners of, *The Nautical Almanac and Astronomical Ephemeris, for the year 1767,* London, 1766.

Longitude, Commissioners of, *Tables requisite to be used with the Nautical Ephemeris, for finding Latitude and Longitude at Sea,* London, 1781.

Mackenzie, M., *A Treatise on Marine Surveying, Corrected and republished by James Horsburgh*, London, 1819.

——, *Orcades: or a geographic and hydrographic survey of the Orkney and Lewis Islands &c.. ,* 1750.

MacPike, E. F., *Correspondence and Papers of Edmond Halley,* Oxford, 1932.

Mead, H. P., *Trinity House*, London, n.d. (c. 1946).

Michell, J., 'A Recommendation of Hadley's Quadrant for surveying, especially the surveying of harbours, together with a particular Application of it in some Cases of Pilotage', *Philosophical Transactions*, 55, London, The Royal Society, 1765, pp. 70–78, Figs 1 & 2.

Miers, J., *Travels in Chile and La Plata*, 2 vols, London, 1826.

Mill, H. R., *The Siege of the South Pole,* London, 1905.

Moore, J. H., *The New Practical Navigator being a complete Epitome of Navigation*, 19th edn, London, 1814.

Moskowitz, S., 'The World's First Sextants', *Journal of the Institute of Navigation*, 34, 1987, pp. 22–42.

Murphy, R. C., *Oceanic Birds of South America*, New York, 1936.

Murschel, A. and Andrews W. J. H., 'Translations of the Earliest Documents Describing the Principal Methods Used to Find Longitude at Sea', in Andrews, W. J. H., *The Quest for Longitude*, Cambridge, Mass., 1996, pp. 375–92

Norie, J. W., *Piloting Directions for the East and West Coasts of South America . . &c. also for the South Shetland, Falkland Galapagos and other Islands, etc.* London, 1825.

O'Brien, H. D., *My Adventures during the Late War*, 2 vols, London, 1839.

O'Byrne, W. R., *A Naval Biographical Dictionary*, Polstead, 1849 (reprinted 1990).

Parry, Commander W. E., *Journal of a voyage for the discovery of the North-west Passage from the Atlantic to the Pacific performed in the years 1819–20 in His Majesty's Ships Hecla and Gripper,* London, 1821.

Phipps, C. J., *A voyage towards the North Pole undertaken by His Majesty's Command, 1773,* London, 1774.

Popham, H., *A Damned Cunning Fellow, The Eventful Life of Rear-Admiral Sir Home Popham KCB, KCH, KM, FRS 1762–1820,* Tywardreath, Cornwall, 1991.

Powell, G., *Notes on South-Shetland, &c. Printed to accompany the Chart of these Newly Discovered Lands*, London, 1822.

Purchas, S., *Purchas his Pilgrims,* 4 vols, London, 1625.

Purdy, J., *Memoir, descriptive and explanatory to accompany the new chart of the Ethiopic or Southern Atlantic Ocean &c.* London, 1822.

———, *The New Sailing Directory for the Ethiopic or Southern Atlantic Ocean &c.*, London, 1822, 1837, 1845 and 1855.

Robertson, J., *The Elements of Navigation containing the Theory and Practice with all the necessary Tables,* 2 vols, London, 1764.

Robson, T. C., *A Treatise on Marine Surveying,* London, 1834.

Ross, J., *A Voyage of Discovery made under the orders of the Admiralty in His Majesty's Ships Isabella and Alexander &c.,* London, 1819.

Sadler, D. H., *Man is not Lost. A Record of Two Hundred Years of Astronomical Navigation with the Nautical Almanac 1767–1967,* London, 1968.

Schouten, William Cornelison, *The Relation of a Wonderful Voyage made by William Cornelison Schouten of Horne, 1619* (reprinted World Publishing Company, Cleveland, Ohio, 1966).

South America Pilot, Part I, London, 1874, 1893, 1902 and 1916.

South America Pilot, Vol. II, HMSO, 1993.

Smyth, W. H., *The Sailor's Word-book,* London, 1867.

Spears, J. R., *Captain Nathaniel Brown Palmer,* New York, 1922.

Stackpole, E. A., *The Voyage of The Huron and The Huntress,* Mystic, Connecticut, 1955.

Stehberg, R. L., 'En Torno a la Autenticidad de las Puntas de Proyectil Aborigenes descubiertas en las Ilas Shetland del Sur', *Boletin Antártico Chileno,* 3, 1, 1983, pp. 21–2.

Stehberg, R. L and Lucero, V., 'Evidencias de coexistencia entre cazadores de lobos y aborígenes fueguinos en isla Desolación, Shetland del Sur, Antártica, a principios del siglo XIX', in *Boletin del Instituto Antártico Chileno, serie* científica, 45, 1995, pp. 67–88.

Stehberg, R. L. and Nilo, L. F., 'Procedencia antártica inexacta de los puntas de proyectil', *Boletín del Instituto Antártico Chileno,* serie científica, 30, 1983, pp. 61–76.

Stevens, T. A., *The First American Sealers in the Antarctic 1812–1819 and the First Voyage of The Brig Hersilia of Stonington, Conn., 1819–1820,* U.S. Department of State, 1954.

Stommel, H., *Lost Islands,* Vancouver, 1984.

Taylor, E. G. R., *The Haven-Finding Art: A History of Navigation from Odysseus to Captain Cook,* London, 1956.

Taylor, W. A., 'A History of Antarctic Discovery', *Scottish Geographical Magazine,* 14, 1898, pp. 535–59.

Tooley, R. V., *Maps of Antarctica,* Map Collectors Circle, London, 1963.

Waters, D. W., *The Art of Navigation in England in Elizabethan and Early Stuart Times,* London, 1958.

Webb, W., *Coastguard! An Official History of HM Coastguard*, HMSO, 1976.

Webster, W. H. B., *Narrative of a Voyage to the Southern Atlantic Ocean in the years 1828, 29, 30, performed in HM Sloop Chanticleer, Captain Henry Foster FRS.*, 2 vols, London, 1834.

Weddell, J., *A Voyage towards the South Pole,* London, 1825.

BRITISH ADMIRALTY CHARTS

[not numbered] *A Chart of New or South Shetland etc....surveyed by E Bransfield, Master R.N. in 1820. Published according to Act of Parliament by Capt. Hurd R.N. Hydrographer to the Admiralty 30th Novr 1822.* [Plate 31]

[not numbered] *A General Chart of South America from a drawing by Lieut. A. B. Becher, R. N. combined with the best English and Spanish Surveys in the Hydrographical Office,* dated 4th November 1824.

1238 *The South Shetland and South Orkney Islands with the tracks of the several Discoverers 1819–1843. Published according to Act of Parliament at the Hydrographic Office of the Admiralty Septr 7th 1839 – Additions to 1844.*

3205 *South Shetland Islands,* 1901 and Taunton, 1991.

4214 *Approaches to Graham Land,* Taunton, 1991.

PRIVATELY PUBLISHED CHARTS

Norrie, J. W., *A Chart of New Shetland with the Tracks of Mr Bransfield, HMS Andromache, 1820. Published 1 January 1822.* [Plate 8]

Laurie, R. H., *Chart of South Shetland, including Coronation Island from the Exploration of the Sloop Dove in the years 1821 and 1822 by George Powell, Commander of the same, 1822.* Published 1 November 1822.

INDEX

Names of features are given with the proper name first followed by the generic term e.g. Horn, Cape.
Lists are used for the following headings: albatross, Bransfield's voyage in the *Williams*, penguin, petrel, pipit, seal,
shag, ships, skua and whale.
No attempt has been made to index every mention of a bird, seal or whale. A number of these are, however,
included under the generic term; specific types are indexed as above.